ENDORSEMENTS FOR

M000117396

You hold in your hands the fruit of many years of scholarship, wedded to the reality of present persecution. The promises of God, so desperately needed in Isaiah's time, come alive for us in these pages at a time when Christianity is marginalised, and Islam is permitted to enact its supremacist agenda. We are encouraged to learn that followers of the Lord in Isaiah's time also had to remain firm in the face of dwindling numbers and fierce opposition. Please do yourself a favor—read this book and share it with a friend!
Erwin Lutzer, Moody Church, Chicago

Elizabeth Kendal states the persecution of the Church is 'at the gate.' She summons the Church and the individual believer to be aware of the ensuing spiritual battle. We must repent and 'trust not in horses and chariots but in the Lord Our God.' For armaments she offers faith and prayer. As a witness to the persecution of the Christ's Church and Christians in the Sudan for over nine years, I commend *Turn Back the Battle* to readers. Read it as if the Church and your spiritual life depended upon it. Heed the call to mobilise, and the declaration of victory in and through the Word of God.
Heidi McGinness, Modern-Day Abolitionist and Director of Outreach, Christian Solidarity International, usa.

In *Turn Back the Battle* Isaiah's message comes through loud and clear. A society which does not acknowledge the laws of God will bring judgement on itself: it will decline and perish. To flourish, a nation needs authentic spiritual identity and a sense of destiny. Without these there will be increasing reliance on coercion, authoritarianism, the intolerance of the 'tolerant', and persecution of those who disagree with the godless consensus. A city can be either built on rebellion against God—Babel—or fulfil God's purposes—Jerusalem. A proper balance needs to be struck between a missionary engagement with culture and prophetic witness to the culture. Suffering for the Faith is itself prophetic and the ultimate counter-cultural criticism. The lesson to be drawn for Christian work is not to rely on compromised human institutions to bring justice and freedom to a beleaguered humanity but to rely on God alone.
Michael Nazir-Ali, former Bishop of Rochester and Director of the Oxford Centre for Training, Research, Advocacy and Dialogue.

What on earth have events in the Middle East over 2700 years ago got to do with what is ahead of us today? Everything! God hasn't changed and neither has humankind. Through careful research and analysis Elizabeth Kendal brings to life the past to unravel the present. Read and be forewarned about what may be about to happen—if we don't return to God.

STUART ROBINSON, Founding Pastor, Crossway Church.

Turn Back the Battle will strengthen your faith. It helps us see that God is not about to surrender the lives and destiny of his people to the evil intentions of a mean and despicable humanity at war with itself. Elizabeth Kendal puts the current awful outpouring of violence, aggression and terrorism against the Body of Christ in its biblical context. She shines the light of God's Word onto the pain, the anguish and the disdain that God's people suffer. This book will reinforce your confidence in God's commitment to liberate his people. It explains why we need to focus on him in our darkest hour. I commend it to all who seek to find reassurance of the unfailing hand of God during the current horrendous siege which is being unleashed on the global Body of Christ.

TIMOTHY O. OLONADE, Executive Secretary and CEO, Nigeria Evangelical Missions Association.

Religious freedom is one of the most urgent, pressing issues for the global human rights movement. Among those who analyse and comment on religious oppression, perhaps no one is more keenly aware of the underlying issues and root causes than Elizabeth Kendal. This outstanding study demonstrates her mastery of this subject. Her engaging writing style makes this book a must-read for anyone concerned about religious freedom today.

MARK ALBRECHT, author of the *Restricted World Ministry Handbook*, the first country-by-country study on Christian persecution.

Turn Back the Battle is a timely antidote against the belief that more activism, more United Nations, more international legislation, more international pressure, more democracy, or Washington can substantially change the situation of persecuted Christians. Elizabeth Kendal's very readable book applies the message of Isaiah to believers today, to show that our faith must be in God alone, and our focus on obeying him before anything else. This is valuable advice and I plan to apply it to the situation of my own congregations here in Egypt.

JOS M. STRENGHOLT, Anglican priest in Cairo, Egypt.

This book challenged my faith. I have a passion for persecuted believers and studying the book of Isaiah with an eye on today's world helped me to focus on the way forward for them and for us. It caused me to remember God's great deeds in the past and trust him for the future. It made me feel ashamed for being so easily influenced by the 'ways of the world'. It gave me hope for the future, since Jesus is Victor. 'Prayer is the highest form of advocacy' is my favourite sentence of this book. May I not just believe it but live it.

ANNEKE COMPANJEN, author of *Hidden Sorrow, Lasting Joy* and *Singing Through the Night*, on the women of the persecuted church.

What you have in your hand is powerful, provocative and essential reading for today's world. Elizabeth Kendal has written a classic. Her many years of research into the subject matter of this must-read book challenge us to not look to man for our help, but to God. *Turn Back the Battle* is theologically sound, historically and culturally savvy, prophetically insightful and geopolitically intuitive. It is desperately needed. This is not one to put back on the shelf. Buy it, read it, live it. Now.

RAY WADELEY, National Deputations Director, Voice of the Martyrs Australia.

With clear spiritual insight, impressive scholarship and intellectual integrity, Elizabeth Kendal explores Isaiah's revelation of God's timeless wisdom, compassion and anguish over the suffering caused by humanity's embrace of the alluring, deceptive philosophies of the world. *Turn Back the Battle* will inspire and empower all who value God-given freedom and yearn to see his righteousness upheld.

KAREN BOS, Christian Faith and Freedom.

Turn Back the Battle is an outstandingly insightful book which exposes global threats to Christian faith, religious liberty and human rights. As the foundation of our civilisation is shaken, and the Church faces life-endangering challenges from within and without, it calls us to ask ourselves in what and in whom do we trust. It proclaims that our ultimate security rests in Christ alone. It invites readers to a radical faith in God. The message of this passionate and prophetically astute book should be heeded by all Christ's faithful witnesses in this the 21st Century.

ALBRECHT HAUSER, Mission Secretary and Canon of the Evangelical-Lutheran Church in Württemberg and a Trustee of the Barnabas Fund.

Elizabeth Kendal has issued a clear prophetic call to the church: 'It is better to take refuge in the Lord than to trust in man. It is better to take refuge in the Lord than to trust in princes' (Psalm 118:8–9). This book will inspire and draw you into a more intimate reliance upon our Almighty Heavenly Father.
NIGEL ROOKE, CEO, Open Doors Australia.

In this careful biblical, theological, exegetical and pastoral study, Elizabeth Kendal uses the book of Isaiah to offer hope and comfort to believers the world over, especially the persecuted church. Kendal has mined Isaiah deeply to bring forth its treasures, and we all owe her our heartfelt thanks for doing so.
BILL MUEHLENBERG, apologist, lecturer, writer, commentator, and CultureWatch blogger.

In this superbly written book, Elizabeth Kendal shows how the wisdom of the prophet Isaiah can equip today's Christians. It serves as a wake-up call for believers tempted by the attractions of an increasingly God-less world, and Christians living under oppression will draw great inspiration from it.
PETER RIDDELL, Vice-Principal (Academic), and Dean of the Centre for the Study of Islam and Other Faiths, Melbourne School of Theology.

Turn Back the Battle accurately applies the message of Isaiah to our day. This excellent historical and theological analysis removes indifference and deception from our eyes to reveal our sins and the state of our global society. It is a call to do something compassionate, to 'suffer-with' those in need. But primarily it is a call to faith, as only God can provide the help needed. Kendal is honest, faithful and qualified in what she writes. For the last five years we have personally witnessed severe persecution against the church in Jos, Nigeria. We have looked to God daily for answers and have seen his church greatly strengthened and many come to know Jesus. We applaud the exceptional prophetic call in *Turn Back the Battle*. This is a radical message, calling us to radical trust, the only response worthy of the gift of Christ who died and rose for us.
KENT HODGE, Christian Faith Institute, Jos, Nigeria.

Turn Back the Battle

ISAIAH SPEAKS TO CHRISTIANS TODAY

Elizabeth Kendal

db

deror books

Elizabeth Kendal, 1962–
Turn back the battle: Isaiah speaks to Christians today.
Published by Deror Books, Melbourne, Australia.
ISBN: 978-0-9807223-6-9

For sales inquiries contact:
inquiries@derorbooks.com

www.derorbooks.com

TABLE OF CONTENTS

Questions for Discussion

At the end of each chapter there are questions for discussion, which can be used by small groups or for individual reflection.

Leaders of discussion groups might wish to start by asking, 'What did you find challenging, confronting and convicting?' and 'What did you find enlightening, comforting and faith-energising?

For further examples of religious persecution and discussions of challenges faced by the church today, consult these sites:

Turn Back the Battle website:

www.elizabethkendal.com

(Resources to help people understand and endure persecution)

Religious Liberty Prayer Bulletin website:

rlprayerbulletin.blogspot.com

Religious Liberty Monitoring website:

elizabethkendal.blogspot.com

Prayers

A carefully crafted prayer is also included after each chapter. This can be used for individual or group prayers.

INTRODUCTION

You will have tribulation

John 16:33

The status quo never lasts.

This is the first rule of history.

Empires rise and fall. The balance of power is permanently in flux. Fortunes come and go. New trends are constantly emerging. Only those who have no concept of history find it unthinkable that the status quo—which they imagine to be normative and rock–solid—could dissolve before their very eyes.

While change is inevitable, catastrophe need not be. More often than not, catastrophe is the consequence of strategic failure: failure to observe, to understand, to adapt or to manage. This is as true for individuals as it is for nations.

In his March 2008 editorial for *Defense & Foreign Affairs Strategic Policy* magazine, Gregory Copley observed:

> It is the confluence of individual events and trends—each separately manageable—which transforms strategic situations. Modern society in the post–Cold War period, however, began to focus down microscopically onto individual issues, as the complexity of advanced societies demanded specialisation.
>
> The ability to raise our eyes from the intense micro–focus became limited, so the collision of separate trends looms

unseen, or is seen only when it becomes overwhelming. Cataclysms, otherwise unavoidable, become inevitable.[1]

Copley had previously forecast that several global strategic trends could converge in the early 21st century to produce a 'dilemma of global proportions'.[2] By March 2008, six months before the global economic collapse of 2008, he was convinced the confluence of trends was already emerging:

> It rides into history as the cavalry unit of the four horsemen of the Apocalypse: Pestilence, War, Famine and Death. It does not spell the biblical end of humanity, but it portends difficult times.

Copley warned that economic distress—including a deep protracted recession in the United States and Western Europe and a major economic downturn in the People's Republic of China—would converge with trends such as population pressure, uncontrollable urban growth, energy shortages and food insecurity, to drive up nationalist zeal and empower authoritarian forces. As economic distress took its toll, relief and development, healthcare and nutrition would all suffer, causing infant mortality to increase while life expectancies decreased.

> The situation will be ripe for emergent pandemics, a number of which wait now in the wings …
>
> National plans for almost all countries … would be thrown into limbo, and all societies would be laid open to strenuous social dislocation, whether from poverty, health issues, or from political uncertainty. The value of all currencies would be thrown into question.
>
> The siege under which the major industrial economies will find themselves would suddenly diminish the differences in capabilities—or options—between those advanced powers and the smaller ones. Countries such as Iran would be freed to act upon the impulses of, or perceived opportunities seen opened to, their leaders …[3]

---

1 Gregory R. Copley (ed.), 'Early warning. Here comes the cavalry', *Defense & Foreign Affairs Strategic Policy*, issue 3, 2008, p. 2, The International Strategic Studies Association, www.strategicstudies.org.

2 Ibid., citing G. Copley, *The Art of Victory*, Simon & Schuster, New York, 2006.

3 Ibid.

The forecast, warned Copley, is for 'a perfect strategic storm'.

How the 'perfect strategic storm' will impact the church

Many Christians fail to appreciate the degree to which even totally non–religious global strategic trends will impact international religious liberty and Christian security. However, consider the events of August 2008. At that time, two totally non–religious trends climaxed and converged, striking a devastating blow for international religious liberty.

Trends: Economic distress and US decline

In August 2008, not only did the US housing bubble burst, triggering domestic and global economic collapse, but the US, being over-extended in Afghanistan and Iraq, proved unwilling and/or unable to come to the rescue of its ally Georgia, which found itself at war with Russia. On the eve of the Beijing Olympics, Georgia had invaded its semi–autonomous province of South Ossetia in an effort to restore Georgian sovereignty over the territory. This was on the expectation— or maybe even the understanding—that it would receive US and possibly even NATO (North Atlantic Treaty Organization) aid. However, when Russia responded militarily in defense of ethnic Russians, no US or NATO aid materialised. Russia subsequently recognised South Ossetia's independence.

After decades of economic and military supremacy, the US suddenly looked quite impotent.

US decline has had a direct and devastating impact on international religious liberty. Since its enactment in October 1998, the US International Freedom from Religious Persecution Act had cast a veil of protection over multitudes of the world's vulnerable religious minorities. By mandating that economic sanctions be levelled against regimes identified as severe violators of religious liberty, this Act gave dictators a reason to reign in their most belligerent elements.

But this Act only had teeth as long as the US had economic leverage. Thus the financial collapse of 2008 seriously undermined its power.

As soon as US weakness was exposed, dictators no longer had any reason to risk domestic tensions in pursuit of US–appeasing reforms. It was as if the veil of protection that US economic and military leverage had provided was stripped away in a moment, leaving minority Christians exposed and vulnerable before a rising tide of militant religious nationalism, intolerant Islamic fundamentalism and brutal, atheistic totalitarianism.

Furthermore, as the global financial crisis spread, domestic unrest erupted in non-free states as local economic distress took hold. Abusive regimes responded to the challenge by ramping up repression and cracking down on dissent, while scapegoating despised and expendable elements, such as the Christian minority, and playing the religion card for political gain—all with complete impunity.

Example 1: China

The Tiananmen Square massacre of 4 June 1989 sent shock waves through China's educated elite, who subsequently rose to become the ruling Communist Party's most ardent and vocal critics. However, as the Chinese Communist Party rightly assessed, most Chinese wanted prosperity far more than they wanted political reform. So to combat the anger and disillusionment, Beijing devoted its energies to appeasing and satiating the emerging middle class by advancing middle-class prosperity. Sure enough, as prosperity increased, middle-class dissent diminished. Feeling more secure and relaxed, the regime responded with tentative steps towards greater openness. For many China-watchers, this fuelled hope that social and political reform might follow.

However, in its determination not to be humiliated by terrorism or protests, the party markedly escalated repression in the lead up to the '08-08-08' Beijing Olympics. Many observers believed that the measures were so Games-specific, that once the Games were over things would settle down. But August 2008 turned out to be a pivotal month in global geopolitics with profound implications for international religious liberty.

After the global financial collapse of August 2008, demand for Chinese exports plummeted. In China, economic distress triggered widespread dissent, including from amongst those who had become the Communist Party's main supporter base: the pacified, increasingly prosperous, emerging middle class. This time, the Communist regime opted for reactionary measures: scaling back openness, escalating repression and cracking down against all real or perceived threats, including pro–democracy demonstrators, lawyers, politicians, union activists, artists and film makers, writers, journalists and Christians.[1] And as the communist party tightened its suffocating grip, there was absolutely nothing the economically distressed US could do about it—and the Chinese Communists knew it.

Example 2: Iran

Through the 1990s, Iran's young educated elite exploited the relative openness of the Khatami era to gain a greater awareness of the outside world. However, this inadvertently fuelled disillusionment, dissatisfaction and restlessness. Ultimately, Iran's minority educated urban elite and emerging middle class started demanding greater social freedoms and increased prosperity via global engagement. They were distraught when Mahmoud Ahmadinejad was elected president in 2005 and re-elected in 2009, because they knew that his regime's belligerence would only deepen their isolation, prolong their hardship and frustrate their progress.

Whereas China's ruling Communists subdued the restless middle classes with the drug of capitalist prosperity, Ahmadinejad's socialist Shi'ite revolutionary regime drowned out middle–class dissent by courting, via generous subsidies, the affection of Iran's majority impoverished masses.

But in 2009, in the wake of the global financial collapse, a dramatic post–budget decline in the price of oil triggered local economic distress and forced the regime to renege on the subsidies it had promised its supporter base. As disillusionment and resentment boiled, the regime intensified repression against any and all real or perceived threats, including (once again) pro–democracy demonstrators, lawyers, politicians, union activists, artists and film makers, writers, journalists and Christians.[2]

Furthermore, to bolster its Islamic credentials and pacify pious Muslims across all levels of society, the regime played the religion card. Claiming 'defence' of Islam, the Islamic revolution and the Islamic state, the regime launched a crackdown on everything un-

---

1 Elizabeth Kendal, 'China: persecution to escalate in 2009', WEA RLPB 517, 18 February 2009 (see RLPB or RLM); E. Kendal, 'China ascendant: persecution intensifying', RLPB 031, 18 November 2009.
2 See E. Kendal, 'Iran: how best to pray', RLPB 010, 24 June 2009.

Islamic, including local Farsi–speaking Protestant congregations. After describing evangelical Christianity as corrupt and deviant and likening Christians to the Taliban, the governor of Tehran province, Morteza Tamadon, went on to accuse the church of conspiring to wage a cultural invasion on Iran.[1]

Christmas 2009 was followed by a wave of arrests. By the end of January 2010, 14 Iranian Christians, virtually all of them converts to Christianity, were in prison simply on account of their faith in Jesus Christ.[2] And that was just the beginning. During the first six months of 2011, at least 285 Christians were arrested in 35 cities in Iran.[3] As the Iranian regime tightened its suffocating grip, there was nothing the US could do about it, and the regime knew it.

Just as Copley had forecast, with the confluence of global trends 'countries such as Iran would be freed to act upon the impulses of, or perceived opportunities seen opened to, their leaders'.

Trend: Rapid population growth and urbanisation

Another trend Copley identified in his March 2008 column was 'uncontrollable urban growth'.

In February 2010, the Foreign Policy Research Institute published a report by Professors P. H. Liotta and James F. Miskel titled *The 'Mega–Eights': Urban Leviathans and International Instability*.[4] Their report highlights

The United Nations Population Division classifies populations in excess of 10 million as *megacities*.

1 AFP Tehran, 'Iran arrests Christian missionaries: official', Al Arabiya News, 4 January 2011, www.alarabiya.net/articles/2011/01/04/132214.html.
2 See E. Kendal, 'Iran: Christians imprisoned amidst mounting repression', RLPB 041, 3 February 2010.
3 See E. Kendal, 'Iran: state violence & persecution escalating', RLPB, 126, 22 September 2011. Figures from the American Centre for Law and Justice, 'Judgment Day: will Pastor Youcef Nadarkhani be Iran's next Christian martyr?', aclj.org/iran/judgment-day-will-pastor-youcef-nadarkhani-be-iran%E2%80%99s-next-christian-martyr.
4 P. H. Liotta & James F. Miskel, 'The "Mega–Eights": urban leviathans and international instability', an excerpt from *The Leviathan Returns: The Rise of the Megacity and Its Threat to Global Security*, Foreign Policy Research Institute, February 2010, www.fpri.org/enotes/201002.liottamiskel.megaeights.html.

the extreme danger inherent in this trend of rapid urbanisation.

Professors Liotta and Miskel regard the rise of '10/40 window' *megacities* as a serious threat to international stability, human security and environmental degradation. The 10/40 window is the area running from West Africa, through the Middle East to East Asia between latitudes 10 and 40 degrees north of the equator. For Christians, the 10/40 window represents a major mission field. 'Over 90 percent of all the least–reached peoples on earth either live within [the 10/40 widow] or have migrated [from there] to other parts of the world.'[1] What happens in the 10/40 window will not only directly impact the local church, it will also impact missionary–sending churches, international Bible colleges, and Western churches receiving 10/40 widow asylum–seekers, immigrants and refugees.

In 2009 I was invited to Sydney, to speak at Moore Theological College's annual mission week. At one point, a group of students delivered a surprise skit, organised with myself and the speaker of the day, Calvin Ma of OMF. While Calvin was speaking, the group of students burst in dressed in green fatigues. They role–played what is a routine event in China: a police raid on an unregistered fellowship. They manhandled and abused the students and confiscated wallets and Bibles while taking photographs for later reference. Then they seized the speaker, Calvin Ma, and abused him for returning to preaching even after his last imprisonment. As they dragged him away, some students started to giggle. In a second, the chapel was full of laughter—that is, until a young Chinese international student rose to her feet and, with tears streaming down her face, cried: 'It's not funny! This really happens! This is happening to my parents even now!' All of a sudden, something new, foreign and alien had become very real, local and personal. The tears of distress the young student from the 10/40 window shed in that powerful, emotion-charged moment had a greater impact on the staff and students of Sydney's Moore College than anything Calvin or I or anyone else contributed that whole week.

Liotta and Miskel write:

> The '10/40 window' demarks regions of the world where
> socioeconomic challenges are the most daunting; where two–

---

1 Patrick Johnstone, Jason Mandryk & Robyn Johnstone, *Operation World 21st Century Edition*, WEC International, Paternoster Lifestyle, Carlisle, 2001 p. 15.

thirds of the world's population and four–fifths of the world's poor live. This 'window' is a veritable stew of competing religious identities and ethnic groups. This part of the world has been resistant to western political and social culture in general—yet mass media make the people there keenly aware of the advantages of the materialism associated with western modernity.

The friction between traditional cultures and the tangible appeal of western modernity (better hospitals, longer life spans, healthier children, more comfortable homes) has yet to yield a new synthesis in many parts of the 10/40 window. Until it does, turmoil and violence are unavoidable. Without doubt, unchecked growth in the '10/40 window' will change the face of the global map in the twenty-first century.

As the authors note, while megacities in the developed world might struggle with aging infrastructure, at least their institutions of governance were well established before the population boom. This is not the case in the developing world.

A handful of megacities have already reached, or may well soon exceed, their carrying capacity for effective governance and control … New York and many of the 'established' megacities of the world avoided the sudden, population tsunamis that Dhaka, Karachi and some other cities have had to face; they were able to take their present shape after the parent national government had secured itself and had developed the major muscle groups needed to govern large populations and expansive tracts of land.

Regarding the megacities of the developing world, Liotta and Miskel write:

Left to their own devices, (as they have been and likely will be) by inept or uncaring governments, these urban populations must eventually erupt in turmoil—destabilising all around them. All the while, these unmanageable cities will continue to pollute their environs, provide bases for organized crime and private militias, and export their residents in the form of

8

human migrations as well as terrorist recruits and desperate terrorist operatives.[1]

They quote Jeffrey Tayler who, writing in the *Atlantic Monthly*, characterised Nigeria, and Lagos in particular, as 'de-developing' in the sense that their infrastructure is collapsing beneath the weight of neglect and corruption.

Liotta and Miskel warn that the conditions in increasingly ungovernable megacities such as Lagos, Cairo, Kinshasa, Dhaka, Karachi, Lahore, Mumbai and Jakarta 'have created fertile earth for terrorist, criminal and extremist organizations', many of which are 'virtually invulnerable to the power of the governments of their respective states'. Furthermore, they note, there is always the possibility that some terrorist and criminal organisations may actually manage to run parallel power structures or seize control of states as urban security collapses.

They conclude with the ominous assessment that the world is simply 'not prepared for these major shifts in the global landscape that megacity growth portends'.[2]

In addition, I would contend that the church is not ready for such an eventuality. Already, violence, corruption and impunity in these ungovernable, lawless cities are inflating the cost of gospel witness, which is increasingly being made at the risk of one's life. For while non–Christian religious zealots do not appreciate Christian missionary endeavours, neither do drug dealers or gun runners, mafia bosses or crime lords.

Trend: Hardship and intolerance are escalating together

While some of the non–religious strategic trends that Copley identifies will directly impact religious liberty, some will not—for example, energy shortages and food insecurity. However, these trends will still impact the church, and the church will have to respond.

God calls churches and individual Christians to live as his witnesses and ambassadors at all times, including through times of immense hardship. During times of famine, disasters of natural and human origin, pandemics, economic collapse and social decay, Christians are

---

1 Liotta & Miskel, 'The 'Mega-Eights'.
2 Ibid.

9

to bring glory to God by faithfully witnessing to the gospel in word and deed. 'Amen', we all say.

Yet trends indicate that hardship will be increasing at the same time as anti-Christian intolerance and persecution will be escalating and religious liberty and Christian security will be declining. In other words, as the world's needs increase, so too will the cost of Christian witness.

By 2010, this trend was already evident as Christian humanitarian aid and charity workers were finding themselves being expelled and assassinated in ever-increasing numbers from states as diverse as modernising Morocco and Talibanised Afghanistan.[1]

Trend: Religious liberty is in decline globally

Unfortunately, the church too has 'focused down microscopically onto individual issues'[2]—so intently and exclusively that it has largely failed to notice the grand narrative that has been unfolding with regards to Christian security and international religious liberty.

The church is only now waking up to the problem of *religious nationalism* in post-colonial emerging democracies, decades after the end of the colonial era saw newly independent states moving to redefine themselves along traditional, pre-colonial, distinctly non-Judeo-Christian lines. While most newly independent states started out as secular constitutional democracies (a gift of their colonial masters), ambitious politicians learned quickly how to play the religion card for political gain. And while it might be a political winner, religious nationalism breeds communalism and fuels religious discrimination and persecution.

The church is only now waking up to the problem of *fundamentalist Islam* decades after Saudi Arabia committed itself to investing billions of petro-dollars per annum in the global dissemination of pro-Sharia, pro-jihad, anti-Shi'ite, anti-Semitic, anti-Christian, intolerant fundamentalist Islam. While the church has been otherwise occupied,

---

1 See E. Kendal, 'Morocco: up to 70 foreign Christians expelled', RLM, 14 March 2010; 'Fitna in Morocco', RLM, 26 March 2010; 'Afghanistan: Christians menaced as Karzai woos Taliban', RLPB 059, 09 June 2010; 'Afghanistan: aid workers executed as Taliban consolidates', RLPB 070, 25 August 2010.
2 See Copley, 'Early warning'.

the Saudis have been funding Islamic jihads all across the world everywhere, that is, except at home. They have also been advancing intolerant fundamentalist Islam across Africa and Asia—training locals and sending missionaries—as well as into the West (especially into Western universities). Indeed, a whole generation has already been thoroughly radicalised and is now hard at work radicalising the next generation. When it comes to countering the spread of intolerant fundamentalist Islam, the church is at least three decades behind the game.

The church is only now waking up to the problem of *mass immigration without integration*, decades after our political elites, for various economic, ideological and political or geopolitical reasons, opened the floodgates.[1] Yet even now, as our suburbs fracture with volatile cultural and religious fault lines, many in the church who are reluctant to witness (especially not sacrificially) prefer to desperately cling to the false hope that humanity will prove to be inherently good and that in time, politics and quiet diplomacy will fix everything.

The church in the West is only now waking up to the problem of rising *fundamentalist secularism* and its consequences. The growth in evangelicalism has not offset the decline in the mainstream denominations, especially in terms of cultural influence.

Trend: culture change in the West

Western culture is evolving from Judeo–Christian to 'post–Christian' (i.e. non–Christian). In terms of religious liberty, that means the West is becoming just like the rest of the world—that is, hostile to the Gospel and less humanitarian. Western Christians who feel secure, thinking that crippling discrimination and persecution simply will not or cannot touch them, are either terribly ignorant, living in denial, or desperately clinging to unrealistic wishful thinking.

Most Western Christians do not realise that the only reason they have not suffered systematic discrimination and violent persecution is because they have been protected from it by the respect for the individual inherent in Judeo–Christian culture, and by the religious liberty provisions inherent in Judeo–Christian law. Religious liberty is not a fruit of 'Western' culture per se, but of Judeo–Christian

1 See Christopher Caldwell, *Reflections on the Revolution in Europe*, Doubleday, New York, 2009.

culture specifically. Human dignity and religious liberty are biblical principles. As the rich biblical foundational soil is eroded away, the culture becomes as unstable and fruitless as a stunted tree on a rapidly eroding bank.

Further, when internal restraint (self-control) is jettisoned, supposedly in the name of 'liberty', external restraints (laws and law enforcers) become essential for the maintenance of 'harmony'. Consequently, authoritarianism is increasing in the emerging 'post-Christian' West, as laws (external restraints) are 'broadened' (to cover an ever expanding list of problematic and unacceptable behaviours and opinions) and 'tightened' (through the removal of exemptions, thereby removing the right to conscientious objection) to reflect and protect the new 'post-Christian' reality.

Do not be naive! It does not take a Communist, Islamic or religious nationalist revolution to destroy religious liberty. Democratically elected secular governments struggling to cope with rising levels of violence, religious and secular fundamentalism, and the complexities and volatility of multiculturalism, are already discovering the political value of pragmatism and appeasement.[1]

Example: the United Kingdom

Consider this excerpt from a Religious Liberty Prayer Bulletin dated 21 October 2009, titled *United Kingdom: Religious liberty fading fast.*[2]

> All Nations Church in Kennington, South London, was
> recently ordered not to use its sound system for its sermons
> or music so as to avoid offending its (Muslim) neighbours.
> A Christian office worker from South London, Denise Haye
> (25), was recently sacked for expressing her disapproval of
> homosexuality. A Christian nurse from Exeter, Shirley Chaplin
> (54), was recently threatened with disciplinary action after she
> refused to remove the cross from her necklace that she had
> worn without a complaint throughout 30 years of nursing. A
> Deputy Registrar with Islington Borough Council, Theresa
> Davies (59), was demoted because she refused to preside over
> same-sex civil partnership ceremonies. A Christian nurse

---

1 See E. Kendal, 'Understanding religious liberty', RLM, 15 April 2010.
2 E. Kendal, 'United Kingdom: religious liberty fading fast', RLPB 027, 21 October 2009.

with 40 years' experience, Anand Rao (71), was sacked after he
suggested to a training seminar that distressed palliative care
patients could try going to church. A Christian community
nurse and professional foster mother (with 80 children's–
worth of experience) was recently struck off the register for
failing to prevent a 16-year-old Muslim girl converting to
Christianity. A Christian homelessness prevention officer
with 18 years' experience, Duke Amachree (53), was sacked
by Wandsworth Council for sharing his faith with a client
who had lost hope. Reverend Noble Samuel of Heston United
Reformed Church, West London, who debates Muslims on his
TV Gospel program, was hijacked in his car by three Urdu–
speaking assailants who grabbed him by the hair, ripped off
his cross and threatened to break his legs if he continued
broadcasting. These cases (all in 2009) are just the tip of the
iceberg. If the Equality Bill that is now making its way through
parliament passes (as expected), then persecution will increase
dramatically.[1]

While Christians are being silenced, Islamisation is advancing,
with Islamic fundamentalists appeased at every turn by short–
sighted politicians who lack political courage and hanker after
political gain.[2] While Christians are fined, sacked and sued for
expressing their faith, Anjem Choudary's Islam4UK is free to
run its Islamic Roadshows all across the country.[3] Independent
think tank Civitas recently reported that Britain already has
some 85 Sharia Courts operating openly, advising illegal
actions and transgressing human rights with impunity ...[4]

---

1 The Equality Bill subsequently passed through the parliament on 6 April
   2010.
2 For examples see 'UK' label, RLM.
3 Young convert to Islam in UK—During a dawah action by Anjem Choudary
   and Al-Muhajiroun. Produced by Islam4UK in association with London
   School of Sharia, June 2009, www.youtube.com/watch?v=fMN76BTMkdY.
   Note: Islam4UK (formerly Al-Muhajiroun, before that group was banned)
   was proscribed under the UK's counter terrorism laws in January 2010. It re-
   grouped as Muslims Against Crusades, which was subsequently proscribed
   in November 2011.
4 Sharia courts should not be recognised under the Arbitration Act. See
   Civitas, 29 June 2009, www.civitas.org.uk/press/prcs91.php.

As long as the various anti–Christian lobby groups can silence Christians and shut down debate through anti–defamation, anti–vilification and anti–discrimination laws along with threats of violence, they will be on a winning trajectory with little resistance—that is, until violent conflict erupts. Violent 'race' clashes are already on the increase, mostly in response to protests against Islamisation. The UK is in trouble.

As culture change progresses and Western culture evolves to become 'post–Christian', Christian witness is increasingly being deemed offensive, intolerant and even criminal—in the West.

The scene in the courtroom is changing. Increasingly, Christ's ambassadors no longer represent the majority. Increasingly, the Lord's righteous are the ones in the dock, standing accused of being intolerant, divisive, a threat to social cohesion and harmony, and even of undermining 'human rights'. As soon as anti–Christian elements find they can commit violence against Christians with impunity, then violent persecution will escalate—in the West. And countries that will not defend religious freedom at home will not defend it abroad.[1]

Under attack: the concept of religious freedom as a universal human right

The Universal Declaration of Human Rights (UDHR)[2] is built on biblical foundations. The creation of humankind in the image of God and the incarnation provide the rationale for human dignity and human rights.[3]

This is why Islam does not recognise the UDHR, but dismisses it as a Judeo–Christian construct. Muslims refer instead to the Cairo Declaration of Human Rights in Islam[4] which the Organisation of Islamic Cooperation (OIC, formerly the Organisation of Islamic Conference) adopted in 1990 specifically to put forward the Islamic

---

1 See E. Kendal, 'USA' label, RLM.
2 See The Universal Declaration of Human Rights, www.un.org/en/ documents/udhr/.
3 See Vishal Mangalwadi, *The Book That Made Your World: How the Bible Created the Soul of Western Civilization*, Thomas Nelson, Nashville TN, 2011, part 3, ch 5, 'Humanity: what is the West's greatest discovery?'.
4 See The Cairo Declaration of Human Rights in Islam: www.religlaw.org/ interdocs/docs/cairohrislam1990.htm.

view of religious freedom. This declaration subjects all rights, including religious freedom, to the Sharia. According to Islam, humanity is only free to convert to a 'higher' religion. Muslims believe that Islam is the natural religion of unspoiled nature and therefore the highest religion of all. So, you can convert (or 'revert') up into Islam, but no one may convert down out of Islam. Nor may anyone attempt to convert another down out of Islam. Apostasy (leaving Islam) is a capital offense. Apart from this, each person is free to hold the religion of their birth, as long as they submit to Islamic rule and the Islamic social order that mandates non–Muslims be humiliated, subjugated and treated as second–class citizens (Qur'an, Sura 9:29).

As the church grows phenomenally across Asia, reactionary Hindu and Buddhist groups have started voicing similar concerns over the UDHR's religious freedom provisions. In 2007, Senegal's Doudou Diene, the United Nations Human Rights Council's Special Rapporteur on contemporary forms of racism, racial discrimination, xenophobia and related intolerance, recommended that the UDHR be amended to address Muslim, Hindu and Buddhist concerns regarding missionary activity, conversions to Christianity, and 'defamation [read: criticism] of religion'. He recommended that 'In the light of the polarised and confrontational readings of these articles' (on religious freedom, freedom of speech and freedom of association), the United Nations Human Rights Council (UNHRC) should 'promote a more profound reflection on their interpretation' and 'consider the possibility of adopting complementary standards on the interrelations between freedom of expression, freedom of religion and non–discrimination'.[1]

The OIC took this a step further, recommending that 'deterrent punishments' be prescribed and enforced through international legal instruments to put an end to 'defamation' (read: 'criticism') of religion, in particular Islam.

As resistance to anti–defamation measures grew through 2008, the OIC fine–tuned its strategy. Since April 2009 the OIC has been working on getting criticism of religion recast as incitement to discrimination, hostility or violence (as per the International Covenant on Civil and

---

1 E. Kendal, 'UNHRC: Watershed Days', World Evangelical Alliance Religious Liberty Commission News & Analysis,18 September 2007 (analyses the 21 August 2007 UNHRC report A/HRC/6/6 to the sixth session of the UNHRC), http://web.archive.org/web/20090612233545/http://www2.ohchr.org/english/bodies/hrcouncil/6session/reports.htm.

Political Rights Article 20.2[1]), so that criticism of religion could be criminalised and punished as incitement.

Success came in March 2011, with the passing of Human Rights Council Resolution 16/18: 'Combating intolerance, negative stereotyping and stigmatization of, and discrimination, incitement to violence, and violence against persons based on religion or belief.' The OIC and the US are currently working through issues pertaining to the resolution's implementation.[2]

In reality, these measures have far more to do with *apostaphobia*[3] than Islamophobia, for the dictators of Islam know that religious liberty is indeed an existential threat to Islam.

Apostaphobia or 'fear of apostasy' is a term I invented in 2008 to focus attention on the true root of all Islam's abuses. The dictators of Islam have a manic fear of apostasy, and the real reason they want criticism of Islam silenced and rejection of Islam eliminated, is their own apostaphobia—their fear that criticism and rejection of Islam will open the door to mass apostasy.

—◦◦◦—

Confronting reality

The church has to come to terms with reality: we are embroiled in a spiritual battle whether we want to be or not. We are fools if we deny it. We cannot avoid it. Will we retreat? Will we stand firm? Will we stumble? Will we endure? This is important, as a lot of people suffer when we stumble.

Jesus mercifully warned us that persecution would come, so that when it did, we would not be shocked, disillusioned or taken by surprise: 'I have said all these things to you [i.e. warned you of the inevitability of persecution] to keep you from falling away' (John 16:1).

---

1 International Covenant on Civil and Political Rights, Article 20.2: 'Any advocacy of national, racial or religious hatred that constitutes incitement to discrimination, hostility or violence shall be prohibited by law.'
2 See E. Kendal, 'UNHRC Resolution 16/18—the OIC, the UN and Apostaphobia', RLM, 21 August 2011.
3 See 'Apostaphobia' label, RLM.

For humanity in general and the church in particular, dark days lie ahead. Some mainstream strategic analysts are even suggesting that an era of relative peace and development is coming to an end and that global strategic trends threaten to launch us into a new Dark Age. Is the church, especially the prosperous, long–comfortable Western church, prepared for such an eventuality?

And while it is wonderful that the church is finally waking up to reality, there is no time for congratulations. For while we have been occupied elsewhere, mighty waters of hostility have been rising, gathering momentum, surging and spilling over the banks that have long held it back. Indeed, we are awaking to the reality that a mighty flood of persecution is upon us whether we would risk it or not.

God's people are under siege.

But as Isaiah will show us, the battle may yet be turned back at the gate (28:6).

Turn Back the Battle is essentially a call to faith. It is a book that examines faithlessness, along with its causes and consequences, and juxtaposes this with radical faith in a faithful sovereign God. Spoken into a context of gross geopolitical and military insecurity, with God's people facing intense pressure, profound hardship and existential threat, Isaiah's prophetic word is profoundly relevant to Christians in our own faith–testing times.

While this book has been written particularly for Christian peacemakers, religious liberty advocates and Christians whose lives and liberties are immediately threatened and imminently imperilled, it is in reality a book for all Christians. For, whether you are facing persecution now or not, 'all who desire to live a godly life in Christ Jesus will be persecuted' (2 Timothy 3:12). As Jesus said, 'I have said these things to you [i.e. I have forewarned you that persecution will come—John 15:18–16:32], that in me you may have peace. In this world you will have tribulation. But take heart; I have overcome the world.' (John 16:33).

The call to radical faith is not a call to inaction. The question is not about whether we should witness, be a voice for the voiceless, pursue excellence or advocate for justice. Of course we should! The Lord commands us to do so.[1] Rather, the question is this: in what or in whom should we trust? What or who should be the object of our hope?

Isaiah was fully cognisant of the times in which he lived and the turbulent geopolitical situation into which he spoke. He knew he was not preaching radical faith to a people comfortably secure—a people who could easily say 'yes, yes, sounds good' before retreating to their sofas and entertainments. This was a message that cried out to be applied—immediately! The Judeans were at war! Their country was targeted for annexation, their city for destruction, and their king for regime change. Their towns were being occupied and their compatriots were being captured and killed.

Yet into this complex political and military crisis, Isaiah preached a simple and uncompromising message: 'Trust God, not man!' The simplicity of the message made it hard to swallow. In fact, Isaiah was mocked and derided for preaching such a simple, unsophisticated solution into such a complex political and military situation.

Not much has changed. It is the same today. For radical faith is not commonly found in our churches, neither is it widely respected. And when it does manifest, it is most frequently mocked and derided, discarded as simplistic, unsophisticated and unrealistic. Yet radical faith is exactly what God calls for.

While this book is essentially a call to radical faith, it is also a call to repentance. For God looks upon the heart (1 Samuel 16:7),[2] and 'without faith it is impossible to please him ...' (Hebrews 11:6a).[3] So may we cry like him who cried, 'I believe; help my unbelief!' (Mark 9:24).

We have all failed and are all imperfect, which is why we need a Saviour. Praise God that the prophecy of Isaiah is as much about redemption and restoration as it is about judgement. For our God

---

1 E.g. Isaiah 1:16–17; 58:6–12.1

2 'But the Lord said to Samuel, "Do not look on his appearance or on the height of his stature, because I have rejected him. For the Lord sees not as man sees: man looks on the outward appearance, but the Lord looks on the heart"' (1 Samuel 16:7).2

3 'And without faith it is impossible to please him, for whoever would draw near to God must believe that he exists and that he rewards those who seek him' (Hebrews 11:6).3

might be a 'consuming fire' (Hebrews 12:29), but he is also a gracious, compassionate Saviour compelled by everlasting love (Hebrew: *hesed*).

It is concerning this everlasting love (*hesed*) that Isaiah commentator John N. Oswalt writes:

> According to the Biblical writers it is his hesed, that gracious, giving loyalty that, if given half a chance, will beggar itself for the beloved. It is not a spineless sentimentality that is blind to our human condition. Rather, it calls us into the mutual commitment of covenant. But it is that 'love [that] never fails' of which Paul knew (1 Corinthians 13:8 NIV), and it is the comfort of the psalmist that allows him to live in security even when everything this world believes to be certain is sliding away or departing (*môt*, as here) into the raging sea of chaos (Psalm 46:3 [Eng. 2]).[1]

As life becomes more challenging and as persecution escalates, Christians will find the threats to their life and liberty more confronting and their security more tenuous. It is therefore absolutely imperative that individual believers and the church as a body be prepared for faith-testing times. For when believers or churches are taken by surprise, hit hard with persecution while in a state of unpreparedness, they tend to reel like a ship caught in that 'raging sea of chaos' without an anchor and a long way from the harbour. With understanding and strategy, shipwrecks of the kind that leave multitudes of believers confused, disillusioned, struggling or dead, might be avoided.

Today in the 21st century, just as in the 8th century BC, God calls us to 'walk in the light of the LORD' (2:5), 'stop regarding man' (2:22), be 'firm in faith' (7:9) and counter-cultural (8:11–14).

When tribulation strikes, we need to look to him (9:13; 22:11), remember him (17:10), find peace and security in him (26:1–4), rest in him (28:12), and not invest our faith in limited flesh, but in him— the Sovereign Creator of heaven and earth (30–31).

If we insist on putting our hopes and faith in human beings, then we will end up with desolation and destruction (34). But if we will trust

---

1 John N. Oswalt, *The Book of Isaiah: Chapters 40–66*, The New International Commentary on the Old Testament, Eerdmans, Grand Rapids MI, 1998, p. 423.

in God and put our faith in him, then the future will be one of great blessing (35).

Today, if we are investing our faith in someone or something other than God—a person, money, organisations, institutions, politics, weapons … (the list could be very long)—then God simply calls us to 'return' and 'rest' (30:15) in him.

In the meantime, 'the LORD waits to be gracious to you …' (30:18a).

CHAPTER 1

Who will we trust when our lives and liberties are on the line?

Isaiah 2:1–4:6

Never has the issue of truth been so challenging as in this 21st century Information Age. Not only do we suffer the burden of information overload, but as Winston Churchill once famously said, 'A lie gets halfway around the world before the truth has a chance to get its pants on.'[1] Without discernment—the ability to sort the truth from the lies and propaganda—the 'gift' of information is really no blessing at all. Faced with multitudes of conflicting narratives, humanity's ageless cry rings out: *Who will we trust?*

Trust: the foundational issue

Men and women have been confronting the issues of truth and trust since the dawn of creation. As soon as God told Adam, 'You may surely eat of every tree of the garden, but of the tree of the knowledge of good and evil you shall not eat, for in the day that you eat of it you shall surely die' (Genesis 2:16–17), the issue for Adam—and subsequently for Eve—was trust. For only if they believed God to be truthful and acting in their interests, would they trust him and obey his word in faith.

When the serpent appeared offering a conflicting narrative, one that rested on the premise that God was lying in order to withhold from Adam and Eve something that would actually profit them (Genesis 3:1–5), Adam and Eve had to make a choice. *Who would they trust?*

---

1 See www.brainyquote.com/quotes/authors/w/winston_churchill.html.

Tempted by the promise of exaltation ('you will be like God'—v. 5), they chose to trust the serpent. But God had indeed been speaking the truth in love. For as soon as they disobeyed, sin and its consequence—separation from God and death—were introduced to a world that until then had been good. Until that pivotal moment evil had been unknown in the earth.

The poison was not in the fruit; it was in the lie that said God should not be trusted. Only after they ingested the lie did Adam and Eve take and eat the fruit in an act of faithless disobedience that instantly alienated them from God as only a breach of faith can.

It is the same today: the poison in the lie continues to disarm humanity to the devil's wicked schemes. And so the question of *Who will we trust?* is not trivial or secondary, but fundamental and foundational. We need to settle this matter in our minds in preparation for faith-testing times, for the question of *Who will we trust?* is never more fraught than when we and those in our care face serious suffering and violent persecution.

It is unsurprising therefore, that the question that divided the imperilled Judeans in the latter part of the 8th century BC as their society crumbled and their enemies advanced, is the very same question that is dividing the church today: *In whom or in what should we trust when our lives and liberties are on the line?*

The prophecy of Isaiah: a book about trust

God was fully cognisant of the social situation, fully appreciative of the military realities, and fully aware of the local and regional political complexities when he sent Isaiah into the fray to answer the question on everyone's lips. Isaiah was to call God's imperilled covenant people—kings and commoners alike—to trust in the Lord rather than in humanity.

It was an unpopular call then and it is an unpopular call today, for it offends all who, in pride and arrogance, believe that humanity can live and possibly even do better without God.

For many years now, as I have read and studied the book of Isaiah, I have been struck by the degree to which Isaiah speaks directly into the situations I am confronting as an international religious liberty analyst and advocate for the persecuted church.

Isaiah's prophetic words of wisdom, spoken as they were into a historic setting of social decay, political turmoil, regional tensions, gross insecurity and existential threat, are as relevant today as they were in the 8th century BC. Now, as then, Isaiah's words offer an absolutely unambiguous treatise on how the people of God should respond to affliction, persecution, insecurity and existential threat.

Despite this, the ageless question of *Who will we trust?* continues to generate considerable division within the church, especially as persecution and insecurity escalate. But while Isaiah condemns faithlessness, especially as it occurs amongst the Lord's own people, he always 'holds out hope for those who repent. In fact, his book serves as a call to such repentance.'[1]

—*∿∿*—

Isaiah commentator J. Alec Motyer describes Isaiah 1–5 as 'an author's preface', where Isaiah presents 'an 'anatomy' of Judah at the commencement of his prophetic ministry'[2]

As a classically trained musician, I think of Isaiah chapters 1 to 5 as the 'overture' of Isaiah's great 'opera'. Here Isaiah sets the scene and introduces his foundational themes—themes that once established will be built upon and developed throughout the remainder of the work.[3]

The scene being set is eerily familiar. Modernise the costumes, replacing cloaks with suits, and the props, replacing swords with guns, and the scene becomes reminiscent of that confronting much of the 21st-century church today. Indeed, social decay, political chaos, regional tensions, geopolitical turmoil, military threat, ethnic-religious violence, impunity and gross insecurity are nothing new at all. This explains why the 21st-century church is asking the very same question that God's people asked more than 26 centuries ago. This is why the prophecy of Isaiah remains so profoundly relevant.

Within Isaiah's preface, or overture, chapters 2 to 4 form a complete

---

1 Avraham Gileadi, *The Literary Message of Isaiah*, Hebraeus Press, New York, 1994, p. 2.

2 J. Alec Motyer, *The Prophecy of Isaiah: An Introduction and Commentary*, InterVarsity Press, Downers Grove IL, 1993, p. 40.

3 Gileadi, p. 57.

unit or 'subsection'[1]. Opening with a superscription—'The vision of Isaiah the son of Amoz, which he saw concerning Judah and Jerusalem'—and bracketed by the two Zion poems of 2:2–4 and 4:2–6, commentators surmise that Isaiah may have produced this subsection for publishing as a separate 'broadsheet' for circulation or for posting to a public place as a 'wall newspaper' before incorporating it into his finished work.[2]

This subsection is in many ways the prophecy of Isaiah in miniature. It presents us with an overview, after which the details will be fleshed out in the historic narrative and oracles of Isaiah 6–39. As such, it deserves close inspection.

Verses 5 and 22 of Isaiah chapter 2 are lynchpins. Both verses are exhortations that arise from what has preceded and are justified by what follows. Together these two exhortations form a foundation upon which the whole prophecy of Isaiah will stand.

Isaiah 2–4 can be divided up like this:

> The Promise: the ideal Zion—2:1–4
>
> > *Exhortation*: 'Come, let us walk in the light of Lord'—2:5
>
> The Problem: the reality! Faithlessness and its consequences—2:6–4:1
>
> > For you are in a mess and totally ruined!—2:6–21
> >
> > *Exhortation*: 'Stop regarding [exalting] man!'—2:22
> >
> > For judgement is imminent, and humans cannot save you —3:1–4:1
>
> The Promise: the new Jerusalem—4:2–6

The promise

It shall come to pass ... (Isaiah 2:1–4)

The promise of God in Isaiah 2:1–4 is 'it shall come to pass' that Zion will be exalted and established as the centre of world pilgrimage and the source of universal blessing. The picture is of nations flowing into Zion in order to be taught by the Lord so they can walk in his ways. At

---

1 Motyer, p. 40.
2 Ibid. p. 53.

the same time, the law and word of the Lord goes out from Zion, and the rule of the Lord brings peace.

What this means is that 'it shall come to pass' that the nations of the world will be supernaturally drawn to Zion. They will recognise that the God of Abraham, Isaac and Jacob—the God of Zion—is *the* God and that his law is good and his word is truth. False religion and nationalism will be rejected as the peoples seek the Lord to learn from his word so they can walk in his light. And the result will be peace— not an enforced peace, but the true peace that is a natural consequence of widespread spiritual transformation.

With this, Isaiah establishes the paradigm: spiritual transformation comes before social transformation. Social transformation is a consequence of spiritual transformation. It is not the other way around. People come to the Lord and then they beat their swords into ploughshares. Consequently, mission (which deals with the human heart and human nature) is integral to economic or political reform (which deals only with surface/administrative matters).

Holding out the promise of transformation as his foundation and motivation, Isaiah exhorts God's people to get on board (so to speak): 'O house of Jacob, come, let us walk in the light of the Lord' (2:5).

This exhortation would not have been necessary were it not for the fact that in their prosperity, the people had forgotten God and taken to walking in darkness.

The problem

You are ruined—the opposite of what you should be (Isaiah 2:6–9)

God had commissioned Israel to be a light to the nations and promised them a glorious future. But instead they had actually become the opposite of what they should be, worldly and faithless to the point of apostasy. Indeed, by 740 BC those who remained faithful to Yahweh were little more than a marginalised minority. Irritatingly counter-cultural, they were scorned by a society that worshipped worldliness, excelled at exploitation, was devoted to decadence and committed to living life without God.

Isaiah laments that the Lord has 'rejected' or forsaken his people on account of their willful and persistent rebellion (2:6–9). The word 'rejected' here does not mean ultimate abandonment or eternal damnation, but a turning away, a letting go at this particular time, so that they might suffer the consequences of their folly.[1] As commentator Raymond Ortlund explains:

> It is not that God doesn't love them any more. But if any
> generation of his people along the way becomes full of pride,
> he would do them no favour by visiting them with a blessing. It
> would only reinforce their self-salvation. Their first need is to
> be emptied of their fullness.[2]

Isaiah laments that God's people have become the opposite of what they are supposed to be. For while the promise is, 'It shall come to pass' that the nations will flow to Zion seeking the Lord and his word (2:3), the Lord's people are only interested in worldliness and prosperity (2:7a). While the promise is, 'It shall come to pass' that in the spiritually transformed world there will be peace (2:4b), the Lord's land is full of weapons of war (2:7b). While the promise is, 'It shall come to pass' that the nations will commit to walking in God's ways (2:3), the Lord's people are walking in the ways of the world and worshipping idols (2:8). While the promise is, 'It shall come to pass' that the nations will be received in the courts of the Lord (2:4b), the Lord's own people have been deemed guilty, rejected and given over to their rebellion (2:6a, 9).

They are 'full of' and 'filled with' (2:6–8) the things of the world—things from the east and things from the west—including barbaric pagan occultic practices—things they should be ashamed of. They 'strike hands with foreigners' (v. 6c), that is, they happily broker deals and enter partnerships and alliances with idolaters and pagans without discrimination, for not only are they proudly cosmopolitan, they are also politically correct and infinitely tolerant. They revel in their prosperity (v. 7a), in which they feel very secure, for they have great faith in their fortifications, weapons and powerful alliances (v. 7b). Furthermore, they have gods galore, just like their neighbours (v. 8).

Instead of being a counter-cultural, magnetic light to the nations and

---

1 Allan Harman, *Isaiah*, Christian Focus Publications, Fearn, Ross-shire, 2005, p. 49.
2 Raymond C. Ortlund Jr, *Isaiah: God Saves Sinners*, Preaching the Word series, Crossway Books, Wheaton IL, 2005, p. 53.

blessing to the world, God's people have joined the world! Indeed, they have been swallowed up and devoured by it. Isaiah acknowledges (2:9) that forgiveness, in the absence of repentance, would be unthinkable from a just and holy God.[1]

Warning: God will bring down all that is false (Isaiah 2:10–21)

Addressing the people directly, Isaiah warns (2:10–21) that God's judgement is at hand and that when 'the splendour of his majesty' (v. 10d) is revealed, everything the people have exalted and trusted in will be brought low 'and the Lord alone will be exalted' (v. 11c). Their shameful sinfulness will be uncovered. The folly and futility of their misplaced pride will be exposed as their great cities, impressive defences, flourishing commerce, booming economy and beautiful crafts will be brought low. In the face of such awesome majesty and terror there will be nothing left for the people to do but to abandon their useless idols and hide.

Driven by the knowledge that dark heavy storm clouds of disaster and judgement are materialising on the horizon, Isaiah unleashes his second great exhortation: 'Stop regarding man in whose nostrils is breath, for of what account is he?' (2:22)

It is not that humans are worthless or of no account. It is just that the human creature is dependent upon God the Creator for its very life and every breath.[2] So why would anyone, let alone the people of God, put their faith in fallen, mortal, limited, created beings and the works of their hands, rather than the eternal, divine, author and sustainer of life, the Creator himself? Faith in humans and their works is always misplaced and futile. As Ortlund notes, 'We think of ourselves as sophisticated, but the fact is, we are too easily impressed.'[3]

Not only is it folly for God's covenant people to regard and exalt human beings and human institutions as the objects of their hope—it is sin. It is a choice made in faithlessness, and it invariably culminates in covenantal betrayal.

The sin of faithlessness is both misunderstood and underestimated in

---

1 Harman, p. 50.
2 'Then the LORD God formed the man of dust from the ground and breathed into his nostrils the breath of life, and man became a living creature' (Genesis 2:7).
3 Ortlund, p. 55.

the church today. While we understand the wisdom and rightness of rejecting adultery, theft, violence, drunkenness and other 'official' sins, the sin of faithlessness generally goes unrecognised and unremarked. Sometimes it is trivialised, sometimes it is excused, but rarely is it treated as a serious failing with calamitous consequences. Because of this, the proud, arrogant self-sufficiency and rebellious independence that stem from faithlessness go unchallenged. Sometimes they are even misconstrued as strength: as a sign that we have progressed beyond dependence on God. The world lauds and applauds while Christians, churches and Christian organisations alienate themselves from God. Excelling in activism and works, they dismiss prayer as passive and unproductive, if not outright superstitious.

But faithlessness always culminates in disaster. This is not because God is a belligerent dictator who delights in making unreasonable demands so he can torture us if we fail or dare to display any initiative or independent thinking. No! It is because God is a loving Father who, when he speaks and acts, has our best interests at heart. It is so often the case that the faithless will reject the path offered by the Lord, but then blame God when they subsequently stumble into a pit. The disastrous consequences of faithlessness are nothing more than basic cause and effect: the inevitable consequence of misplaced trust, of refusing the truth in preference for the lie.

Meanwhile, the church's post-modernist ideologues assure us that noble ends—such as conversions and improved security—will justify any means. 'After all', they say, 'it's the end that matters.' Yet one thing Isaiah 2:6–21 makes very clear is that means matter! For God has determined the means, and he calls us to trust him and walk in his light by faith.

Post-modernists in the church seem unaware that it is because of faithlessness—including the faithlessness of far too many senior Christian leaders—that multitudes of Christians are courting, or being led into, disaster and that God's anger is being furiously provoked. And though it might be understandable, easy and even natural for people—including God's people—to put faith in the visible over the invisible, that is the first step on the slippery slope that leads into darkness, disaster and ultimately—if discipline fails to produce repentance—apostasy and judgement. And so Isaiah exhorts the people of God to stop regarding and exalting humanity (2:22)—now—before it is too late.

Judgement on society (Isaiah 3:1–7)

To gain an appreciation of how serious the state of apostasy is, we only need to look at the judgement described in Isaiah 3:1–4:1. If it is true that the God of justice will always issue a penalty befitting the crime, then apostasy is clearly serious indeed, for God's judgement will be devastating.[1]

Isaiah 3:1–7 describes the crisis that will hit Jerusalem and all Judah: a crisis that will come from God's own hand; a crisis that the righteous remnant will have to live through as well. 'For behold, the Lord GOD of hosts is taking away from Jerusalem and Judah support and supply' … bread, water, national leaders, local officials, tradespeople, advisors, and those in the military of every rank. In short: everything the people have exalted, trusted in, hoped in, placed their faith in, and rested on will be stripped away (3:1–3).

Then the Lord will fill the leadership vacuum with immature incompetents—'infants' (v. 4)—and the very fabric of society will unravel. The people will oppress one another and youths will be insolent toward their elders. Society will yearn for leadership but none will be found. In desperation they will grab anyone! The mere possession of a cloak (or suit) will be enough to make someone a candidate for leadership. However, with the nation in such a state of decay, no one is going to want the job (3:4–7).

When we think of God's judgement, we tend to think of those 'acts of God' that our insurance policies rarely cover: earthquakes, floods, cyclones, wars, famines, plagues and maybe even economic meltdowns. Rarely do we consider poor leadership and social decay as judgements from the hand of God.

Social decay: the product of spiritual rebellion (Isaiah 3:8–12)

Isaiah 3:8–9 makes it clear that the social collapse Judah will suffer will be a direct consequence of her spiritual rebellion—a willful rebellion of which she is absolutely unashamed. This is very confronting, especially as the above paragraph (which paraphrases Isaiah 3:4–7) comes close to describing much of where modern society is headed. We bring the consequence and judgement of social decay upon ourselves, not primarily through a lack of attention to politics, but through a lack

---

1 See also Hebrews 10:26–31.

of attention to the Lord. The remedy is not more authoritarianism or political activism, but spiritual transformation through repentance, reformation and revival.

Comfort in the midst of woe

Then Isaiah gives a most comforting message: in the midst of 'woe' there is comfort.

> Woe to them!
>   For they have brought evil on themselves.
> Tell the righteous that it shall be well with them,
>   for they shall eat the fruit of their deeds.
> Woe to the wicked! It shall be ill with him,
>   for what his hands have dealt out shall be done to him
>   (3:9c–11).

In absolute justice, the wicked will reap what they have sown, but so too will the righteous. Here is a beautiful picture of a righteous remnant. They are about to be caught up in a catastrophic flood of suffering not of their making. It is not their fault that disaster and judgement are coming upon the nation. But even within the 'woe' of the flood there will be comfort for the faithful minority. The Judge of all the earth distinguishes between the righteous and the wicked. 'Shall not the Judge of all the earth do what is just?' (Genesis 18:25).

Rage and sorrow commingle in God's heart as he laments that his people are oppressed and ruled over by immature young men and by women[1] who mislead them while obliterating[2] the right paths (3:12), leaving them lost and helpless, like sheep without a shepherd.

---

1 The reference to women here is not sexist. As Harman notes (p. 57): 'In mentioning the women, cases like Jezebel (1 Kings 18:4; 21:1–15) or Athaliah (2 Kings 11:1) could well be in mind.' Motyer (p. 62) also considers the scenario of a dominant, demanding, manipulative royal harem being the real power behind the throne. Oswalt (p. 138) meanwhile regards the context as giving no grounds for any specific application. Rather, he says, 'It is much more likely that a general figure is being used here to express Isaiah's contempt for men who are not leading.'

2 Harman, p. 57: 'Here the verb "to swallow" is used in the sense of "obliterate".'

The citizens and their judgement described (Isaiah 3:13–4:1)

Suddenly the doors of the divine courtroom swing open and Isaiah leads us in to where God has taken his place as judge (3:13).

First, society's leaders—the 'elders and princes'—stand accused of injustice, oppression and corruption. They are guilty and the Lord is furious (3:14–15).

'What do you mean by crushing my people, by grinding the faces of the poor?' he roars.

Then the 'daughters of Zion' are charged with being haughty, proud, covetous, idolatrous and worldly; obsessed with fashion, accessories and appearances (3:16–23). The 'daughters of Zion' are literally the women of Jerusalem and figuratively the citizens (male and female) of Jerusalem. While the literal sense is true—Jerusalem's women are accurately described—the figurative sense is also true. The citizens of Jerusalem have become obsessed with worldliness, wealth, prosperity and appearances. They are consumers and materialists extraordinaire! She (Jerusalem) is 'full of' whatever is fashionable in the world. She is opulent, extravagant, self-obsessed. Bedecked in fine jewellery and all manner of accessories, she is dressed to impress. But not for much longer—for God is about to turn everything on its head. Judgement will bring about a reversal of fortunes: the exalted shall be humbled and pretence will be replaced with reality.

> Instead of perfume there will be rottenness;
> and instead of a belt, a rope;
> and instead of well-set hair, baldness;
> and instead of a rich robe, a skirt of sackcloth;
> and branding instead of beauty (3:24).

Rottenness, ropes, shaved heads, sackcloth and branding: this is a portrait of devastation, conquest, enslavement and exile. Further, Jerusalem's men shall die in battle and there will be much mourning and desperation with only one man left alive for every seven women. And so the women (in the literal sense) and Jerusalem (in the figurative sense) will be transformed from models of opulence into tragic captives and desperate 'scabrous hags begging to belong to someone'.[1]

---

1 Oswalt, p. 140.

The promise

The new Jerusalem (Isaiah 4:2–6)

Praise God, the story does not end there. For with a turn of the page, Isaiah transports us from this scene of total ruin into a world that is wholly different, the world that the righteous faithful will inherit—the promised new Jerusalem.

Here again there will be a reversal of fortunes: the humble shall be exalted and instead of 'filth' (i.e. vomit: pollution on the inside) and 'bloodstains' (pollution on the outside) there will be cleansing and all the muck will be washed away. Instead of war and insecurity there will be peace and absolute security in the presence of the Redeemer. Instead of displacement, homelessness, hardship and desperation there will be shelter, refuge, provision and rest.

The corrupt Jerusalem, which was filled with pride, haughtiness, arrogance, corruption, exploitation, wealth, weapons and idols, has been brought low and demolished. And, like barnacles on a sinking ship, those determined to cling to the city to the end have gone down with it.

Meanwhile, the new Jerusalem, filled with the beauty and glory of the Messiah, has been exalted as the eternal home of the humble, faithful, holy remnant. As those wed to the king, they will be fully provided for, and the promise of Isaiah 3:10—'Tell the righteous that it shall be well with them, for they shall eat the fruit of their deeds'—will be fulfilled.

Should not this glory, which God has promised, be enough to motivate the people of God to examine their hearts, repent of their sins, return and walk in the light of the Lord? And should not the prophetic word concerning the storm visibly gathering on the horizon, a storm propelled not by wind but by divine wrath, a storm of judgement that will burst through the nation, overturning life as they know it—should not this be enough to motivate the people to give up their idols and vain hopes in limited mortals and turn to the God of their salvation, the Rock of their refuge?

It should!

But will it?

—◈—

Who will we trust?

And what of us? Will the promises of God be enough to motivate the 21st-century church to stay faithful as that 'perfect strategic storm',[1] which has been gathering and building for decades, bursts over us?

Who will we trust, as global strategic trends converge to usher in an era of escalating hardship, repression, persecution and insecurity? Will we rise to the occasions that these faith-testing times will present? Will we cling to God or to those things that are under judgement, which have been exposed as false and are destined to pass away? Will we walk by faith in the light of the Lord, or by sight, regarding and exalting humanity? As the storm clouds roll in, as society crumbles and the mighty river of persecution rises, will we put our trust and hope in God, or, forsaking and forgetting him, follow the ways of the world and place our faith in someone or something else?

Praise God, he is a gracious Redeemer. When we are tempted, he warns us. When we diverge, he calls us to repent and return. Only those who defiantly 'pay regard to vain idols', and refuse to repent and trust their God, 'forsake their hope of steadfast love.' Or, as the NIV puts it, 'Those who cling to worthless idols forfeit the grace that could be theirs' (Jonah 2:8).

Relinquishing worthless idols: the experience of Jonah

The above words, prayed by the prophet Jonah as he repented of his rebellion in the belly of the fish, fit perfectly with the message of Isaiah. Jonah was a prophet who came to ruin on account of rebellion. Yet the God of all grace did not abandon him. Instead, God the great healer gave Jonah a dose of redemptive affliction, which took him into depths of the ocean and into the belly of the great fish. It was there, shrouded in thick darkness, that Jonah realised his folly and repented. There, in the darkness and stench of the fish's belly, Jonah contemplated not only the mystery of divine sovereignty and the horror of divine judgement, but also the profound loss that a person inherits when they refuse to trust the Lord. Then, as a prophet 'reborn' (regurgitated!), Jonah obeyed the Lord, preached to the Assyrians in Nineveh, and witnessed one of the greatest revivals of all time while learning a profound lesson on divine love.

---

1 Copley, 'Early warning'. See Introduction.

God is committed to bringing down all that is worthless, false and cannot save. So if we are clinging to worthless idols—such as money, weapons, material possessions, status or self; human institutions, human wisdom, human strength or human strategies—we must let them go lest we fall along with them. Let them go! Relinquish them all! Trust the Lord! And do so with confidence. Never underestimate the power of radical faith in a sovereign God.

The power of radical faith (Hebrews 11)

Faith is not passive or weak, desperate or ridiculous. Faith in God is both reasonable and dynamic. Though the walk of faith commences with and is sustained by humble and seemingly inconsequential means—specifically prayer—

The Assyrians of Nineveh, who repented at the preaching of Jonah, subsequently became followers of Jesus Christ in the days after his resurrection. The Assyrian Church of the East is the world's oldest Christian denomination. With conversion to Christianity, this once great warrior nation became a great missionary nation. The Assyrians fought alongside the allies during WWI on the assurance that they would be granted their own state. However, they were betrayed and abandoned to their fate at the hands of vengeful Arabs, Turks and Kurds, who massacred them mercilessly in the 1920's. The Assyrians of the Nineveh Plains of Northern Iraq of today are, in the early 21st century, facing genocide again. This genocide will be the legacy not only of Islamic jihad, but of Western betrayal post-WWI and the naivety, incompetence and strategic failures of the US-led Iraq War which commenced in 2003.

it advances in supernatural power with surprise after surprise after surprise.

'By faith' the Red Sea was parted, the walls of Jericho fell and the prostitute Rahab found salvation (Hebrews 11:29–31). 'Through faith' men and women of God have

> conquered kingdoms, enforced justice, obtained promises, stopped the mouths of lions, quenched the power of fire, escaped the edge of the sword, were made strong out of weakness, became mighty in war, put foreign armies to flight (Hebrews 11:32–34).

'Through faith' the dead have been raised and saints have been victorious over torture, mocking, flogging, imprisonment, stoning, execution and all manner of persecution and affliction (Hebrews 11:35–38).

Who or what is the object of your faith?

Faith does not imply inactivity! But similarly, activity does not imply success.

> Unless the LORD builds the house,
>   those who build it labour in vain.
> Unless the LORD watches over the city,
>   the watchman stays awake in vain (Psalm 127:1).

The issue is this: who or what is the object of your faith?

Isaiah was politically active: he petitioned kings! Yet Isaiah's hope did not reside in humans, and specifically not in those kings. Nor did Isaiah's hope reside in works and techniques—not diplomatic, not political, not military. Isaiah's hope resided wholly in his faithful sovereign God. Consequently, he never felt tempted to compromise the message for the sake of political gain or personal security, and could speak prophetically into politics with full integrity.

Today however, far too many Christians from amongst the persecuted and their advocates in the free world are, following the manner of the world, trusting (frantically) in the US, the European Union (EU) and the UN, as well as various other governments, worldly powers, institutions, Christian organisations and lobby groups, and various Christian personalities and leaders to deliver them from their trials.

But the US cannot save the church. During the decade between 1998 and 2008, the US wielded its International Freedom from Religious Persecution Act to the benefit of many persecuted minority Christians. But those days are over! Without economic leverage, this Act simply has no teeth.[1]

Neither can the EU save the church. Cursed with confusion, the EU cannot even save itself!

---

1 See Introduction. America's loss of leverage and influence in no way diminishes her role as a prophetic voice, should she wish to exercise it.

Despite the fact that the UN is now totally dominated by rogue and un-free states, Christians continue to invest their hopes—hopelessly—there.

In early 2009, I attended a peaceful demonstration organised by Diaspora Copts to draw attention to the plight of Christian Copts being persecuted and massacred in Egypt. The event was organised in the wake of the 7 January 2009 massacre in Nag Hammadi, Upper Egypt, where Muslim gunmen fired into young Copts, killing eight and wounding many more, as they left the Church of St John the Baptist after attending Christmas Eve midnight mass.[1] The demonstration was an excellent event. Commencing with worship, proceeding with banners, crosses and hymns, the event drew thousands and did a wonderful job of raising awareness of a terrible situation. (God had used a similar event in August 1998, run by the same group, to call me into full-time religious liberty ministry, so they hold a special place in my heart.)

In the course of the afternoon, I overheard one young boy aged around 10 to 12 years ask his young friend, 'Do you know what the UN is?' His eyes were wide and the intonation in his voice indicated excitement.

'No, I don't,' answered his young friend.

'It is the United Nations,' explained the older boy, 'and they are the ones who can save us!'

But I promise you, any Christian who has the UN as the object of their hope is destined for profound confusion, frustration, disappointment, disillusionment and possibly even total despair.

Furthermore, decoupled from its biblical foundations, 'democracy'—now reduced to mere majoritarianism—cannot save the church. The extreme faith invested by many in majoritarianism is merely an expression of their profound faith in humanity. This faith, however, is based on the false presupposition that humanity is essentially good! 'Give people liberty,' they say, 'and they will choose good over evil, benevolence over greed, egalitarianism over selfish ambition, justice over corruption, and so on.' This might be the position of proud, arrogant fallen humanity which believes it is good, but it is not the position of the Bible, which describes humanity as fallen and in need of spiritual transformation. To trust in humanity is misplaced and

1 See www.youtube.com/watch?v=a7LmAxclgR0.

futile; so 'Stop regarding man!' (2:22).

On the other hand, radical faith in a sovereign God is powerful and effective because the object of faith—the Almighty Creator God—is supremely powerful and absolutely faithful. Trusting God over humanity in the face of social decay, political decline, regional chaos, international instability, military threat and escalating religious repression and persecution, really is the most reasonable thing on earth!

A call to faith

This book is essentially a call to faith—a vehicle to give fresh impetus to the cry of the prophet at a time when the church is facing essentially the same scene that confronted Jerusalem's faithful remnant in the latter part of the 8th century BC.

We have listened to the overture.

The scene has been set: society is crumbling and enemies are advancing.

The foundational themes have been presented: God is at work in his world, bringing down that which is false so that he alone might be exalted. So 'stop regarding man'; repent and come—'walk in the light of the LORD'—for only through faith will you be saved.

Now we move into the grand opera itself, with its dramatic historic narrative, its heart-melting arias, its challenging recitatives and magnificent choruses. It is a classic opera: an opera for all peoples, an opera for all times. Yet it is an opera that resonates with particular relevance at those faith-testing times when the people of God are under siege.

Because hope and faith can be extremely difficult to muster when the odds appear overwhelming and the battle is literally *at the gate*—when conquest, subjugation and death seem inevitable—God, through this divine opera, not only tells us but shows us (providing theology and precedent), that the battle may indeed be turned back at the gate.

It is my heart-felt prayer that the 21st-century church will embrace the narrative of Isaiah 7–39 and incorporate it into her imagination so that it might give her the strength and faith to heed the call of the prophet and see the battle turned back at the gate in our own day.

Questions for Discussion and Reflection

1. While peace and economic growth brought Judah great prosperity, they also contributed to her ruin. By 735 BC extravagant worldliness, idolatry, faithlessness, drunkenness, cruelty, corruption, arrogance and militarisation had become the order of the day (2:6–8; 3:14–15).

   Could Judah be regarded as typical of the nations of the world in any age?

2. In judgement and to aid Judah's rebirth/return/renewal, God took away all the things the people had come to depend upon and glory in (3:1–7; 3:18–4:1). He did this so that false idols might be cast down and the Lord alone might be exalted (2:11, 17 and 20).

   Was God's intervention as much about mercy as it was about judgement?

3. Using Isaiah 2:2–4, discuss:
   (a) the path/route/process that leads to radical social transformation (v2–3a);
   (b) the pivotal element that enables radical social transformation (v3);
   (c) the features of a radically transformed society (v4).

4. Isaiah chapters 2–4 contains two exhortations: one positive, 'Come . . . walk in the light of the Lord' (2:5); and one negative, 'Stop regarding [exalting / trusting in] man [humanity]. . .' (2:22).

   In short: 'Trust God, not man.'

   How might you put this into practice in your own situation?

Prayer

That I might exalt the Lord, who alone is worthy and able to save.

My Lord and God,
You created this world and everything in it: seen and unseen.
All the wisdom necessary for life in this world is found in you,
    as is the strength to apply that wisdom and put it into practice.

Yet the world rejects you as Lord and scoffs at your wisdom.
Trusting in its own wisdom and strength,
    humanity creates one disaster after another.
The world is shrouded in human failure:
    conflict, corruption, chaos and collapse.
Despite this, humanity, being too arrogant to admit
    that it is flailing and failing,
    arrogantly and stubbornly marches on to destruction.

Forgive me Lord for the times I resisted the wisdom of your word,
    simply because it didn't suit me.

Forgive me Lord for the times I hid myself in the crowd,
    or even denied you, to save myself from persecution,
    or even just a little embarrassment.

Forgive me Lord for the times I put my faith in human beings,
    human institutions, human means and various false idols
    devoted to destruction—rather than in you.

Having suffered the consequences of my foolish choices,
    having seen the error of my ways;
I now repent of my lack of faith,
    of my folly and short-sightedness,
    and of my failure to give witness to your truth—
    the remedy this world so desperately needs.

I commit to walk in the light of the Lord,
    not only for my own benefit,
    but so that through my witness others might come to see
    that the way of the Lord is good and right and true,
    and that you O Lord can be trusted.

I commit to exalting, not humanity, but the Lord who alone is worthy and able to save.

Lord bless my witness, so that through my words and my life, my family, my neighbours and others might be inspired to seek you and to trust you: this world's only hope and only Saviour.

'That the earth might be filled with the knowledge and glory of the Lord as the waters cover the sea.' (Isaiah 11:9b; Habakkuk 2:14)

Amen.

CHAPTER 2

Stand or stumble: the choice is yours
Faith tested at the upper pool

Isaiah 7:1–13

We are in Jerusalem.

It is 735 BC.

Judah is at war.

Where is Ahaz, king of Judah?

Syria and Israel are allied in a conspiracy. They plan to reverse Judean foreign policy by effecting regime change in Jerusalem. Ahaz, king of Judah, is out at the conduit of the upper pool on the highway to the Washer's Field, just south of Jerusalem.[1] He is inspecting the city's water supply, assessing the water security situation. Jerusalem does not have a natural water supply within its city walls, and so water has to be brought in via an aqueduct from the Gihon Spring. With invading Syro-Ephraimite forces advancing across Judah with Jerusalem in their sights, King Ahaz must prepare for the eventuality that the city could come under siege.

Previously …

Throughout the preceding century, virtually every time Assyrian imperialism flared, Syria (also known as Aram) found itself on the frontline. Damascus had been ravished by Assyrian armies repeatedly,

---

1 Commentators generally agree that while the exact location of this particular pool is unknown, it is believed to be south of Jerusalem, possibly at the confluence of the Tyropeon (Central) and Kidron Valleys.

41

and Tyre, Sidon and Israel had all been forced to pay tribute to Nineveh (Assyria's capital city). Assyrian imperialism had posed a great threat to the region—so much so that Syria and Israel (also known as the Northern Kingdom, or Ephraim after its largest tribe) had regularly been forced to put aside their historic enmity, rest their border squabbles, and stand united in defense of northern Palestine.

In the days when Ahab was king of Israel (869–850 BC) and Ben-hadad II ruled in Damascus (870–842 BC), Israel and Syria formed a coalition to defend the region against Assyrian expansion. At Qarqar in 853 BC, their coalition—which included various states of northern and western Palestine and was backed by Egypt—successfully repelled an Assyrian offensive led by King Shalmaneser III.[1] That victory secured the region some fifty years of peace.

In 805 BC, King Adad-nirari III of Assyria led his forces into the Levant. Once again, Damascus was crushed and tribute was extracted from Israel, Tyre, Sidon, Edom and others. For the next fifty years, Assyria's domestic and local troubles prevented it from launching tribute-gathering adventures west of the Euphrates. During that time, Syria and Ephraim made peace with each other. In fact, peace reigned across the whole region west of the Euphrates, facilitating economic growth and enabling a period of great prosperity.

In 745 BC, the accession to the throne in Nineveh, Assyria, of Tiglath-pileser III, heralded a new era of Assyrian revival complete with a more aggressive policy of Assyrian expansion. As historian John Bright notes, Assyria had long

> coveted the lands beyond the Euphrates, both because of their valuable timber and mineral resources, and because they were the gateway to Egypt, to southwestern Asia Minor, and to the commerce of the Mediterranean.[2]

Bright describes Tiglath-pileser III as 'an exceedingly vigorous and able ruler', who moved quickly to

> reassert Assyrian power against the Aramean (Chaldean) peoples of Babylonia to the south, and against the kingdom

1 John Bright, *A History of Israel*, 4th edn, Westminster John Knox Press, Louisville KY, 2000, p. 243.
2 Bright, p. 270.

of Urartu to the north, as well as of realizing the Assyrian potentialities in the west. [1]

Over the next five or so years, King Tiglath-pileser III of Assyria took tribute from all the northern and western Palestinian states. But, as Bright explains, 'The campaigns of Tiglath-pileser differed from those of his predecessors in that they were not tribute-gathering expeditions, but permanent conquests.'[2] Furthermore, Tiglath-pileser III had zero-tolerance for rebellion. Rather than repress rebellion by means of reprisal, he would annex rebellious states and eliminate the threat through forced migrations: deporting indigenes and replacing them with imported foreigners, thereby destroying social cohesion and national identity.

Throughout the region, the hottest political issue had long been whether a people should be pro-Assyria or anti-Assyria. That is, should they pay tribute, submit and live in relative peace but without independence, or should they fight for independence despite the risks? No state could fight alone, for Assyria was the regional superpower and hegemon. It was imperative, therefore, that those electing to fight for independence first assemble the strongest coalition they could muster.

In 745 BC, Menahem ben Gadi seized power in Israel by means of political assassination. He then volunteered an excessively generous tribute to Tiglath-pileser III thereby securing Assyrian favour and his own position on the throne in Samaria. Israel's nationalists—especially those in the military—were horrified. When Menahem died in 737 BC, his son Pekahiah succeeded him—but not for long. In yet another bloody coup, Pekahiah was assassinated by one of his own military officers: the son of Remaliah. Immediately upon seizing power, this 'son of Remaliah' reversed Israel's foreign policy and realigned it once again with the anti-Assyrian policy of neighbouring Syria.[3]

Together, the son of Remaliah (also known as King Pekah of Israel) and King Rezin of Syria, resolved to assemble a regional coalition to resist Assyrian aggression. They put pressure on Judah to join. However, King Jotham of Judah (742–735 BC) was not interested, and Judah maintained a policy of independence.

---

1 Ibid.
2 Ibid., p. 271.
3 2 Kings 15:25.

Pekah and Rezin, however, would not take 'No!' for an answer. They needed Judah in their military coalition. And so they conspired to use military force to pressure Judah into reversing its Assyria policy. Meanwhile, Jotham died and was succeeded by his son, Ahaz, who inherited not only the crown but the impending Syro-Ephramite war.

Early in 735 BC, Syria launched a devastating military invasion into Judah. Thousands of Judeans were captured and transported to Damascus. Ephraim also invaded, killing 120,000 Judean 'men of valor' in just one day and transporting around 200,000 captives to Samaria. Fortunately, a prophet of the Lord in Israel named Oded courageously and boldly intervened, and Ephraim's captives were returned.[1] Fortunately, for those in Jerusalem, the Syro-Ephramite forces were not able at that time to mount an attack on their city.

With Judah busy defending her northern border, her traditional enemies to the south grasped their opportunity and exploited the situation. Philistines invaded from the west and Edomites invaded from the south-east, raiding cities and taking captives.[2] Furthermore, in what was a devastating blow, Syrian forces seized the strategic southern port city of Elath (Ezion-geber) on the Gulf of Aqaba. After ethnically cleansing it of Judeans, Syrian forces utterly destroyed it. Subsequently, Edomites occupied Elath and settled there.[3] This was territory that had been annexed by King David, bringing peace, and developed by King Solomon, bringing wealth. Alas, now Elath was lost.

In desperation King Ahaz prayed and offered sacrifices to the gods of Damascus in the vain hope that the gods that were favouring Syria might favour him also.[4] But to no avail.

It is 735 BC

It is the height of the Syro-Ephramite war.

The Judean Army has suffered heavy casualties. The strategic southern port city of Elath is lost. Hundreds of thousands of Judeans have been killed and captured. King Ahaz is being forced to fight a war on three fronts. And to top it off, Judean intelligence is reporting that an assault

---

1   2 Chronicles 28:1–15.
2   2 Chronicles 28:16–19.
3   2 Kings 16:6.
4   2 Chronicles 28:22–23.

on Jerusalem is imminent. According to reports, the Syro-Ephramite coalition is determined to annex the city, vowing to tear it to pieces if necessary.

Pekah, the son of Remaliah, king of Israel, and King Rezin of Syria, have decided that they have given King Ahaz long enough. For despite all the terror Syro-Ephramite forces have unleashed on Judah, Ahaz has still not yielded to their demands. So in order to reverse Judean foreign policy, Pekah and Rezin plan to annex Jerusalem and effect regime change, removing the obstructionist Ahaz and installing a compliant puppet—the son of Tabeel—in his place. As we know, King Pekah of Israel has plenty of experience in conspiracies of this sort, having already reversed Ephraim's foreign policy through a violent coup d'état.

And so King Ahaz is extremely anxious—this is personal! His life and liberty are on the line. And he is not the only one in terror for his life—the whole city is in a state of panic. As Isaiah observed: 'the heart of Ahaz and the heart of his people shook as the trees of the forest shake before the wind' (7:2).

So, with Judah at war and hemorrhaging on three fronts, and Jerusalem staring down the barrel at impending siege and regime change, King Ahaz is out inspecting the water supply. For as any military strategist will tell you, in the event of siege, if the city is without water then she is without hope.

Enter Isaiah

> [3]And the LORD said to Isaiah, 'Go out to meet Ahaz, you and Shear-jashub[1] your son, at the end of the conduit of the upper pool on the highway to the Washer's Field. [4]And say to him, 'Be careful, be quiet, do not fear, and do not let your heart be faint because of these two smoldering stumps of firebrands, at the fierce anger of Rezin and Syria and the son of Remaliah. [5]Because Syria, with Ephraim and the son of Remaliah, has devised evil against you, saying, [6]'Let us go up against Judah and terrify it, and let us conquer it for ourselves, and set up the son of Tabeel as king in the midst of it,' [7]thus says the Lord GOD:

---

1 Shear-jashub: the name means 'A remnant shall return'.

'It shall not stand,
  and it shall not come to pass.
For the head of Syria is Damascus,
  and the head of Damascus is Rezin.
And within sixty-five years
  Ephraim will be shattered from being a people.
And the head of Ephraim is Samaria,
  and the head of Samaria is the son of Remaliah.
If you are not firm in faith,
  you will not be firm at all' (7:3–9).

God has given the prophet Isaiah a message for King Ahaz. The message contains:

- a word of **advice** (7:4) in the face of apparent threat (7:5–6)

- a **promise** (7:7) along with explanation (7:8–9a)

- a **warning** (7:9b)

God's **advice** to Ahaz—'Be careful, be quiet, do not fear, and do not let your heart be faint'—seems strange considering Jerusalem is facing invasion, conquest and annexation, and King Ahaz's life is at risk from enemies plotting regime change.

However, if we are prepared to see things from God's perspective and believe his word, then the advice makes perfect sense. Clearly, while Ahaz sees Syria and Israel's hostile intentions as a serious, existential threat, God sees King Rezin of Syria and King Pekah of Israel, as 'smoldering stumps of firebrands' (7:4), that is, as spent forces, fading lights that will soon fizzle out.

Commentator John Oswalt notes:

In every circumstance there are two perspectives, the human and the divine, and, as here, the two are frequently in conflict. From Ahaz's point of view Syria and Ephraim constitute a major threat, but from God's point of view they are negligible and need not occupy the king's time. It is not always easy to gain the divine perspective. Yet, unless we seek it, we are always in danger of paying too much attention to the passing and paying too little attention to the significant. Furthermore, apart from a diligent search for God's perspective in every circumstance, we conclude too easily that God is concerned only about spiritual affairs and not about practical matters, a fallacy which leads eventually to the loss of God in all affairs.[1]

God then makes a **promise** concerning the Syro-Ephramite conspiracy: 'It shall not stand, and it shall not come to pass …'

God could quite reasonably expect or even demand that Ahaz simply accept his word on the matter, but he does not. God generously gives Ahaz both an explanation and a forecast, which show the reasonableness of his advice to be careful, quiet and confident.

For the head of Syria is Damascus,
  and the head of Damascus is Rezin.
And within sixty-five years
  Ephraim will be shattered from being a people.
And the head of Ephraim is Samaria,
  and the head of Samaria is the son of Remaliah (7:8–9).

The punchline of the prophet's message actually exists in what is left unsaid. Unlike Syria and Ephraim, whose capitals are just cities and kings are just men, Judah's capital is no ordinary city and her king is no ordinary man. For the capital of Judah is Jerusalem and the king in Jerusalem is of David's line. The point is: Jerusalem—the City of David—is a city of promise, and the Davidic dynasty is guaranteed by God, unconditionally! For after King David (1000–961 BC) conquered Jerusalem and established the city as his stronghold, God made a covenant (agreement) with him there, saying: 'Your house and your kingdom shall be made sure forever before me. Your throne shall be established forever' (2 Samuel 7:16). Thus, Ahaz's security is not primarily an issue of power or politics—it is primarily an issue of faith.

Then comes God's **warning**, and it is a profound warning indeed. 'If you are not firm in faith, you will not be firm at all.' In other words, your salvation will come through faith, or not at all. As Raymond Ortlund points out: 'God is offering Ahaz the opportunity of a lifetime to experience what it means to be saved by God. But that means Ahaz must treat God as God.'[2]

So Ahaz has a choice: either he can stand firm in faith, being still and quiet, knowing that Yahweh is God and trusting him to keep his

---

1 Oswalt, p. 196.
2 Ortlund, p. 89.

promises, or he can stumble in panic, making poor decisions with tragic consequences.

Ahaz's choice

Unfortunately for the Judeans, King Ahaz is a faithless man. He practises the idolatrous paganism of the neighbouring peoples, even going so far as to sacrifice his own sons in fire.[1] So King Ahaz not will be consulting God about this threat to Jerusalem. Like most Judeans, King Ahaz sees himself as far too sophisticated for that. Like most Jerusalemites, his whole life is lived on a horizontal, worldly level. Ahaz does not honour God as holy, nor does he fear him. Ahaz is only interested in elevating his own status and image.

And now, as the people face the horrors of war, as they quake with fear contemplating the horrors of siege, now, when faith is needed more than ever—there is none! While luxuriating in peace and prosperity, the ungrateful Judeans have carelessly let faith drain away. For who wants God and who needs faith when everything you want is in this world and at your fingertips?

While King Ahaz listened to Isaiah, he obviously was not convinced, because the next thing we see is God offering Ahaz a second chance. Isaiah's record does not reveal how much time had passed. The second chance might have immediately followed the first, while Ahaz was still at the aqueduct, or it might have been days later. We do not know. All we do know is that Ahaz was in need of a second chance, and God, in a demonstration of longsuffering patience and amazing grace, offered it to him.

> [10]Again the LORD addressed Ahaz, and said, [11]'Ask a sign for yourself from the LORD your God, whether in the depths below or the heights above.' [12]But Ahaz said, 'I will not. I will not put the LORD to the test.' [13]Then Isaiah said, 'Take heed, O house of David! Is it not enough for you to try the patience of men? Must you also try the patience of my God?' (7:10–13).[2]

God asks Ahaz to test him, and to not hold back but to make the test as hard as he likes. God is offering to perform for Ahaz whatever sign or miracle it would take to convince him to trust God. God is not

---

1 2 Chronicles 28:3.
2 Avraham Gileadi's translation, *Gileadi*, p. 286.

expecting Ahaz to leap into the dark with his fingers crossed. Even though God has already parted the Red Sea, delivered his people from slavery, made Mount Sinai tremble, brought down the walls of Jericho, and so on, he is still willing to endure Ahaz's faithlessness a little longer if he might only have an opportunity to prove personally to Ahaz that he is absolutely worthy of his trust, and that faith in God is totally rational and reasonable. But Ahaz declines the offer.

Raymond Ortlund comments:

> God hands him [Ahaz] a blank cheque, but Ahaz refuses to cash it. Why? He doesn't want to trust God. Sure he puts it in pious language (Deuteronomy 6:16). But it's all quick-thinking diplomatic hypocrisy. He knows there are strings attached. If he lets God in, God will take control. And for Ahaz, that would mean using God's strategies to get through the crisis and giving God the glory for the outcome. Ahaz proves here that faith can be refused by the will, no matter how strong the evidences. If we don't want God, we can find a way to make our unbelief sound plausible, even pious.[1]

While God was literally saying 'test me!', it was actually Ahaz who was being tested. Ahaz declines God's offer (v. 12) because he knows that if God comes through then he will have to trust him, and he does not want to do that, for his mind is made up. He wants to do things his way. He will ask Assyria for help against the Syro-Ephramite conspiracy. Assyria is the strongest force in the region. 'Assyria will save me,' Ahaz reasoned. 'Assyria will cut Pekah and Rezin down to size. And then, instead of them looking down their noses at me, it will be me looking down on them! I wouldn't want God getting in the way of this!'

Notice that in verse 11, God exhorts Ahaz to test '*your* God', but by verse 13 Isaiah is rebuking Ahaz for wearying '*my* God'. Ahaz's rejection of God in verse 12 changed everything! God is no longer Ahaz's God. This was indeed a pivotal moment in the history of God's people.

Ahaz rejected the warning: 'If you are not firm in faith, you will not be firm at all' (7:9b) for he clearly did not believe it. Instead, Ahaz believed he was quite capable of standing firm in his own wisdom.

---

1 Ortlund, p. 90.

So Ahaz sent messengers to Tiglath-pileser king of Assyria, saying, 'I am your servant and your son. Come up and rescue me from the hand of the king of Syria and from the hand of the king of Israel, who are attacking me.' Ahaz also took the silver and gold that was found in the house of the LORD and in the treasures of the king's house and sent a present to the king of Assyria. And the king of Assyria listened to him ... (2 Kings 16:7–9).

The king of Assyria rescues Ahaz

During the following year (734 BC), Tiglath-pileser III led a military campaign down the Mediterranean Coast as far south as Gaza. He punished the Philistines for their rebellion and cut the supply lines between Egypt and the Palestinian states.

The next year (733 BC), Tilgath-pileser III led his Assyrian forces against Israel. Invading via the Huleh Basin, north of the Sea of Galilee, the Assyrian Army swept through northern Israel, capturing and fortifying key cities as they advanced:

In the days of Pekah king of Israel, Tiglath-pileser king of Assyria came and captured Ijon, Abel-beth-maacah, Janoah, Kedesh, Hazor, Gilead, and Galilee, all the land of Naphtali, and he carried the people captive to Assyria. Then Hoshea the son of Elah made a conspiracy against Pekah the son of Remaliah and struck him down and put him to death and reigned in his place ... (2 Kings 15:29–30)

Tiglath-pileser III annexed eighty percent of Israel, converting it into four new Assyrian provinces: Dor, Megiddo, Gilead and Karnaim. Israel survived, but only as a greatly diminished entity. While Samaria was still its capital, Hoshea, having seized power in yet another violent coup, was now its king.

Then, in the following year (732 BC), Tiglath-pileser III's forces invaded and conquered Damascus, and converted Syria into an Assyrian province:

The king of Assyria marched up against Damascus and took it, carrying its people captive to Kir, and he killed Rezin (2 Kings 16:9).

As King Ahaz travelled to meet the victorious Tiglath-pileser III in

50

Damascus, he must have felt vindicated and very proud. The reality was, however, that he had sold Judah's sovereignty and was up to his neck in debt to King Tiglath-pileser III of Assyria, who 'afflicted him instead of strengthening him' (2 Chronicles 28:20). For even though Ahaz gave gifts of gold and silver to Tiglath-pileser III, 'it did not help him' (v. 21).

Evidently Ahaz had believed the myth: 'the enemy of my enemy is my friend'. He believed he could guarantee his security by allying with the regional superpower. Driven by naivety, short-term considerations and political expediency, Ahaz did not think about the long-term implications of his actions—of what might be the consequences of opening the floodgates to an aggressive, imperialistic superpower so that it might advance right up to Judah's northern border.

Eventually Judah too would fall prey to Assyria's imperialistic aggression. (Assyria invaded Judah in 701 BC). Ortlund writes:

> Someone has said that this whole episode was like a mouse attacked by two rats, squeaking for the cat to come and save him. The cat did (2 Kings 16:5–9) but the mouse ended up as dessert.[1]

―――

The church's choice

There are some timeless truths here that we should consider in relation to the global church, the local church and the scattered church (Christian individuals). The only way to have God as your God is to trust him. If we are not firm in faith, we will not be firm at all. But what does this mean for us in practice?

Contrary to popular thinking, trusting God is not passive: it is not resignation! Trusting God involves actively and diligently seeking God's perspective and will, with a commitment to actively and diligently walking in the light of the Lord (2:5).

We seek God's perspective and will by actively and diligently studying God's word so we are familiar with how God has worked throughout history (or 'his-story'); so we might come to know more of God's

―――――――

1 Ortlund, p. 91.

character, his promises and what he demands of us; and so we might understand more about his eternal plan.

Further, we must always seek God's perspective and will through persistent, diligent prayer. This is not 'dictator prayer', where we arrogantly tell God what we are doing in order to invoke or command a blessing. Neither is it 'Matrix prayer', where we ask God for guidance and then just passively wait for God to download all required knowledge and understanding into our brain (as in the movie, *The Matrix*). Those genuinely seeking God's perspective and direction must pray the humble prayer of a trusting dependant. We must let God's word and Spirit take our every thought captive.[1] Then we must obey in faith.

As we diligently pray and study God's word in search of God's perspective and will, we must remain alert and open to the fact that God's ways are not our ways.[2] Invariably, God's ways are not the ways of the world, and walking in his ways invariably requires radical faith. Furthermore, God's plans invariably (and thankfully) reveal his character and his glory—not ours. So if our plans depend on people and elevate humanity, then, regardless of good intentions and despite earthly praise, they are doubtless plans of human origin and are not of God.

Do not imagine that the walk of faith will be easy. We are fallen, mortal and fragile 'jars of clay'[3] with hearts that cannot be trusted.[4] We mean well but struggle with sin—particularly pride—and are prone to error.[5] And so the walk of faith can be a slow and tentative walk: two steps forward (rejoice!), one step back (repent!). But as long as we are motivated by a heart that is humble, trusting, and committed to obedience, then it will be a forward progression. Pride, and an addiction to human praise, will ruin everything—so 'stop regarding man' (2:22).

Our daily devotions should include a rejection of pride and a commitment to, and affirmation of, humble trust. The hands we lift up to God should be empty of human boastings and personal agendas,

---

1 2 Corinthians 10:3–6.
2 Isaiah 55:8–9.
3 2 Corinthians 4:7.
4 Jeremiah 17:9.
5 Romans 7:18–25.

while our minds should be convinced that trusting God is the most reasonable thing on earth. Of course, the greatest reason of all to trust God is that he has shown us the extent of his love, in that 'while we were still sinners, Christ died for us' (Romans 5:8).

As the church, as local churches, as Christian organisations and Christian individuals, we need to examine ourselves, asking: do we really trust God and his word? Do we routinely seek God's perspective? Are we prepared to take God's advice, believe his promises and heed his warnings? Or do we routinely choose to go our own way and put our trust in someone or something else?

Are we prepared to submit to God's will for our lives even if it means running a race[1] that we would not have chosen for ourselves—a race that takes us through singleness, poverty, chronic illness, mission in a hostile land, persecution or war?

If you had a suspicion that God might be calling you to step out in radical faith for the gospel's sake, would you want him to confirm that to you so you could obediently walk in his ways? After all, God's perspective on the matter would no doubt be that a life lived in obedience to him would bring you more satisfaction and God more glory than anything you could ever imagine. Or would you, like Ahaz, rather not know, preferring to make your own plans because according to your perspective, enduring singleness, poverty, chronic ill health, the trials of mission, persecution or war, could surely be nothing other than miserable and you have other ideas?

God has demonstrated his power, wisdom, love and faithfulness over and over and over again. We have no excuses. God does not usually fill us in on all the details of what he is doing, but he does ask us to trust him. And trust demonstrates itself in obedience. If Adam and Eve had trusted God in the Garden of Eden, then they would not have believed the devil's lie and fallen into temptation.

When faith-testing times come upon us—and they will come (John 16:33)—will we trust God enough to seek his perspective and will (James 1:5[2]), and then obey in faith that he will be true to his character and faithful to his promises?

---

1 Hebrews 12:2.

2 'If any of you lacks wisdom, let him ask God, who gives generously to all without reproach, and it will be given him' (James 1:5).

If we will not trust God, then we will ultimately trust someone or something else.

It is essential that we actively build up faith now in preparation for faith-testing times. It is urgent, for the principle that applied to Ahaz also applies to us: 'If you are not firm in faith, you will not be firm at all.'

Questions for contemplation or discussion

1. Have you experienced testing times when trusting God and following his word seemed exceeding difficult, but in hindsight you are very glad you did trust and obey for God proved faithful and his word proved true?

   Write down one such account as a testimony to how trusting God and walking by faith is worth it, even when circumstances make it difficult. (If in a group: share your testimony.)

2. God's advice to King Ahaz—be quiet, fear not and stand firm; and his promise—'it [the Syro-Ephraimite plot] will not come to pass'; were both based on God's heavenly perspective—that Kings Rezin and Pekah were fading lights; and on his promise (the Davidic covenant) which guaranteed the security of David's heir.

   Consider some of the worst threats facing the Church today.

   (a) What might God's perspective be—of the enemy?

   —of their Christian victims?

   (b) To what promises might we anchor our hopes and prayers?

   Here are a few to start with.
   Add to this list as many helpful promises as you can:

   Isaiah 40:31; Psalm 146:7–9; Habakkuk 2:14; Matthew 28:20b; John 16:33; Romans 16:20.

3. The key verse in God's advice to King Ahaz is Isaiah 7:9b.

   'If you are not firm in faith, you will not be firm at all.' (ESV)

   'If you do not stand firm in your faith, you will not stand at all.' (NIV)

   What exactly is God saying?

   How might this apply to your own situation?

Prayer

I believe, help my unbelief.

My Lord and God,
You alone are sovereign over all principalities and powers—
    in heaven and on the earth.
You are not intimidated by any amount of human bluster,
or any threat that any man or woman or army or nation might issue.
Indeed the nations are like 'a drop from a bucket' to you,
    like 'dust on the scales' (Isaiah 40:15).

I praise you Father for you are not a God who is far off and removed,
    but one who is near and profoundly interested in every single
    aspect of my life:
        material, political and economical;
        physical, emotional and spiritual.

Forgive me Lord, for the times I failed to seek your perspective on
    these matters.

Forgive me Lord, for the times I forgot or resisted your promises,
    and responded in fear of what I saw
    rather than in faith in what I knew.

I thank you Lord for your long-suffering patience and grace.
I humbly thank you for the countless second chances and for your
    willingness to forgive.
I praise you for your faithfulness;
    indeed, you are absolutely worthy of my trust.
Great is your faithfulness!

May your Holy Spirit work powerfully in me to increase my faith,
so that I might be deeply rooted and firmly established in you my
    Rock (Psalm 1; Mattthew 7:24–27; Psalm 18:2).
For I do not want to wither, topple, collapse or be swept away when
    hard-times flood in.
I want to be a witness that stands firm in faith, not only for my own
    sake, but for the Church's sake, so your grace, power and glory
    might be revealed to the world.

Lord, you have assured me that
'All things are possible for one who believes.' (Mark 9:23)
And so it is in earnestness that I cry to you,
'I believe, help my unbelief!' (Mark 9:24)

For the sake of your Church and for glory of the Lord,

Amen.

CHAPTER 3

A paradigm for threatened Christians

Isaiah 8:5–17

With Judah at war and haemorrhaging from three fronts and Jerusalem facing the prospect of imminent siege, God invites King Ahaz of Judah to rest and trust in him, while warning that salvation will come through faith or not at all.

> Be careful, be quiet, do not fear, and do not let your heart be faint … If you are not firm in faith, you will not be firm at all (Isaiah to Ahaz, king of Judah, Isaiah 7:4a, 9b).

After weighing up his options—faithful, covenant God or regional superpower—Ahaz elects to put his faith in the regional superpower, Assyria. In doing so, Ahaz opens the floodgates for aggressive, imperialist Assyria to sweep into the Levant.

With their enemies subdued and the conspirators dead, the Judeans rejoice over Ahaz's foreign policy success, his diplomatic coup d'état. How Ahaz must have reveled and gloried in it! Yet once again, the divine perspective—the view from timeless heaven—was quite different. As far as Ahaz was concerned, his foreign policy initiatives and his skillful, strategic diplomacy had saved Jerusalem and guaranteed her security. From God's perspective however, Ahaz's faithless act of covenantal betrayal had opened Judah up to disaster (the consequence of folly) and judgement (the consequence of rebellion and sin).

How God must have grieved, for he knew the extent to which Ahaz was deceiving himself and all Judah. Isaiah must also have grieved, for he knew full well what the consequences would be. And so, while Ahaz reveled in his perceived gains—fame, glory, political security through success in war, national security through an alliance with the regional superpower—Isaiah contemplated covenant curses in the light of the fact that it is the nature of aggressive imperialism to keep moving forward, advancing and consolidating, stage by stage.

If Isaiah and his message of radical faith in a faithful God had a following in 735 BC, it doubtless shrank to a very small remnant as the post-war years of peace and security rolled by. It is hard to imagine Judeans thinking, 'Oh dear, what have we done?' For on the surface, everything looked just fine. Only those who dared look deeper and think harder could have perceived that the peace they were enjoying was nothing other than the calm before the storm.

A mighty flood of trouble is on its way

When God addresses Isaiah again, it is to paint a very bleak picture indeed—a picture of catastrophe and judgement in the form of Assyrian invasion.

> The LORD spoke to me again: 'Because this people has refused the waters of Shiloah that flow gently, and rejoice over Rezin and the son of Remaliah, therefore, behold, the Lord is bringing up against them the waters of the River, mighty and many, the king of Assyria and all his glory. And it will rise over all its channels and go over all its banks, and it will sweep on into Judah, it will overflow and pass on, reaching even to the neck, and its outspread wings will fill the breadth of your land, O Immanuel' (8:5–8).

What God is saying here, is that because this people have refused to walk by faith and accept God's help (i.e. the waters of Shiloah that flow gently) and because they are rejoicing over the violent deaths of Rezin and the son of Remaliah (unlike God, who takes no pleasure in the death of anyone[1]) therefore they will have the object of their hope, the military power of Assyria (i.e. 'the waters of the River', the Euphrates 'mighty and many') all the way up to their necks! For like most raging floodwaters, the torrents sweeping in from the north will not be easily controlled or contained. Eventually 'the River' (the Euphrates, 'the king of Assyria and all his glory') will spill over its banks and flood into Judah, overwhelming Immanuel's land.

---

1 Ezekiel 18:32.

But God is with us

Then, fired up with indignation and burning with zeal, Isaiah lifts his voice, and no doubt his fist, and shouts in defiance to the surrounding enemies:

> Be broken, you peoples, and be shattered;
>   give ear, all you far countries;
> strap on your armour and be shattered;
>   strap on your armour and be shattered.
> Take counsel together, but it will come to nothing;
>   speak a word, but it will not stand,
>   for God is with us (8:9–10).

And so Isaiah passionately attests to that which God has already promised, that despite all their military might and worldly wisdom, the plots and schemes of enemy nations cannot and 'will not stand' (7:7), because 'God is with us' (8:10). All God's faithful need to do is stand firm in faith.

Terrible days lie ahead for all in Judah, including the faithful. However, while the faithful will be caught up in suffering alongside the rebellious, they will not suffer as the rebellious. God has an important and very specific word for them—it is a paradigm for threatened believers, and it comes with the promise that they will have sanctuary amidst the flood.

And so, as seriously faith-testing times loom, God delivers this hugely important word to Isaiah, impressing it upon him through an especially profound experience. It was as if the Almighty came to Isaiah, placed his hands firmly on his shoulders, looked into his eyes with piercing firmness and spoken in tones of firm resolve:

> For the LORD spoke thus to me with his strong hand upon me,
> and warned me not to walk in the way of this people, saying:
> 'Do not call conspiracy all that this people calls conspiracy, and
> do not fear what they fear, nor be in dread. But the LORD of
> hosts, him you shall honour as holy. Let him be your fear, and
> let him be your dread. And he will become a sanctuary and
> a stone of offense and a rock of stumbling to both houses of
> Israel, a trap and a snare to the inhabitants of Jerusalem. And
> many shall stumble on it. They shall fall and be broken; they
> shall be snared and taken' (8:11–15).

A paradigm for threatened believers

God warns Isaiah 'not to walk in the way of this people' (v. 11). Rather, Isaiah is to remain firm in his commitment to walk by faith, in the light of the Lord, even though it appears that everyone else has chosen to walk by sight, trusting in limited human strength and questionable human wisdom from dubious human sources.

Jerusalem was abuzz with rumours and accusations of conspiracy, and the people's hearts were shaking with fear, like trees in the wind (7:2). And because they had come to regard their sovereign Redeemer God as irrelevant, they had invested all their hope in fallen, limited, mortal, worldly 'saviours' that would eventually either fail or devour them.

And so, with compelling power and sense of great urgency, God warns Isaiah not to walk the way they walk, not to think the way they think, and not to feel the way they feel. God's faithful remnant is to be different. Though the tide of popular opinion rise against them, they are to stand firm in faith.

Then God warns Isaiah: 'Do not call conspiracy [Hebrew = *qešer*] all that this people calls conspiracy…' (8:12). But what might the people have been calling a conspiracy? Judah's neighbours were conspiring to capture and annex Jerusalem and replace Ahaz with a puppet. That was clearly a conspiracy, so why would God caution Isaiah not to call it that?

In commenting on the Hebrew text, Motyer notes: 'On all its other thirteen occurrences (e.g. 2 Samuel 15:12; 2 Kings 11:14) *qešer* (conspiracy) means internal treason', as distinct from foreign plot.[1]

But as Motyer observes, as far as we know there was no internal conspiracy posing a threat to Ahaz. Of course, it is quite possible that a 'fifth column' did exist inside Judah, of dissidents who supported an anti-Assyrian position and who might have even backed the Syro-Ephramite plan to bring about regime change in Jerusalem. Or maybe the pro-Assyrian Judean majority, keen to see Syria and Israel humbled and subjugated, was accusing Isaiah of being a traitor and conspirator on account of his opposition. But this is all pure conjecture, for the Bible does not report any such thing.

There is however, another conspiracy afoot here—one that is going

---

1 Internal/domestic conspiracy (i.e. treason) = *qešer* (as in Isaiah 8:12).
  External/foreign conspiracy = *qašar* (as in Nehemiah 4:8) (Motyer, p. 94).

unnoticed. And it is this unrecognised, unremarked conspiracy—the supreme conspiracy, the supreme treason—that God warns Isaiah to reject.

To understand this conspiracy, we need to understand the nature of covenants: what it meant for a vassal (a weaker, lesser king) to be in a covenant relationship with a suzerain (a stronger, overlord, protector king), and what it meant for Israel/Judah to be in a covenant relationship with God.

The conspiracy against the Lord

Examining suzerain-vassal treaties

Theologian Michael Horton comments:

> One of the remarkable examples of God's providence is the rise of the international treaty ... Before a single word of the Bible was penned, the ancient Near East already had in place a secular version of the covenant in the form of suzerain-vassal treaties. A suzerain was a great king, like an emperor, while a vassal was what we would today call a 'client state' ... The treaties from the Hittite Empire (1450–1180 BC) are especially similar to what we find in the Bible.[1]

It was a time when the primary political unit was the city-state, and treaties were the main means of organising inter-city affairs on various issues from trade relations to border disputes. Delbert Hillers writes:

> In this atmosphere of lively, and formal, diplomatic interchange, it was inevitable that there should be fixed forms for concluding alliances. The major problem faced was one of enforcement, which makes it only half-correct to think of ancient treaties as belonging to 'international law' ... In the desire to achieve some kind of good faith among nations, to replace a state of constant war by peace, recourse was to oath, to the gods.

Thus, the

> ancient use of the oath made sense; it filled important gaps in the network of law.

---

1 Michael Horton, *Introducing Covenant Theology*, Baker Books, Grand Rapids MI, 2006, pp. 23–4.

An ancient treaty, then, is essentially an elaborate oath. There are two fundamental components: the thing to be performed, and the oath, the invoking of divine vengeance in case the promise is not kept.[1]

Today, when the strong exploit an opportunity to expand their empire by rescuing a weaker force today, they generally do it under the cover of 'humanitarian intervention'. Consider the US-NATO intervention in Kosovo, Serbia, in 2000, and the Russian intervention in South Ossetia, Georgia, in 2008.

In ancient times, a vulnerable or threatened king of a weak state would appeal to a great king, usually an emperor, for protection through incorporation into his empire. Usually, a great king would be eager to exploit any opportunity to expand his empire by 'rescuing' a besieged or threatened weaker king. The relationship between the suzerain and the vassal was then defined and codified in a written treaty, sworn before the gods.

These Near-Eastern suzerain treaties always included the following elements:

- *The preamble:* 'thus saith' the suzerain's name and title—as in contemporary international politics, the stronger power—the suzerain—always set the terms.

- *The historical prologue:* '… who rescued you from …'—a recounting of the historical situation that justified the suzerain's demands.

- *The stipulations:* '… you shall … you shall not…'

- *The sanctions:* the proscribed penalties for rebellion—for example, eviction from homes and exile from lands.

- *The blessings and curses* from the gods, to be delivered in response to the vassal's keeping or breaking of faith. These gods were always on the side of the strongman (the suzerain), and the punishments they could deliver (i.e. total annihilation) were always unreasonably disproportionate to the alleged crimes but proportional to the alleged greatness of the god being offended.

- The *list of witnesses.*

---

1 Delbert R. Hillers, *Covenant: The History of a Biblical Idea,* The Johns Hopkins Press, Baltimore & London 1969, pp. 27–28.

- *The provision* for the deposit of the treaty texts into the temples of both parties for the benefit of the peoples and their gods.

While vassals were authorised to call upon the suzerain for protection, they were also obliged to maintain loyalty and the payment of tribute. Horton writes:

> Far from being arbitrary, merely legal dos and don'ts, the stipulations were an utterly reasonable duty. They fit the character of the liberation these ancient people had experienced. Typically they involved the following: no backroom alliances with other kings, no murmuring against the suzerain, and payment of an annual tribute tax to the great king.[1]

Examining the Sinai and Davidic covenants

At Mount Sinai, the nation of Israel entered into such a covenant relationship with God. The Sinai covenant followed the pattern of a Near-Eastern suzerain treaty. The Lord God, as suzerain, made a unilateral covenant (agreement) with this people whom he rescued out of Egypt, out of the land of slavery,[2] promising that if they would obey his laws then they would be his treasured possession and he would be with them as their God to protect and bless them.[3]

Isaiah scholar Avraham Gileadi notes that the Sinai Covenant required the loyalty of the people, the entire people, to a person, making it a difficult covenant to keep. Gileadi explains:

> After the conquest of Canaan, when Israel's loyalty to the Lord lapses, the Lord's protection of his people also lapses, and by the time of Samuel and Saul, the Philistines threaten Israel's very existence. When Israel demands a king, Samuel reminds them that the Lord is their King—their suzerain (1 Samuel 8:4–10; 12:12).[4]

Samuel reminded the people that if they only obeyed the Lord's covenant, then he would protect and bless them as promised. But the people demanded to have a king who would fight their battles for

1 Horton, p. 27.
2 Exodus 20:2.
3 Exodus 19:5–6.
4 Gileadi, p. 69.

them—just like the other nations. And so the Lord granted the people a king.

Once they had a king, God's protection would be on the same basis as in ancient Near-Eastern treaties: that is, not by virtue of the people's agreement with the suzerain (God)—as in the case of the Sinai covenant—but because a vassal, their king, demonstrated loyalty towards the suzerain (God). 'All that is now required of the people,' writes Gileadi,

> is to exercise loyalty toward their king. A human king, in effect, stands in for the Lord as the people's suzerain, while he himself serves as the Lord's vassal. With the advent of human kingship, the Sinai covenant thus grows less prominent because it follows the pattern of a separate and secondary agreement between a suzerain and a people.[1]

Then, through the Davidic covenant, God added a further dimension to the relationship. Firstly, the Davidic covenant included the conditional element:

> Those who are loyal to the Davidic king obtain the Lord's protection by proxy so long as the king maintains loyalty towards the Lord. The suzerain (the Lord) is bound [by the covenant] to protect the people of the vassal (King David) when the vassal fulfils the terms of the covenant.[2]

In Near-Eastern treaties, when a vassal proved themselves faithful and loyal, the suzerain could symbolically 'adopt' them as an heir, guaranteeing dynastic succession, preserving the name on the throne. Likewise, God covenanted with loyal David concerning his heir: 'I shall be to him a father, and he shall be to me a son' (2 Samuel 7:14).

Secondly, the Davidic Covenant's promise of an enduring dynasty was absolutely unconditional: '... your house and your kingdom shall be made sure forever before me. Your throne shall be established forever' (2 Samuel 7:16; see also 2 Samuel 7:1–17 and Psalm 89:3–4, 20–37).

So, herein lies the supreme conspiracy: King Ahaz, the Lord's vassal, has pledged his allegiance to another king—to King Tiglath-pileser III of Assyria. Furthermore, when Ahaz appeals to Tiglath-pileser III he presents himself as 'your servant and your son' (2 Kings 16:7),

---

1 Gileadi, pp. 69–70.
2 Gileadi, p. 71.

betraying God not only as his Lord (king and suzerain) but as his Father. This is the *real* conspiracy. It is unnoticed and unremarked, and *it is a conspiracy against the Lord.*

Examining Jesus Christ our King

As Christians, we are servants and adopted sons and daughters of God.[1] Our Saviour, Jesus Christ—son of David, Son of God—fulfilled the covenant on our behalf and now sits on David's throne as our king for all eternity over a kingdom that can never be shaken.[2]

Far too many Christians today think that to have Jesus as Lord means to have him merely as a friend, life-coach or role model. But to have Jesus as Lord is to have him as king. And to have Jesus as king is a privilege not to be underestimated: it is the most awesome blessing available to humanity. For Jesus Christ is not like worldly kings: 'The King of love my Shepherd is, whose goodness faileth never. I nothing lack if I am his, and he is mine forever.'[3] He reigns for our benefit.[4]

So, when our faith is tested; when we are challenged, persecuted, threatened or besieged by troubles or hostile forces; to whom or to what should we turn, and in whom or in what should we trust? We have a mighty, loving king—Jesus Christ the son of David and King of Kings—who is faithful and worthy of our absolute trust.

So, could it ever be acceptable for Christians to refuse him in order to invest their hopes elsewhere? Post-modernists would say that each person has to determine the pathway or strategy that works best for them. But surely, when Christians decide to turn from the Lord in order to invest their hopes in political powers, military might and the worldly wisdom, then this is nothing less than *a conspiracy against the Lord* inspired by nothing other than sheer faithlessness. And nothing tempts Christian men and women, even great Christian leaders, to conspire against the Lord like hardship or persecution or existential threat.

In fact, it is quite common to find Christians, when faced with hardship or persecution, jumping immediately into activism, quick-as-a-flash,

---

1 1 John 3:1.
2 Hebrews 12:28–29.
3 Hymn: 'The King of love my Shepherd is' (Psalm 23), Henry William Baker (1821–1877).
4 Ephesians 1:22.

in order to fix things. 'No time to think,' they reason, 'for we gotta act! And there's no time to pray—but never mind, there's no need to pray, for we can fix this all by ourselves. And if God has plans of his own [which of course he does], then we don't want to know about it, for our minds are already made up. We'll tell God our plans—not the other way around! "Assyria" is available, so we'll go to "Assyria" for help, despite the fact that we'll be obliged to subjugate ourselves as servants and sons to liars, dictators and aggressors.'

As someone who has spent more than a dozen years engaged in full-time religious liberty analysis and advocacy for the persecuted church, I can attest that this is far more common than many loyal believers would care to imagine. In fact, it was the growing prevalence and acceptance of conspiracies against the Lord—in our churches and Christian organisations—that provided the impetus for this book.

Fear not!

It is not inconsequential that the very next thing God warns Isaiah against is misplaced fear, for nothing drives Christians to make very bad choices and conspire against the Lord, like misplaced fear: 'and do not fear what they fear, nor be in dread. But the LORD of hosts, him you shall honour as holy. Let him be your fear, and let him be your dread' (8:12–13).

More than 700 years later, Jesus would use similar words when speaking about persecution and the hostile forces that would rail against the church (Matthew 10:16–39): '... have no fear of them...' (v. 26), '... do not fear those who kill the body but cannot kill the soul. Rather fear him who can destroy both soul and body in hell' (v. 28).

Likewise, the apostle Peter speaks to those suffering for righteousness' sake, saying: 'Have no fear of them, nor be troubled, but in your hearts honour Christ the Lord as holy ...' (1 Peter 3:14–15).

We are not to fear hardship or the forces that persecute and threaten us. We are only to fear (reverence, honour) the Lord. This is why 'looking to Jesus' or 'eyes fixed on Jesus' as both the founder and the perfecter of our faith (Hebrews 12:2) must be the motto of all believers, but especially of struggling, troubled, threatened, besieged and persecuted believers.

We are not to fear what the world fears—we are to be different. While the world is fixated on and terrified by what it sees, God's children are to be fixated on and comforted by what they know. And we should remember that our God, who is faithful by nature, is both willing and able to care for our every need. He is motivated by everlasting love (*hesed*), and enabled by sovereign power. Equipped with this knowledge and energised by this memory, true believers can find peace amidst any storm.

It is a person's attitude towards or belief concerning the Lord that determines whether, when confronted by tribulation, they will look to the world and panic, or look to the Lord and find peace. If we believe God is irrelevant, or unwilling or unable to save, then all we have is what we see—and that could be devastating and terrifying. But if we sanctify God by honouring him as holy, then we will look to him in faith and find a perspective that calms us, enabling peace despite circumstances. Gileadi's translation of Isaiah 8:12–13 is clear and beautiful: 'be not afraid or awed by the thing they fear. But sanctify the Lord of Hosts, making him your fear, him your awe.'[1]

Promise: the Lord will be to you a sanctuary

God then gives Isaiah an awesome promise and an amazing insight (Gileadi's translation):

> And to you [who honour and fear him] he will be a sanctuary,
> but to the two houses of Israel a stumbling block or obstruction
> rock, and a snare, catching unawares the inhabitants of
> Jerusalem. Many will stumble into them, and when they fall
> shall be broken, and when they become ensnared shall be
> taken captive (8:14–15).[2]

The promise is that to those who faithfully honour, fear and trust him, the Lord will be to them a *sanctuary*. Meanwhile, faithless rebels do not just travel merrily down their own path. For the Lord is a reality: he is there whether we acknowledge him or not. Those who refuse to acknowledge him inevitably stumble over him, with devastating consequences.

In days of hardship and escalating persecution, the concept of the Lord as sanctuary can be very comforting and appealing. But it is

---

1 Gileadi, p. 288.
2 Gileadi, pp. 288–9.

essential that we understand what this means, for misunderstandings elicit unrealistic expectations that, when not fulfilled, leave people dismayed, disappointed, disconcerted and disillusioned.

Clearly, not everyone who trusts God and honours him as holy is physically delivered from worldly troubles. Those who preach that God delivers the faithful from all their worldly troubles not only elevate those whom God has healed or delivered as faith-giants—giving men and women the glory that should be God's—but they judge every sick, disabled, poor, marginalised, abused, bereaved or persecuted believer as undeserving due to insufficient faith. They preach faith as a work that merits materialistic reward in this life, when the Bible teaches us that faith is the free gift of a gracious God, not a work in which anyone can boast.[1] Furthermore, the Bible is unambiguous in its assertion that tribulations are inevitable, and that faith can be very costly.

The facts speak for themselves: many a faithful saint was serving the Lord in humble trust when they succumbed to terminal disease or some other tragedy. Likewise, many a faithful missionary—from the first apostles to the modern day—was obeying God in faith when they were unjustly imprisoned or violently martyred. God does not decry the abused, mistreated, tortured and martyred saints of Hebrews 11 as men and women not worthy of blessings in this world. Rather, God exalts them as those of whom the world was not worthy.[2]

So what does it mean to have God as our 'sanctuary'? The Hebrew word found in Isaiah 8:14 is, *miqdāš*—sanctuary—that is, a holy place, a sacred place, the place where God dwells amongst the people in all his holiness.[3] And is not this the mark of true believers—that God is with us? The promise is that faithful believers, who trust God enough to walk in his light, will find God with them in the midst of their troubles. Furthermore, God will be working in and through them according to his sovereign plan and purpose. This sanctuary, this place of intimate communion with God in the midst of earthly troubles, is a place of supernatural peace and strength. It is a spiritual refuge where the faithful, regardless of how physically weak or inherently powerless they may appear, receive divine strength to soar as if on eagles' wings.[4]

---

1 Ephesians 2:8.
2 Hebrews 11:35–38.
3 Motyer, p. 95.
4 Isaiah 40:29–31.

Most of us dread hardship, illness, persecution or conflict, fearing we will not have the strength to stand firm in the face of it. But here is God's promise: to those who sanctify God by honouring him as holy—that is, those who let God be God and trust him—he will be to them a sanctuary. He will draw them into his holy presence, into his holy of holies, into a wholly and holy other realm, before he shuts the door behind them. God does all the work and makes all the provision, which is why we do not need to fear, we need only trust and obey.

Surely this is one of the most beautiful promises in all scripture. Prosperity theology—'God wants you to be rich healthy and perpetually happy' theology—not only defies reality, it corrupts, disappoints and ruins lives. Meanwhile, biblical theology addresses reality head on, while opening the door to supernatural peace and strength amidst the storms of life.

And so the paradigm for threatened believers is this:

Do not *walk* the way the world walks (as if God were irrelevant) (8:11).

Do not *think* as the world thinks (only materially and politically) (8:12a).

Do not *fear* what the world fears (pain, poverty, persecution, etc.) (8:12b).

Think differently (spiritually, honouring the Lord as holy) (8:13a).

Fear differently (fear only the Lord) (8:13b,c).

Walk differently (by faith not by sight), knowing the Lord is with you (8:14a).

God gave this paradigm to Isaiah so he could prepare and fortify himself ahead of seriously faith-testing times (the Assyrian invasion). Isaiah shared this paradigm with his band of disciples to likewise prepare and fortify them. The Holy Spirit had these words immortalised in Scripture for our benefit. But what is the church doing with them?

Isaiah is preaching the radical faith of Psalm 46

Isaiah was not presenting his disciples with a radical new concept. Consider Psalm 46, which opens with the declaration that in the midst of all the chaos of the world: 'God is our refuge and strength, a very present help trouble' (v. 1). 'Therefore,' the psalmist says, 'we will not fear' (v. 2), no matter what (v. 3).

That magnificent theme of God as 'a very present' provider, sustainer, Sovereign and sanctuary is then developed in the psalm's second stanza: 'There is a river whose streams make glad the city of God ...' (v. 4). What river is the psalmist talking about? There is no river running through Jerusalem! Then the psalmist identifies the river: 'God is in the midst of her' (Jerusalem). The Spirit of God himself is the 'river whose streams make glad the city of God'. The gently flowing waters of Shiloah (8:6) are the waters that flow from 'the throne of God and of the Lamb, through the middle of the street of the city [the heavenly Jerusalem] ...' (Revelation 22:1–2). It is because God is in the midst of her (Jerusalem) that 'she shall not be moved'(v. 5a). Every day, though nations rage and kingdoms totter, God is sovereign over all the earth (vv. 5a–6). 'The LORD of hosts is with us,' declares the psalmist. 'The God Jacob is our fortress' (v. 7).

The psalm's third stanza opens with the exhortation to come and see (behold and remember) 'the works of the Lord' (vv. 8–9). Only when God's people are equipped with this knowledge—this memory—can they rise to the occasion and do as God exhorts: 'Be still and know that I am God' (v. 10a). Does that exhortation sound familiar? It sounds very much like Isaiah's 'Be still, be quiet' (7:4) and 'Sanctify the Lord of hosts', or 'honour him as holy' (8:13). And God crowns his exhortation with a promise: 'I will be exalted amongst the nations, I will be exalted in the earth!' (v. 10b,c). And so, with either a sigh of relief and the peace that comes from faith, or with joy and the exhilaration that comes with a proclamation of victory (or maybe both) the psalmist concludes by reinforcing the theme: 'The Lord of hosts is with us; the God of Jacob is our fortress' (v. 11).

And so Isaiah is merely embodying the faith of the psalmist when he elects to stand firm in faith with the Lord as his sanctuary. 'I will wait for the LORD, who is hiding his face from the house of Jacob, and I will hope in him' (8:17).

A paradigm for faith-testing times

It is the most wonderful grace that the King of Kings should love and care for us.

Whenever we feel besieged, challenged or confronted—and even when we do not—God invites us to draw on the same 'waters of Shiloh that flow gently' that were rejected by King Ahaz but which have empowered and sustained the faithful through the ages. It is not a burdensome thing to do—no travelling or carting is required and there is no cost. 'Come, everyone who thirsts, come to the waters … without money and without price' (55:1). For all who are thirsty for the Spirit of God only have to look to God who promises to freely provide us with living water that will become in us 'a spring of water welling up to eternal life' (John 4:14).

Today, as hardship escalates, as global volatility and insecurity increase, and as persecution intensifies, the church (generally) does not seem prepared for faith-testing times. This is serious, for when believers or churches are taken by surprise, hit hard while in a state of unpreparedness, they tend to reel like a like ship caught in a storm without an anchor and a long way from the harbour. Many will suffer a shipwreck experience as a consequence of poor decisions made in haste on account of misplaced fear. And while these unprepared believers might learn much through their experience, unfortunately they are usually not the only ones battered and shaken—so too are all their 'passengers' and all those following in their wake.

As the tide of popular opinion rose in opposition to the prophet, and as the Assyrian 'floodwaters' rose and streamed into the northern Levant, God took great pains to prepare and fortify Isaiah for the faith-testing times ahead. He warned Isaiah not to walk and think and fear as the world does, but to walk and think and fear differently. And to those who live according to this paradigm of radical faith, God promises to be to them a sanctuary, a *miqdāš*.

God gave this paradigm to Isaiah so that he could be braced, anchored, fortified and at peace ahead of the impending calamity. Isaiah shared God's words with his band of disciples so they too might be prepared in advance. The Holy Spirit of God immortalised these words in Scripture for the benefit of all believers throughout the world for all of time.

Ideally the church should be teaching this paradigm to all believers in preparation for faith-testing times.

It is not too late to begin!

Questions for Discussion and Reflection

1. Memorise God's paradigm for threatened believers (Isaiah 8:11–14a):

   - Don't *walk* the way the world walks (as if God were irrelevant) (v11).
   - Don't *think* as the world thinks (only politically and materially) (v12a).
   - Don't *fear* what the world fears (pain, poverty, persecution etc) (v12b).
   - *Think* differently (spiritually, honouring the Lord as holy) (v13a).
   - *Fear* differently (fear only the Lord) (v13b,c).
   - *Walk* differently (by faith not by sight) knowing the Lord is with you (v14a).

2. Do you think knowing this paradigm—which is essentially a guide to counter-cultural living in a hostile world—will help you persevere in faith through testing times?

   Why?

3. Does knowing the Lord's promise—that to those who trust him he will be a sanctuary/*miqdas* (8:14a)—give you confidence that you will be able to endure persecution?

   Why?

4. How does our king, Jesus Christ the Lord, compare to the kings of this world?

   (Consider Psalm 145 and 1 Peter 3:22.)

5. In order to bring you into his marvelous kingdom, Jesus Christ the King of kings came down from heaven and in great humility redeemed you with his own precious blood.

   What is your response to his love?

Prayer

Living for the King.

My God and king,
I praise you as the King of kings and Lord of lords.
    (1 Timothy 6:15–17; Revelation 19:16)
I marvel that you, on account of love, came down and ransomed me,
    rescuing me from the power of sin and death.
Upon the cross of Calvary you shed your blood so that I might live as
    your blessed subject, secure in your unshakable kingdom.
What king on earth ever loved like this?

Lord, forgive me for the times I sought to blend into the world,
    as if I was ashamed of what I am:
    a beloved heir of the awesome and majestic King of glory!

Forgive me for the times I denied you or kept silent
    in order to shield myself from the hostility of the world, even
    after you surrendered to the hostility of the world in order to
    redeem me.

Forgive me for the times I have, in pure carelessness and short-
    sightedness, or even out of misplaced fear, allowed myself to be
    swept up in or devoured by the world
    when you have called me to be different.

Lord, you have been so faithful to me;
    forgive me for the times I have not been faithful to you!

May your Holy Spirit work in me to instill courage and faith enabling
    me to walk, think and fear differently from the world at all times,
    especially in those times when my first inclination would be to
    hide rather than stand out.

I commit to believing and embracing your glorious promise:
    that when I, courageously and in faith,
    walk, think and fear differently from the world,
    then, despite being in the midst of trials,
I *will* know that I am in your midst,
    for your dwelling place *will* be with me,

surrounding and sustaining me in the most remarkable and awesome way.

In this I believe and to this I will cling.

May the devil have no victory over me!

'I will extol you, my God and King,
      and bless your name forever and ever.' (Psalm 145:1)

Amen.

CHAPTER 4

Inquire of the Lord of Hosts:
A radical approach to affliction

Isaiah 9:13

God does not normally reveal to us all the finer details of his plans—thankfully, as that could be very unnerving. Nor, thankfully, does our infinitely wise, just and gracious God ask for our approval or permission before he acts providentially in history. All God asks of us is that we trust him: standing firm in faith,[1] honouring him as holy,[2] walking in his light.[3]

But let us imagine for a moment that God did reveal his plans to us, and that he did seek our approval and permission before proceeding.

Consider these five hypothetical scenarios:

Hypothetical scenario 1: redemptive affliction (personal)
Imagine:

> *God appears before you in all his awesome majesty and reveals that he is going to expose some hidden sin in your life so it can be decisively dealt with—you know, in the same way that a deadly cancer needs to be exposed before it can be decisively dealt with.*
>
> *He warns you that the exposure will be painful and humiliating. 'But,' God assures you, 'this intervention, which arises out of my everlasting love for you, is absolutely necessary if tragedy is to be averted and maturity and sanctification realised.*

---

1 Isaiah 7:9b.
2 Isaiah 8:13.
3 Isaiah 2:5; 2 Corinthians 5:7.

'The grief, anxiety, affliction and humiliation you will experience will stop you in your tracks and shake you to your core. But through it all you will learn much and grow stronger.

'The whole process will take between three days and thirty years— depending on your resistance. But,' he promises, 'the love, joy and peace you find as you repent and draw nearer to me, will more than compensate for your pain.'

But before he departs, God looks you in the eye and asks: 'Is this ok with you?'

There is no doubt about it: sometimes the affliction we suffer is the Lord's anger and tender-loving mercy coming together as redemptive discipline. God strikes us personally, specifically for the purpose of sanctification, that is, that we might become more like Christ. Sometimes, as troubles, shame and threat besiege us, we feel as though life is spinning out of control. Other times we are left feeling as if life's rug has been pulled out from under us (so to speak), leaving us besieged by emptiness and hopelessness. Then, when he has our attention, God calls us to repent of the sin—greed, laziness, lust, anger, pride—that he has exposed.

The godly Elihu spoke to Job of this phenomenon, albeit because he misunderstood Job's situation.

And if they [the righteous] are bound in chains and caught in the cords of affliction, then he declares to them their work and their transgression, that they are behaving arrogantly. He opens their ears to instruction and commands that they return from iniquity (Job 36:8–10).

He delivers the afflicted by their affliction and opens their ears by adversity (Job 36:15).

In other words, sometimes God uses affliction as a bulwark against the advance of sin in a person's life. While this was not the case in Job's affliction, it is doubtless true in many cases. The affliction or humiliation stops the sinner in their tracks and 'opens their ears', making them attentive to God's voice. The divine counsellor—the Holy Spirit[1]—then speaks into the sinner's conscience, piercing shame

---

1 John 16:5–15; Ephesians 6:17; Hebrews 4:12–13.

and trauma to call the sinner to repentance and reconciliation.

Doubtless every Christian has experienced this sort of redemptive affliction to some degree. Though unsought, it is suffering that we nevertheless appreciate greatly in hindsight as we come to recognise its sanctifying, character-building and redemptive nature. Redemptive affliction is indeed a mercy from the hand of God, who loves us so much that he would rather see us afflicted in the short-term than disabled or lost in the long-term.

Jesus knew that pride inhabited Peter's heart. He also knew that this pride would, if left unchecked, become a stumbling block that would prevent Peter from enjoying the fullness that comes through faith. And so the Lord gave the devil permission to test Peter.[1] Proud Peter, confident that he was beyond failure,[2] stood in his own strength and fell, dramatically—denying his beloved Lord three times to save his own skin.[3] The pain Peter felt when the cock crowed and Jesus 'turned and looked at Peter',[4] was like a knife plunging into his heart.[5]

Peter did not want to deny his Lord, for he truly loved him. Jesus knew that. But Jesus also knew that Peter would never 'wait for the Lord'[6] for divine strength so long as he proudly believed his own strength was sufficient. And so, in order to redeem Peter from the crippling, destructive, even deadly sin of pride, God allowed Peter's hidden sin to be exposed through a painful and humiliating failure.

That painful and humiliating confrontation with sin and weakness was an intervention born of divine love and mercy. Through that humiliation, Peter was emptied of the proud self-sufficiency that would have limited him. Peter could now step out into the future fully dependent upon divine empowerment, something Jesus knew Peter would need in large volumes, firstly as a persecuted evangelist in a hostile environment[7] and finally as a martyr. According to tradition, Peter was martyred—crucified upside down—in Nero's Rome in around 34 AD. This was during the great persecution that the Emperor

1 Luke 22:31–32.
2 Luke 22:33.
3 Luke 22:54–60.
4 Luke 22:61.
5 Luke 22:62.
6 Isaiah 40:28–31.
7 Arrested: Acts 4:3; 5:18; 12:2. Threatened: Acts 4:21. Tried: Acts 5:27. Imperilled: Acts 5:33. Imprisoned: Acts 12:4–5.

Nero unleashed against Rome's Christians in the aftermath of his burning of the city.[1]

Hypothetical scenario 2: redemptive affliction (communal)

Imagine:

> God appears before you in all his awesome majesty and reveals that he is going to bring affliction upon your family, your community or your nation 'for their speech and deeds are against the Lord'.[2]

> He warns you that you will see people you love suffering. Furthermore, you will suffer along with them because God is not going to remove you from the situation—he needs you to be there, for as a mortal you have much to learn, and as a Christian you have much to offer.

> However, even though you will suffer along with your brethren, you will not suffer as they suffer, for you will not fear the things they fear. You will be different—or at least you will learn to be. For you are going to learn that through faith, you can have peace, hope and even joy amidst trial.

> God explains that while you stand firm in faith, others around you will be divided. Some will be angry—really angry. They will be angry at God for letting this happen, and they will be angry at you for not being angry. 'Though they reject and hurt you,' says God, 'you are to remain firm in faith. For I will not have finished with them yet!'

> God asks you to trust him and be patient in affliction, because over time some of those around you will come to crave the peace and hope you possess. Opportunities to witness—opportunities like you have never known before and will never know again—will open up to you. You will have unprecedented opportunities to plant gospel seeds of life in the hearts of people you love and care about. For some, your radical response to affliction will be life-changing. For others it will be profoundly thought-provoking. 'Be patient,' God exhorts you, 'for I will not have finished with them yet either.'

---

1 *Foxe's Book of Martyrs*, prepared by W. Grinton Berry, Baker Book House, Grand Rapids MI, USA, 1978, pp 12–13.

2 Isaiah 3:8.

Finally, God assures you that through the trauma, pain and stress—which could take some time—all you need to do is trust him: standing firm in faith, honouring him as holy and walking in his light. He promises to take care of the rest.

But before he departs, God looks you in the eye and asks: 'Is this ok with you?'

There is no doubt about it. Sometimes the Lord judges or strikes a rebellious family, community or nation, and faithful believers are caught up in the midst of it, although not by accident, for our infinitely wise and absolutely trustworthy Sovereign does not have accidents. Believers caught up in such troubles are there by design, for a heavenly purpose.

When God uses affliction to gain the attention of a rebellious people, individuals respond in one of two ways. As Elihu explained to Job (Job 36:5–15), they either listen, repent and return to the Lord in order to serve him—in which case they will be blessed (v. 11); or they get angry and harbour bitterness in their hearts, arrogantly resisting him and stubbornly defying him—in which case they risk dying in their sins (vv. 12–14).

In such cases, God uses affliction to 'sift'[1] or 'winnow'[2] a people. (Winnowing is the process by which threshed (beaten and broken) wheat is tossed into the air by a winnower using a winnowing fork. There the wind then separates the grain from the chaff. The grain returns to be gathered, while the chaff is blown aside to be swept up for the fire.)

This was certainly the case for the citizens of the kingdoms of Israel and Judah during their days of affliction. In Elijah's day, the righteous suffered along with the wicked the full effects of the three-year drought. Likewise in Isaiah's day, the righteous suffered along with the wicked the full trauma of Judah's wars. While the rebellious were offered an opportunity to repent and return to God, the righteous—who were caught up in a disaster not of their making—were assured that if they would just trust him—standing firm in faith, honouring God as holy, walking in his light—then he would be to them a sanctuary.

---

1 Isaiah 30:28.
2 Matthew 3:12; Luke 3:17.

Hypothetical scenario 3: injustice redeemed

Imagine:

> *God appears before you in all his awesome majesty and reveals that a terrible affliction or injustice is about to befall you. However, you are not to fear it. 'For,' God explains, 'I will always be totally in control. I will be at work, redeeming this injustice and using it and you to change the course of history.*
>
> *'Even though you are not without sin (for no one on earth is without sin[1]), this affliction or injustice will have absolutely nothing whatsoever to do with discipline or judgement. You will suffer greatly, and possibly die. But the faith and peace you display as you trust in and love your Sovereign Lord, despite your circumstances, will deeply impact others and bring great glory to God.*
>
> *'On account of your suffering, your unbelieving and indifferent neighbour will take an interest in your testimony. In fact, he will come to faith through your witness. Subsequently he will lead his wife into faith and together they will raise their daughter in the knowledge and memory of God. And I can tell you that this girl, though presently a mere child, will grow into a selfless servant of God whose courageous witness will transform a whole community.*
>
> *'Further to this, on account of your suffering, your rebellious, estranged son will return to you. He will witness your faith and peace amidst trial and it will impact him profoundly. In fact, your example of grace through trial will be foundational in your prodigal child's eventual repentance and salvation. And I can tell you that your son will go on to subsequently establish a godly Christian family that will faithfully pass on the memory of God for generations to come.*
>
> *'Though you will pay a high price for all this through your suffering, you will be greatly compensated. Your relationships with your family and friends will deepen, becoming immeasurably satisfying. You will also discover a more intimate and personal relationship with your Lord than you could ever have imagined, and this will be an absolutely wondrous, precious delight to you, something you would not trade for anything.'*

---

1   1 John 1:8; Romans 3:10.

But before he departs, God looks you in the eye and asks: 'Is this ok with you?'

There is no doubt about it. Sometimes affliction has nothing to do with discipline or judgement. Rather, it is simply the case that God providentially uses for his good purpose what the devil meant for evil.

Joseph might have irritated his older brothers (Genesis 37:1–11) but he certainly did not deserve the evil and unmitigated wickedness they inflicted upon him when they plotted his death and sold him into slavery (Genesis 37:12–36).

However, though evil was at work, God was in control. Though evil had bolted from the stable and was galloping wildly, God put the bit in evil's mouth and the reins over evil's head and rode it to accomplish his own divine purpose.

As Joseph was to later acknowledge to his brothers, while his brothers did sin, God was always in control of the situation, directing history according to his perfect plan. The depth and breadth of Joseph's faith in a just and righteous, sovereign God was demonstrated in his total lack of bitterness.

> I am your brother, Joseph, whom you sold into Egypt. And now do not be distressed or angry with yourselves because you sold me here, for God sent me before you to preserve life. For the famine has been in the land these two years, and there are yet five years in which there will be neither plowing nor harvest. And God sent me before you to preserve for you a remnant on earth, and to keep alive for you many survivors. So it was not you who sent me here, but God (Genesis 45:4–8).

Likewise, the violent persecution that befell the righteous Stephen (Acts 6–7) had nothing to do with discipline. Stephen, described as a man 'full of grace and power',[1] was stoned to death by a jealous, hate-filled mob under the watchful eye of Saul of Tarsus.[2] But God, in sovereign power, redeemed the situation so that this terrible evil proved to be a pivotal moment in church history. For the brutal slaying of Stephen and the subsequent persecution that arose against the church ensured that Jerusalem's growing church could not get comfortable.

---

1 Acts 6:8.
2 Acts 7:54–60.

Instead, the church was forced to pick up its precious gospel message and scatter 'throughout the regions of Judea and Samaria.[1] This was indeed a pivotal moment in the globalisation of Christianity.

Furthermore, Stephen's testimony and grace under siege glorified and continues to glorify God. And God, who is always true to his word, was indeed Stephen's sanctuary to the end, even blessing him with an exhilarating vision of the spiritual reality.[2] Stephen was not abandoned. Rather, even as the stones and rocks rained down on him, pelting his flesh and breaking his bones, Stephen was experiencing God as his sanctuary. The hate-filled mob might have brought him down, but God exalted him to glory. Stephen is a role model and hero of the faith. His example been has immortalised in Scripture for the benefit of the church through the remainder of the age.[3]

Hypothetical scenario 4: suffering as mercy

Imagine:

> *God appears before you in all his awesome majesty and reveals that he is going to let you suffer in order to save you from yourself. He reminds you that you have a fallen nature that is corrupted and weak[4] and a heart that cannot be trusted.[5] So, in order to keep you close and safe, God will limit you through affliction.*

> *God assures you that this affliction is necessary, because without it, your considerable gifts and strengths will only fuel your pride—and 'pride goes before destruction, and a haughty spirit before a fall' (Proverbs 16:18). 'I love you far too much to let that happen,' he assures you.*

> *So while this affliction might seem awful and even cruel, it is not. It will actually be a great mercy through which you will learn to depend upon God who intends to achieve, through you, more than you could even ask or even imagine.[6]*

> *But before he departs, God looks you in the eye and asks: 'Is this ok with you?'*

---

1 Acts 8:1, 4.
2 Acts 7:55–56.
3 Consider also Matthew 10:17–20; Philippians 1:12–14.
4 Romans 7:18.
5 Jeremiah 17:9.
6 Ephesians 3:20–21.

There is no doubt about it. Sometimes our affliction is actually a means of grace. Such was the case with Paul's 'thorn in the flesh', which kept him humble and dependent on the Lord's provision and all-sufficient grace.[1] This 'thorn' provided Paul with a constant reminder of his human frailty, which in turn kept him dependent upon God, who in turn supplied all his needs and provided him with supernatural grace and strength.

And finally …

Hypothetical scenario 5: witnessing to the heavens

Imagine:

God appears before you in all his awesome majesty and reveals that he is about to let the devil test you as he tested Job. You are going to suffer pain, loss and persecution but not on account of discipline. Making matters worse, you will not be able to discern any earthly benefit.

'However,' God explains, 'as you stand firm in faith and honour me as holy, absorbing all the blows that Satan delivers while resisting his temptations, spectacular victories will be won in heavenly places.'

God warns you that the affliction and persecution will be terrible. However, he wants you to know that as you persevere in faith and love, demons will gnash their teeth and beat their heads in frustration, humiliated by failure upon failure. Meanwhile, angels will be amazed by your faith, and will rejoice in wonder and delight that there is such faithfulness and love on earth.

Remember that it is 'through the church' that 'the manifold wisdom of God might now be made known to the rulers and authorities in heavenly places.'[2] 'Your witness,' explains God, 'is never only for the benefit of mortals; and in this case, your witness will actually be specifically for the benefit of spiritual beings.'

---

1 2 Corinthians 12:7–10.
2 Ephesians 3:10. This is the text used by Jonathan Edwards for his most amazing of discourses: 'The Wisdom of God Displayed in the Way of Salvation.'

God warns you that this is a very difficult, misunderstood, and greatly under-rated calling. 'Stay alert,' he warns, 'for Satan will tempt you to anger, bitterness and despair. Do not fear. Trust me, for I am sovereign over all creation, including all principalities and powers.[1] *I will not let you be tempted beyond your ability to endure.*[2] *Memorise 1 Peter 5:6–11*[3] *and be assured, my grace is sufficient for you.'*[4]

But before he departs, God looks you in the eye and asks: 'Is this ok with you?'

There is no doubt about it. Sometimes our affliction is like Job's: it appears to be unfair, unjust, and with no earthly purpose whatsoever. This is exactly how the trial and crucifixion of Jesus appeared to earthly eyes.

We must never lose sight of the fact that we are living in a battleground, not a playground (to quote A. W. Tozer[5]), and the spiritual realm is a reality even if it is invisible. When we faithfully love and trust God for richer for poorer, for better for worse, in sickness and in health, even unto death, then we witness to angels, confound devils and win great spiritual victories in the heavenly realms. This is a high calling indeed.

---

1   1 Peter 3:22: '[Jesus Christ], who has gone into heaven and is at the right hand of God, with angels, authorities, and powers having been subjected to him.'
2   1 Corinthians 10:13.
3   'Humble yourselves, therefore, under the mighty hand of God so that at the proper time he may exalt you, casting all your anxieties on him, because he cares for you. Be sober–minded; be watchful. Your adversary the devil prowls around like a roaring lion, seeking someone to devour. Resist him, firm in your faith, knowing that the same kinds of suffering are being experienced by your brotherhood throughout the world. And after you have suffered a little while, the God of all grace, who has called you to his eternal glory in Christ, will himself restore, confirm, strengthen, and establish you. To him be the dominion forever and ever. Amen (1 Peter 5:6–11).
4   2 Corinthians 12:9.
5   A.W. Tozer, *This World: Playground or Battleground? A Call to the Real World of the Spiritual*, Harry Verploegh (ed.), Christian Publications Inc., Camp Hill PA,1988.

Ephraim's affliction (Isaiah 9:8–10:4)

Clearly it does not require much imagination to see how God can be at work in the midst of suffering and persecution. What it does require is that we think differently: spiritually, not just materially. For when we are afflicted or persecuted, what we need most of all is discernment and insight through the Holy Spirit that we might ascertain God's perspective and will. Because if we can think spiritually, see things from God's perspective and discern his will, then we can 'get on board' (so to speak) and participate in advancing rather than hindering or resisting God's work.

As Saul (Paul) travelled to Damascus in pursuit of Christians to persecute,[1] he was confronted by the risen Christ who appeared to him and said: 'Saul, Saul, why are you persecuting me? It is hard for you to kick against the goads.'[2]

The allusion here is to the ox goad, the instrument used by a farmer or animal handler to move and direct oxen forward. It is basically just a stick with a pointy end used to prick (goad) the ox—usually on the back leg—with the intention of moving it along and getting it to go where the handler wants it to go. Sometimes, however, a resistant ox will kick back against the goad to spite the handler. But in kicking against the goad the ox will be kicking against a sharp object, hurting not the handler, but itself. Still, the persistent handler will goad the ox forward. The more stubbornly rebellious the ox, the more it will kick against the goad and the more it will hurt itself.[3]

By the time of Isaiah, Ephraim (the Northern Kingdom of Israel) had been 'kicking against the goads' for a good long time. In fact, they had kicked so defiantly and stubbornly for so long that they had actually become hardened, calloused and totally desensitised.

As a result, God was about to visit Ephraim and its capital, Samaria, with a final judgement—a judgement to end all judgements.

> [8]The Lord has sent a word against Jacob,
>   and it will fall on Israel;
> [9]and all the people will know,

---

1 Acts 9:1–5.
2 Acts 26:14.
3 See C.H. Spurgeon, 'The conversion of Saul of Tarsus', a sermon delivered on 27 June 1858 at the Music Hall, Royal Surrey Gardens, www.spurgeon.org/ sermons/0202.htm.

> Ephraim and the inhabitants of Samaria,
> who say in pride and in arrogance of heart:
> ¹⁰'The bricks have fallen,
> but we will build with dressed stones;
> the sycamores have been cut down,
> but we will put cedars in their place' (9:8–10).

As commentator J Alec Motyer notes, the Hebrew words for 'pride' and 'arrogance' (v. 9) describe (respectively) 'the "haughtiness" of those who get their own way by their own devices', and the attitude or spirit of those who believe they are 'not beholden to any', 'superior and self–sufficient'. The proud and arrogant of heart will always stubbornly back their own judgments, trust their own responses, depend on their own resources and put their own policies to work.[1]

Some commentators regard verse 10 as metaphoric, saying that it describes how the proud people of Ephraim would have doubtless responded had they been struck by devastating earthquake. However, as commentators also note, it is also quite likely that verse 10 is not metaphoric and that it describes exactly how the Israelites did respond after the earthquake that devastated Israel in the days of King Jeroboam II (793–753 BC). Doubtless Samaria's prosperous and corrupt elite, who had started building 'houses of hewn stone' in the years just prior to the earthquake (Amos 5:11), saw the devastation as a wonderful opportunity for more wide–scale redevelopment.

But the earthquake was not the only affliction to have hit Israel, for the Lord had struck Israel repeatedly as he endeavoured to goad them forward, onto the right path and into line. God was exposing Israel to disciplinary redemptive affliction. But instead of listening, repenting and returning,[2] 'The people did not turn to him who struck them, nor inquire of the LORD of hosts' (9:13).[3]

Even after the earthquake, they just picked themselves up, dusted themselves off, and not only rebuilt but renovated, making great improvements! As Oswalt comments: 'Israel, by her own resilience and resourcefulness, could turn disaster into accomplishment.'[4] An impressive achievement! Except for the fact that, because they 'did not

---

1 Motyer, p .107.
2 Compare Job 36:11.
3 Compare Job 36:12–13.
4 Oswalt, p. 252.

turn to him who struck them, nor inquire of the Lord of hosts', they missed the whole point!

Isaiah's charge that 'The people did not turn to him who struck them, nor inquire of the LORD of hosts' is central to God's complaint in Amos 4:6–11, which provides us with a catalogue of all the times the Lord had struck or afflicted Israel over recent generations specifically with the aim of goading them back to him.

The Lord says in Amos 4:6–11: I gave you famine, yet you did not return to me (v. 6). I withheld rain, resulting in drought and crop failure, yet you did not return to me (vv. 7–8). I struck your gardens and crops with blight and mildew and locusts, yet you did not return to me (v. 9). I sent pandemics and war, yet you did not return to me (v. 10). I rained catastrophic devastation upon you (earthquake?), yet you did to return to me (v. 11).

In his commentary on Amos, J. Alec Motyer notes that while the people of Israel had been ever so busy making money (including by robbing the poor and exploiting the weak) and being very religious (Amos 2:6–4:5), God had also been very busy: 'sending famine (6), and drought (7), blight and locust (9), epidemic (10a), war (10b) and earthquake (11) … seeking to bring his people to repentance.'[1]

> The troubles of life are spread before us here by Amos: troubles caused by deprivation (famine and drought), troubles caused by infliction (blight and endemic), troubles caused by opposition (war and earthquake)—all the troubles of life are there in principle, falling into one category or another … But over them all [is] the first person singular of divine decision and action. Everything on earth comes from a God who rules and reigns in heaven.[2]

The afflictions besetting the people of Israel were nothing other than the curses of the covenant as described in Leviticus 26 and Deuteronomy 28.[3] Even though they repeatedly felt the goad in their flesh, the Israelites did not repent. Rather, they defied the Lord in their

---

1 Motyer (on Amos), p. 98.
2 Motyer (on Amos), p. 97 .
3 E.g. famine and war (Deuteronomy vv. 47, 48); drought and crop failure (vv. 23–24, 39–40; Leviticus 26:3–4; 26:18–19); blight, mildew and locusts (vv. 21–14, 38); war (vv. 25, 41; Exodus 22:24); earthquake (Deuteronomy 29:23); oppression and theft (vv. 29–34); and the diseases of Egypt (vv. 60–61).

hearts and kicked against the goads. It is Ephraim's lack of repentance that Isaiah laments in Isaiah 9:13 as he warns of the judgement to come.

The judgement about to befall Ephraim would be devastating. According to the Lord, Israel had already been devoured by alliances: 'Syria on the east and the Philistines on the west devour Israel with open mouth' (9:12). And this while Assyria was preparing to devour Syria! (9:11). Clearly, when Pekah the son of Remaliah assassinated King Pekaliah of Israel, seized power in a coup, reversed Israel's foreign policy and joined Syria's anti–Assyrian coalition, he only *thought* he was advancing Israel's security. In reality, Pekah was handing little Israel over to be devoured by her bigger neighbour, Syria, who—as God foreknew—was just about to be devoured by an even bigger fish: Assyria!

As if this looming national disaster was not enough, Isaiah warns that God is also going also to 'cut off from Israel' all her leadership, high and low, legitimate and false. There will be political collapse at every level (9:14–17) (compare this with the warning to Judah in 3:1–15). As a result, anarchy, social wickedness, violence and lawlessness will escalate (9:18–21). Morality will decline and corruption and injustice will become pervasive. The most vulnerable members of society will be exploited and abused with impunity (10:1–2). Punishment will come from afar, bringing ruin and captivity. There will be nothing left to do but hide (10:3–4: compare this with the warning to Judah in 2:10–21).

Learn the lessons of history and ask, 'what might God want from us?'

Isaiah presented Judah with this chronology and analysis of the demise of Ephraim and the fall of Samaria so that the Judeans could understand their times, discern God's hand and learn the lessons of Ephraim's history. The Holy Spirit immortalised Isaiah's message in Scripture for us so that we might learn from it also. And the most crucial lesson that must be learned is that when we are struck by or threatened with affliction or persecution, the most important thing we can do—the first thing we must do—is seek our Sovereign and inquire of the Lord of hosts.

This might seem really obvious, but unless we have this listed as 'Step

One' in our 'Strategy for Dealing with Affliction', then we just might, in the panic of the moment and in response to misplaced fear, rush headlong into vain activism without ever seeking the Lord's perspective and will. Such activism, even misguided prayer activism—praying passionately, but contrary to the Lord's will: that is, praying only for relief when what God wants is witness—yields disappointment, disillusionment and despair, and sometimes even serious injury to ourselves, others and the cause of God.

Every mature Christian knows that times of great suffering can be times of immense spiritual growth and sanctification. For example, it is certainly a fact that some of the most common fruits of persecution are:

- *purification* (winnowing or sifting) of the church, which makes it a truer reflection of Christ
- *spiritual growth* (a fruit of learning to depend upon God alone)
- Christian *solidarity* both locally and globally (as in John 17:21)
- Christian *witness and testimony* (as in Matthew 10:16–20)
- *cultural criticism.*

Concerning this last point, very few Christians are aware of the fact that suffering persecution for righteousness' sake is the ultimate act of cultural criticism.

That any society would persecute peaceful, benevolent citizens simply on account of their faith is shocking and unacceptable—so shocking and unacceptable in fact, that virtually every state that does it or condones it, denies it. To cover up what is really happening, these states enshrine religious freedom in their constitutions while enacting laws that devout believers simply cannot abide and denying them the right to conscientiously object.

Faced with such threats, it is not uncommon for Christians to adopt a spirit of denial, whereby they reject the notion that persecution could ever be part of their testimony. They insist that 'It's not happening' (Australian: 'She'll be right mate!'), rather than face the reality that their nation or community might be evolving (or regressing) into a more hostile, less civilised place where persecution of the righteous is systematic. They live in denial to avoid despair. While we can and should lament our loss, despair should never be the Christian response.[1]

Persecuted believers are rarely ever passive victims. Persecuted believers are those who, in the face of corruption, violence, dictatorship, repression and injustice do not shrink back, but stand up and cry out (sometime with words, but mostly with deeds), 'Over my dead body!' It is a cry that resonates, shattering the silence of the deniers. As culture collapses, society degenerates and persecution escalates, the testimony of the persecuted only grows louder, heaping ever more criticism upon the culture.

Sometimes it takes the shocking and shameful cutting down of the righteous to shake a people out of their nonchalance so they cry out in shame and horror: 'What have we become?' 'To what depths have we sunk?' 'How did we come to this?'

All through the Islamic world, there are Muslims questioning and leaving Islam because they have been shocked out of their nonchalance by Islam's violence and repression, particularly its persecution of peaceful, righteous Christian citizens.

The same will happen in the West. Yes, affliction and persecution are escalating and intensifying in the West; but we are not to fear, for God is doing something new—yet old. Once again he is exposing and dealing with sin by taking it upon his own body—only this time his body is the church.[2]

If the Lord, in divine love and wisdom, is goading us in a particular direction, and we resist—kicking against the goads—and 'in pride and arrogance of heart' pursue our own agenda, then we will get hurt. What is worse, if we, in a spirit of defiance or arrogant self-sufficiency, rush into activism as soon as affliction or persecution strike, then we risk hurting not only ourselves, but all those 'riding with us' and following us. By this means, and despite our good intentions, catastrophic trouble is brought upon the church of Jesus Christ.

We do not want to end up like Ephraim, kicking against the goads until we are calloused and totally desensitised, having missed numerous opportunities to participate in God's great plan. God is sovereign. The situation is never out of control. All we need to do is remember that

---

1 See Chapter 3 of this book.
2 1 Corinthians 12:27.

God is infinitely wise, and both willing (on account of his everlasting love—*hesed*) and able (as Almighty Creator and Sovereign) to do through us more than we could ask or even imagine.[1] Our God can be trusted!

So, no matter what our circumstances—but especially when we are facing trial, affliction and persecution—we should never cease to pray:

- that we may be filled with the knowledge of God's will in all spiritual wisdom and understanding

- that the eyes of our hearts might be enlightened, so that we might walk in a manner worthy of the Lord, fully pleasing to him in every way

- that we may be strengthened with power through his Spirit, with all power according to his glorious might, for all endurance and patience with joy, giving thanks to the Father in heaven, who is the God of our Salvation and the Rock of our refuge (see Colossians 1:9–14; Ephesians 1:15–23).

It is no small thing for believer in the midst of severe trial to declare:

> Though the fig tree should not blossom,
>   nor fruit be on the vines,
> the produce of the olive fail
>   and the fields yield no food,
> the flock be cut off from the fold
>   and there be no herd in the stalls,
> yet I will rejoice in the LORD;
>   I will take joy in the God of my salvation.
> (Habakkuk 3:17–18)

Such a declaration can only come from a believer who honours God as holy and trusts him.

May we be such God-fearing, God-honouring, and God-trusting people. May we be amongst those whose first port of call, when affliction and persecution strike, is the port of humble prayer. For only when we are prepared to step out in faith—to stop resisting his will and start trusting him with our lives—will we come to know God as our sanctuary (8:14), strength (40:29–31) and joy (Psalm 46:4).

---

1 Ephesians 3:20–21.

God, the Lord, is my strength;
  he makes my feet like the deer's;
  he makes me tread on my high places (Habakkuk 3:19).

Questions for Discussion and Reflection

1. Can you, with hindsight, see how some of your worst trials have actually resulted in great blessings, such as spiritual growth and sanctification (making you more like Jesus) and/or powerful, effective gospel witness?

   Write down one such case as a testimony to how God can and does redeem our trials and sufferings. (If in a group: share your testimony.)

2. If God can and does redeem trials and sufferings for positive ends, then what should be our first response when we are confronted with trials, suffering, threats and persecution?

   Why?

   Why do we frequently fail to do this?

3. When we are afflicted, perplexed, persecuted and struck down specifically because of our faith—specifically on account of the name of Jesus (John 15:18–21)—we manifest the death of Christ in our bodies before the watching world in what is a powerful form of cultural criticism. And just as Christ's wounds give life, so too can ours! (2 Corinthians 4:7–12)

   Does this Biblical reality help you think differently about the suffering of persecution? Explain.

4. List some of the blessings that can arise out of the evil of persecution?

Prayer

Lord, redeem my suffering.

Dear God my Father,
You are sovereign over all creation and know the end from the
    beginning. (Isaiah 46:9–10)
You can do all things and no purpose of yours can be thwarted.
    (Job 24:2)
You will fulfill your purpose for me. (Psalm 138:8a)

I praise you O Lord, for you are a redeeming God who takes what
    has been ruined by sin and the devil and redeems it
    for the sanctification of your people,
    for witness to the world,
    and for the glory of your name.

Forgive me for the times I have failed to trust you with my trials and
    sufferings.

Forgive me for the times I have responded badly to suffering,
    persecution and affliction by going on the defensive
when you have been standing at the ready,
    eager to work in and through me to advance your truth,
    build your kingdom,
    and achieve great victories on earth and in heaven.

I have missed so many opportunities to grow in faith; to witness to
    your grace, and to glorify your holy name.
Father, for this I am truly sorry.

May your Holy Spirit impart to me spiritual wisdom and insight so
    that I might discern your hand,
    recognise your redemptive work
    and get on board to facilitate rather than frustrate your divine
    will and purpose.

Increase my faith Lord, that I might have that peace and rest that
    comes from faith.
May I have faith to give you, and trust you with, my anxieties (1
    Peter 5:7) and my burdens. (Matthew 11:28)

May I have faith to confidently trust that you are always in control.
May I have faith for assurance that you are working all things for
good according to your divine will and purpose. (Romans 8:28)

Use me for your glory and bless me, not according to the measure of
the world, but as determined by your perfect wisdom and your
everlasting love.

I commit my body and my life to you as a living sacrifice. (Romans
12:1–2)
In God I trust.

Amen.

CHAPTER 5

Forgetting God

Isaiah 17:1–11 & 28:1–6

In the previous chapter we have seen how Ephraim's (Israel's) afflictions were the product of redemptive discipline, by which means God endeavoured to goad his people to repent and return to him. For Ephraim had descended into worldliness and idolatry. In an effort to grab his people's attention, the Lord *roared* with *roars* that shook the nation.[1]

But the Ephraimites resisted, kicking against the goads until they were hardened, calloused and totally desensitised. Ultimately there was nothing left for God to do but, in justice and in accordance with his covenant, burst forth in judgement against his own people.

So we know *why* Ephraim suffered affliction. The question to which we now turn is: *how?* How could a people who had known such divine blessing—a people who had experienced deliverance, mighty interventions, mercy, miracles and provisions directly from the hand of their God—how could they become so worldly and idolatrous, defiant and rebellious?

The answer is very simple: they forgot the God of their salvation and did not remember the Rock of their refuge.

> [1] An oracle concerning Damascus.
>
> Behold, Damascus will cease to be a city
>   and will become a heap of ruins.
> [2] The cities of Aroer are deserted;
>   they will be for flocks,

---

1 Amos 1:2.

which will lie down, and none will make them afraid.
³ The fortress will disappear from Ephraim,
   and the kingdom from Damascus;
and the remnant of Syria will be
   like the glory of the children of Israel,
declares the LORD of hosts.
⁴ And in that day the glory of Jacob will be brought low,
   and the fat of his flesh will grow lean.
⁵ And it shall be as when the reaper gathers standing grain
   and his arm harvests the ears,
and as when one gleans the ears of grain
   in the Valley of Rephaim.
⁶ Gleanings will be left in it,
   as when an olive tree is beaten—
two or three berries in the top of the highest bough,
   four or five on the branches of a fruit tree,
declares the LORD God of Israel.

⁷ In that day man will look to his Maker, and his eyes will look on the Holy One of Israel. ⁸ He will not look to the altars, the work of his hands, and he will not look on what his own fingers have made, either the Asherim or the altars of incense.
⁹ In that day their strong cities will be like the deserted places of the wooded heights and the hilltops, which they deserted because of the children of Israel, and there will be desolation.

¹⁰ For you have forgotten the God of your salvation
   and have not remembered the Rock of your refuge …
   (17:1–10a)

Here we have the Lord's declaration, through his prophet Isaiah, that Damascus—one of the most strategic cities in the region and the object of Ephraim's hope—is about to be devastated. Ephraim, positioned as she is in Syria's belly—having been devoured (9:12) by the Syro–Ephraimite alliance—will consequently share her fate. The cities of 'Aroer' (possibly the Aroer of Numbers 32:34, established by the Israelite tribe of Gad) will be emptied of their human inhabitants (17:1–2). Israel will be left defenseless and Damascus will be left powerless (17:3). This is a picture of violent conquest, destruction, displacement, captivity and exile: a humanitarian catastrophe.

'In that day' (17:4) everything that Ephraim has exalted, gloried in and hoped in will be brought low. Jacob's (Israel's) fatness (health) will vanish, leaving him wasted, a mere shadow of his former self. Ephraim will be like a field that the reaper, and then the gleaner, has swept over—a field stripped bare. A remnant will remain—a few people here and there, clinging to life in the farthest corners of the land (17:4–6).

'In that day' (17:7), as destruction sweeps in and terror takes hold, the eyes of Israel will finally refocus, as those who had rejected God in their prosperity look to him in their adversity.

Is this not so often the case, that when self–reliance fails and the works of our hands cannot save, then hope has nowhere else to go and eyes have nowhere else to look but beyond ourselves to the one who made us?

John Oswalt comments:

> In these verses the author contrasts the gods who are made with the God who has made. In a tone reminiscent of 2:6–22 and 44:9–18, he points out the folly of investing one's own handiwork with ultimate significance. What we have made cannot save us, it is not fundamentally different from us, that is, holy. Yet somehow when life is going well it is very easy to live as if that were so (Hosea 4:7). It is 'When Life Tumbles In' that we are forced to look for One who is other than we, One who is beyond us, who holds us in his hands rather than vice versa.[1]

In the midst of terror, chaos, confusion, wrath and judgement, false religion will fail and prove futile. Meanwhile, those who look to God will find that he remains and proves faithful. Mercy and salvation will be graciously given to those who look to their Maker in humble repentance. But as Oswalt notes:

> Israel's new awareness of God will come only in the destruction and thus will not prevent it. God has called his people in so many ways, hoping to avert the disaster (Hosea 11:1; Mattthew 23:27) but they would not hear until the disaster rips all their false supports from them.[2]

'In that day' (17:9) Israel's cities, woodlands and hills will be left deserted and desolate. 'For you have forgotten the God of your

---

1 Oswalt, p. 352.
2 Oswalt, p. 353.

salvation and have not remembered the Rock of your refuge.' Notice how God, in his explanation of how Israel got into this mess (17:10), does not bother presenting a charge sheet listing all Israel's specific sins, chronicling Israel's decline. For Israel's sinful deeds were merely the outward expression (symptoms or fruits) of their internal rottenness. And so God just goes straight to the heart of the matter: Israel would be left deserted and desolate because they had forgotten the God of their salvation and not remembered the Rock of their refuge.

The Israelites had not heeded Moses' warning

Take care lest you forget the LORD your God by not keeping his commandments and his rules and his statutes, which I command you today, lest, when you have eaten and are full and have built good houses and live in them, and when your herds and flocks multiply and your silver and gold is multiplied and all that you have is multiplied, then your heart be lifted up, and you forget the LORD your God, who brought you out of the land of Egypt, out of the house of slavery, who led you through the great and terrifying wilderness, with its fiery serpents and scorpions and thirsty ground where there was no water, who brought you water out of the flinty rock, who fed you in the wilderness with manna that your fathers did not know, that he might humble you and test you, to do you good in the end. Beware lest you say in your heart, 'My power and the might of my hand have gotten me this wealth.' You shall remember the LORD your God, for it is he who gives you power to get wealth, that he may confirm his covenant that he swore to your fathers, as it is this day. And if you forget the LORD your God and go after other gods and serve them and worship them, I solemnly warn you today that you shall surely perish. Like the nations that the LORD makes to perish before you, so shall you perish, because you would not obey the voice of the LORD your God (Deuteronomy 8:11–20).

Note that according to Moses, the threat to the knowledge and memory of the Lord was not going to come from systematic repression or persecution. Note also that the knowledge and memory of God was not at risk of being discredited by an impotent and unfaithful God. No! The threat would come from the people's prosperity—specifically if, in seeking to credit themselves, they were to forget from whose hand their prosperity came.

Francis Schaeffer has commented:

> I am convinced that the first step in God's people turning away from Him—even while they tenaciously and aggressively defend the orthodox position—is ceasing to be in a relationship with Him with a thankful heart.[1]

And so the free and prosperous, yet profoundly ungrateful and deluded Israelites chose to forget their generous, faithful, redeeming God. They did not want him taking credit for their prosperity or interfering with their plans—so they cast him behind their backs[2] and suppressed the truth.[3] Then, with God conveniently out of the picture, priests, prophets, rulers, teachers, parents and elders gorged their obsession with status and appearance while starving both themselves and the next generation of the knowledge and memory of God. This was a sin of commission as much as omission. '[She, Israel] adorned herself with her ring and jewellery, and went after her lovers, and forgot me, declares the LORD' (Hosea 2:13b).

The Israelites had not heeded the psalmist's advice

Give ear, O my people, to my teaching;
   incline your ears to the words of my mouth!

I will open my mouth in a parable;
   I will utter dark sayings from of old,
things that we have heard and known,
   that our fathers have told us.
We will not hide them from their children,
   but tell to the coming generation
the glorious deeds of the LORD, and his might,
   and the wonders that he has done.
He established a testimony in Jacob
   and appointed a law in Israel,
which he commanded our fathers
   to teach to their children,

1 Francis A. Schaeffer, *Death in the City*, Crossway Books, Wheaton IL, 2002, p. 96.
2 Ezekiel 23:35.
3 Romans 1:18.

> that the next generation might know them,
>> the children yet unborn,
> and arise and tell them to their children ... (Psalm 78:1–6).

In other words, religious and community leaders, teachers and parents are exhorted to dutifully raise the next generation to know— to remember—the words and deeds of the Lord.

> so that they should set their hope in God
> and not forget the works of God,
>> but keep his commandments;
> and that they should not be like their fathers,
>> a stubborn and rebellious generation,
> a generation whose heart was not steadfast,
>> whose spirit was not faithful to God (Psalm 78:7–8).

As C. H. Spurgeon notes concerning Psalm 78:7, the command to teach the next generation was not only reasonable, but purposeful. 'Faith cometh by hearing,' says Spurgeon. 'The design of teaching is practical: holiness towards God is the end we aim at, and not the filling of the head with speculative notions.'[1]

The conquest of the land would require substantial faith for which God in his mercy and wisdom had made provision. For while the Promised Land was yet before them, the Exodus was behind them. Despite God's provision, the Ephraimites (in this case, the tribe of Ephraim) forgot their God and consequentially were hamstrung by lack of faith.

> The Ephraimites, armed with the bow,
>> turned back on the day of battle.
> They did not keep God's covenant,
>> but refused to walk according to his law.
> They forgot his works
>> and the wonders that he had shown them (Psalm 78:9–11).

There was no excuse for this forgetfulness, as the psalmist demonstrates as he catalogues the great works God had done on behalf of his people: the deliverance out of Egypt, the parting of the Red Sea, God's presence and guidance through the wilderness, his provision of water from the rock, his provision of manna from heaven and meat (quail)

---

1 C. H. Spurgeon, *Treasury of David*, vol. 2, MacDonald Publishing Company, McLean VA, n.d., p 332.

from the sky, his wrath at sin and discipline of the rebellious, and his long-suffering patience and grace upon grace upon grace. God had filled their memory banks with riches, making deposit after deposit after deposit. The people had plenty to draw on. Had the Ephraimites only remembered, their memory would have energised their faith and they would have had the courage to lay hold of the Promised Land in the strength of the Lord. But no, their memory was gone and with it, their courage. And so 'they did not drive out the Canaanites who lived in Gezer',[1] leaving Canaanites living in the midst of Ephraim contrary to the Lord's instructions.

And just as memory energises faith which in turn fuels courage, forgetfulness energises arrogance which in turn fuels defiance.

> They tested God again and again
>   and provoked the Holy One of Israel.
> They did not remember his power
>   or the day when he redeemed them from the foe,
> when he performed his signs in Egypt
>   and his marvels in the fields of Zoan (Psalm 78:41–43).

As C. H. Spurgeon notes, the power, signs and marvels listed in Psalm 78:43–55 would actually have been quite difficult to forget.

> Such displays of divine power as those which smote Egypt
> with astonishment, it must have needed some more than usual
> effort to blot from the tablets of memory. It is probably meant
> that they practically, rather than actually, forgot.[2]

So the Israelites forgot the God of their salvation and did not remember the Rock of their refuge. In doing so they ended up just 'like their fathers': stubborn, rebellious, faltering and unfaithful.[3] It is not surprising, therefore, that they also ended up hearing the words their fathers heard: 'You shall not enter my rest.'[4]

—◆◆◆—

---

1 Joshua 16:10; Judges 1:29.
2 Spurgeon, p. 340 (Psalm 78:42).
3 Psalm 78:8.
4 Numbers 14:20–23; Psalm 95:8–11; Hebrews 3:8–11.

The memory that energises faith

If the church is to step forward in obedience to take hold of God's promises in spite of risk, affliction, persecution, insecurity and threat, then we will need to be courageous, having faith that is energised by the knowledge and memory of God. We simply cannot afford to forget him.

Yet how often do Christians, churches, even influential Christian leaders, view the way of faith as a last resort—a sad, desperate choice made in hopelessness after all human efforts have failed? More often than not, their prayers are not even prayers of faith, but works seeking to elicit a response. Such Christians have forgotten God and returned to the way of works, self–sufficiency and independence.

If the church is to pray intelligently and respond faithfully amidst growing insecurity and intensifying persecution, then the church simply must remember our saving God. We must remember how and why God acts in the history of the world, the history of his people Israel and the history of his church—for such memory energises faith.

Furthermore, the challenges facing the church today can be so enormous, with the prospects appearing so hopeless, that unless we have mountain–moving faith[1] energised by memory, then we will be crippled by doubt and will flee the battle as did the tribe of Ephraim.[2] This is as true for intercessory prayer (a spiritual battle) as it is for any other act of responsive faith. Indeed, intercessory prayer is a spiritual battlefield that many churches have already abandoned, thereby deserting their own flesh and blood struggling, bleeding and dying at the frontline.

Memory–energised faith: essential for bold intercessory prayer

Intercessory prayer is not a battle for the weak, unprepared or unarmed. If we are to pray intelligent prayers of 'great power'[3]—that is, 'successful' prayers that 'work' because they are aligned to the will of God—then we will need to be equipped with the whole armour of God: the belt of truth, the breastplate of righteousness, the gospel of peace, 'the shield of faith, with which you can extinguish all the flaming darts of the evil one'; the helmet of salvation, and 'the sword

---

1 Matthew 17:20; 1 Corinthians 13:2.
2 Psalm 78:9–11.
3 James 5:16.

of the Spirit, which is the word of God'.[1]

Oswalt Sanders writes:

> That prayer is one aspect of spiritual warfare is clearly taught
> in scripture (Ephesians 6:11,12,18,19). In this aspect of prayer,
> three and not two are involved. Between God and the devil,
> the god of this world, stands the praying man. Though pitifully
> weak in himself, he occupies a strategic role in this truceless
> warfare. His power and authority as he battles in faith are not
> inherent, but are his through his union with the Victor of
> Calvary.[2]

The devil's goal will always be to prevent us from praying, but if he
cannot stop us praying, then he will aim to subvert our prayers. C. S.
Lewis alluded to this strategy in his classic masterpiece, *The Screwtape
Letters*. In his 27th letter of instruction to the junior devil Wormwood,
Screwtape (Wormwood's uncle and devil mentor) vents his disgust
and frustration over Wormwood's failure to keep his 'patient' (a young
Christian male) from diligent prayer. And what is worse, the 'patient'
has adopted a 'new urgency' in prayer, particularly over the issue of
'the war'.

'Now is the time,' says Screwtape, 'for raising intellectual difficulties
about prayer of that sort.'[3]

The only foothold the devil can
have over our prayers is the one
we give him through ignorance,
forgetfulness or lack of faith. If only
we would know and remember
God—his character, attributes,
words, deeds, promises—then we
could come boldly into the courts
of the Lord with prayers energised
by memory, fuelled with faith,
defended with truth and limited
by nothing!

> 'Then I said, "I will appeal
> to this, to the years of the
> right hand of the Most High."
> I will remember the deeds
> of the LORD; yes, I will
> remember your wonders of old.
> I will ponder all your work, and
> meditate on your mighty deeds.
> Your way, O God, is holy.
> What god is great like our God?'
> (Psalm 77, esp. vv. 10–13)

1 Ephesians 6:10–18.
2 J. Oswald Sanders, *World Prayer*, OMF International, Littleton CO, 1999, pp. 10–11.
3 C. S. Lewis, *The Screwtape Letters*, , Barbour and Company Inc. Uhrichsville OH, pp. 136–7.

'Satan dreads nothing but prayer', wrote Samuel Chadwick.

His one concern is to keep the saints from praying. He fears
nothing from prayerless studies, prayerless work, prayerless
religion. He laughs at our toil, mocks our wisdom, but trembles
when we pray.[1]

And in this increasingly hostile world, the embattled and besieged,
persecuted church of Jesus Christ needs our prayers, for *intercessory
prayer is advocacy to the highest authority.*

We need to pray for Christian pastors who have been kidnapped by
the security forces of brutally repressive totalitarian regimes. No one
knows where these pastors are, or even if they are dead or alive—they
are, in every sense, 'disappeared'.

Praise God, we *can* pray with faith and boldness because we *know* that
these 'disappeared' Christians have not disappeared from God's sight,
for God's word tells us that we can never escape from his Spirit nor
from his presence.[2] And Jesus promised, 'And behold, I am with you
always, to the end of the age.'[3]

We need to pray for churches and individual believers that are
struggling to just survive in corrupt, violent, lawless, warlord-ruled
societies where despairing women self-immolate and where drug
abuse, child trafficking, persecution, kidnapping and extortion
are endemic. In some cases, violent Islamic jihad has succeeded in
purging the visible church from the landscape, forcing the scattered
remnant into hiding.

Praise God, we *can* pray in faith and with boldness for miracles of grace
because we *know* that no matter how dark, devastating and hopeless
things appear, our Almighty God is the one for whom 'nothing will
be impossible'.[4] He is the Creator who turned darkness and chaos into
light and life with the word of his mouth.[5]

We need to pray for those situations where well-supported, well-
armed militants with genocidal intent fuelled by hatred, greed,
bloodlust and syncretised religion, call upon demonic forces to

---

1 Quoted by Sanders, p. 12.
2 Psalm 139:1-12.
3 Matthew 28:20.
4 Luke 1:37.
5 Genesis 1.

empower them in their war against Christian peoples. The demonic power and motivation behind these rebels is not to be mocked or trivialised.

Praise God, we *can* pray with faith and boldness for we *know* that Christ 'disarmed the rulers and authorities and put them to open shame, by triumphing over them' in Christ through the cross.[1] And we *know* he rules from heaven as King with all 'angels, authorities and powers having been subjected to him.'[2]

We need to pray concerning those cruel dictators who rule with seemingly absolute power, oppressing their people and denying them justice. They abuse their power and grow fat on the proceeds of corruption while their people suffer and starve. They harass, incarcerate, abuse, starve, violate, torture and execute humble, peaceful disciples of Jesus Christ with impunity. They seem untouchable!

Praise God, we *can* pray for the liberation of oppressed peoples. We *can* pray for an end to dictatorial regimes. We *can* pray for religious liberty to become a reality in nations where Bibles are banned, churches are closed and believers are imprisoned, exiled and executed. We *can* pray for these things in faith, boldness and confidence because we *know* that 'God has put all things under the authority of Christ, and he gave him this authority for the benefit of the church.'[3]

Prayer of 'great power' is muscular with faith fed on and energised by the knowledge and memory of God. This is real prayer. And real prayer is something profoundly different to exotic spiritual fantasy, religious pious duty and desperate wishful thinking. Real prayer is doing business with the Sovereign God, the King of Kings, in the courts of heaven!

In these darkening days of escalating persecution and insecurity, the church would do well to remember that real prayer is not only a critical and strategic element of the spiritual battle, real prayer is the highest form of advocacy and God's ordained means of unleashing the forces of heaven.

---

1 Colossians 2:15.
2 1 Peter 3:22.
3 Ephesians 1:22, New Living Translation.

111

Can't get access to the President? Who cares! Go over his head to the God who reigns.[1]

Can't get into the UN? So what! Christ has opened the way into the courts of heaven, into the presence of the Lord of Hosts (literally: the Commander of Heaven's hosts or forces).[2]

Does this generation have faith for this? Will the next?

Memory—energised faith: essential amidst social collapse (Hosea 4:1–6)

Hosea, a contemporary of Isaiah, was a prophet to the Northern Kingdom/Israel during its days of decline and conflict before the fall of Samaria. He preached at a time of immense geopolitical turmoil to a people who had grown up in prosperity and security, but who were now faced with decline and conflict.

> Hear the word of the LORD, O children of Israel,
>   for the LORD has a controversy with the inhabitants of the
>   land.
> There is no faithfulness or steadfast love,
>   and no knowledge of God in the land;
> there is swearing, lying, murder, stealing, and committing
>   adultery;
>   they break all bounds, and bloodshed follows bloodshed.
> Therefore the land mourns,
>   and all who dwell in it languish,
> and also the beasts of the field
>   and the birds of the heavens,
>   and even the fish of the sea are taken away (Hosea 4:1–3).

Do you, like me, see here in Hosea's description of Israel, a description of the society in which you live? Declining faith, love and knowledge of God? Increasing violence, crime and immorality? The land exploited and the wildlife depleted? The whole creation mourning? Remember the context of Hosea's message. As commentator Derek Kidner notes, Hosea was preaching to a people whose kingdom would be extinct within a generation.[3]

---

1 Isaiah 52:7.
2 Hebrews 10:19–22.
3 Derek Kidner, *The Message of Hosea*, The Bible Speaks Today series, InterVarsity Press, Nottingham, p. 18.

Who was responsible for Israel's apostasy? God lays the blame squarely on those who were the custodians of knowledge and memory.

> Yet let no one contend,
>   and let none accuse,
>   for with you is my contention, O priest.
> You shall stumble by day;
>   the prophet also shall stumble with you by night;
>   and I will destroy your mother (Hosea 4:4–5).

Today, Christian priests, pastors, youth leaders, teachers, parents and grandparents must recognise that they—we—are the custodians of the knowledge and memory of God. If our society, our culture, has forgotten God, then it is because the church forgot him first. We must repent. We must remember God. The church is God's witness to the world. Can we as local churches really forget God and still expect him to bless us? Might it not be more reasonable to expect that God might freely choose to find himself another witness?

> My people are destroyed for lack of knowledge;
>   because you have rejected knowledge,
>   I reject you from being a priest to me.
> And since you have forgotten the law of your God,
>   I also will forget your children (Hosea 4:6).

Christians of the early 21st century should have little doubt that the Western world—in particular those countries transformed by the Protestant Reformation, great revivals, the Great Awakening and great social reforms—is under divine judgement.

After being blessed with so much from God's hand, the West boasts in pride and arrogance of heart: 'My power and the might of my hand have gotten me this wealth.'[1]

The West would do well to remember Moses' warning (Deuteronomy 8:11–20), the psalmist's advice (Psalm 78) and Ephraim's afflictions (Amos 4:6–11; Isaiah 17:1–10a). For like Ephraim, the free and prosperous yet profoundly ungrateful and deluded West has forgotten God. As a consequence, the 21st century will see Western civilisation struggling for its very survival.[2] And just like Ephraim,

---

1 Deuteronomy 8:17.
2 Consider the situation in the West in terms of the covenantal curse in Deuteronomy 28:43–44.

the West's afflictions will not have been caused by immigration or Islam or homosexuality or fundamentalist secularism or the economy. The West's afflictions will be the consequences of its own poor and rebellious choices along with judgement from the hand of a just and angry God.

Like Ephraim, the West has forgotten God. The trouble is the West's Judeo–Christian culture is so free, open, fruitful and dynamic that, like a living tree, it cannot survive unless it is deeply rooted in the rich deep soil of Judeo–Christian belief—that is, in God's Holy Word. As the foundation is eroded, society's roots (reasonings) wither and the tree (culture) suffers. As the fruits of Judeo–Christian culture—liberty, grace, benevolence and prosperity—become scarce (being without reason), external restraints (law and law enforcers) are increasingly utilised by authorities desperate to prevent cultural collapse.

'The sojourner [foreigner] *who is among you shall rise higher and higher above you, and you shall come down lower and lower. He shall lend to you, and you shall not lend to him. He shall be the head, and you shall be the tail.'*—one of the curses of Deuteronomy 28:43–44.

As Western culture evolves to become 'post–Christian' (i.e. 'non–Christian')—a process we should recognise as culture change—intolerance escalates, authoritarianism emerges, religious liberty fades and persecution intensifies. Beliefs once regarded as foundational and fundamental are increasingly deemed offensive and unacceptable. Such allegedly 'regressive' beliefs may be held (hence the claim to religious freedom), but they may no longer be freely expressed or exercised lest they offend the new gods and threaten the harmony of the new order.

When a society forgets God, the seriousness of the situation is embodied in the persecuted believer. Ultimately this is a spiritual battle, and this battle is already raging at our gate.

The ultimate consequence of forgetting God (Isaiah 28:1–6)

The fall of Samaria (722 bc)

Here in 28:1–6 Isaiah presents us with three pictures that relate to three crowns. The pictures are double-barreled, relating to both the citizens of the city and to the city itself.

The first picture (28:1–3) describes the floral garlands worn by Ephraim's drunken partygoers. The party is coming to an end and the flowers are fading, for the Lord has sent Assyria to gatecrash Ephraim's party. She will sweep in like a destructive hailstorm. Eventually she will burst through Ephraim's glorious strong city, Samaria, like an overwhelming flood. The drunkards will stumble and their floral garlands, like the crown of Ephraim—the magnificent city of Samaria—will be cast down to the earth and trodden underfoot.

> Ah, the proud crown of the drunkards of Ephraim,
>   and the fading flower of its glorious beauty,
>   which is on the head of the rich valley of those overcome
>   with wine!
> Behold, the Lord has one who is mighty and strong;
>   like a storm of hail, a destroying tempest,
>   like a storm of mighty, overflowing waters,
>   he casts down to the earth with his hand.
> The proud crown of the drunkards of Ephraim
>   will be trodden underfoot … (28:1–3).

In the second picture (28:4), the city of Samaria is itself pictured as a garland of fading beauty 'on the head of the rich valley'. The city is described as being ripe for the picking. Her fate will be like that of an early fruit—a first-ripe fig before summer. She will be snatched and devoured without a second thought—delicious! I love J. Alec Motyer's dramatic rendition: 'The Lord has an irresistible foe (2–3) and Samaria will be gobbled up with the same alacrity and unthinkingness as a passer-by picks and swallows a first-ripe fig (4).'[1]

> and the fading flower of its glorious beauty,
>   which is on the head of the rich valley,
>   will be like a first-ripe fig before the summer:

---

1 Motyer, p. 229.

> when someone sees it, he swallows it
> as soon as it is in his hand (28:4)

As Raymond Ortlund notes:

> What Isaiah sees in Ephraim is the script we've played out
> a thousand times in history. Kingdoms rise and fall; wealth
> is accumulated and then stolen; ego climbs up onto some
> pedestal and then falls down to absurdity.[1]

Ephraim had forgotten God. There was 'no faithfulness or steadfast love, and no knowledge of God in the land' (Hosea 4:1b), and so God 'destined [her] for total disappearance'.[2]

The Assyrian invasion of 733 BC left Israel greatly diminished. After some four–fifths of Israeli territory was annexed to Assyria, Israel's new king, Hoshea (732–724 BC), submitted and became an Assyrian vassal.

When, in 724 BC, Hoshea withheld tribute (2 Kings 17:4), Assyria's King Shalameser V (son and heir to Tiglath-pileser III) swept into Israel like a devastating storm of hail. What a shock this would have been for Hoshea, for he thought he had covered his bases. Before he withheld tribute he secured promises of support from Egypt. But this support never came, for Egypt was at that time, in reality, weak and unable to help anyone. The only one who really could have helped— the Holy God of Israel—was never approached. He was forgotten.

And so Assyria invaded and occupied what remained of Israel, except for the capital city, Samaria, which it besieged.[3] King Hoshea was taken captive and imprisoned. The besieged city of Samaria held out against the Assyrians for three long years.

During that time, Shalmaneser V died and was succeeded by Sargon II, to whom Samaria fell in the late summer or autumn of 722/721 BC. Sargon's forces burst through the city like a raging flood. 'Thousands of its citizens—27,290 according to Sargon II—were subsequently deported to Upper Mesopotamia and Media, there ultimately to vanish from the stage of history.'[4]

---

1 Ortlund, p. 153.
2 Motyer, p. 230.
3 2 Kings 17:5.
4 Bright, p. 275.

For you have forgotten the God of your salvation
    and have not remembered the Rock of your refuge …
    (17:10a).

But, there is a third crown.

In that day the LORD of hosts will be a crown of glory,
    and a diadem of beauty, to the remnant of his people,
and a spirit of justice to him who sits in judgement,
    and strength to those who turn back the battle at the gate
    (28:5–6).

Concerning this third picture, Oswalt comments:

Isaiah here depicts what could have been, if the right crown
had been put in place. Nevertheless, despite the present failure,
God will achieve his ultimate purpose. The approach is similar
to that of [Isaiah] 4:2–6, where the true appears after the
false has been done away with. When all the false garlands
have been trampled in the mud, then the real one can appear.
Indulgence must lose its appeal as more and more exotic forms
are sought; the glories of the world's Samarias become so
quickly tarnished by greed and oppression, but God remains.
His beauty will not fade nor can he be defeated. The issue for
us is whether we will remain. In every age there is a remnant
which is part of that great final one. They are characterized by
the ability to see through the tinsel of life, beyond the trappings
of appearances, to those truths which are eternal, which will
prevail.[1]

This crown—'the LORD of hosts'—differs in all aspects to the drunkard's
fading garland and the fruit ripe for picking. This crown is true as
opposed to false, lasting as opposed to fading, divine as opposed to
human.

Furthermore, this crown is not a mere ornament; for *this crown
changes everything*. This crown—'the LORD of hosts'—will be 'strength
to those who turn back the battle at the gate'.

Samaria did not put on this crown and consequently fell in 722 BC.
And so the question for Judah is this: will Jerusalem be wearing this
crown when her time of testing comes? Isaiah is warning Jerusalem
that if she fails to put on the right crown, then she too will fall. Only

---

1 Oswalt, p. 508.

if she remembers the God of her salvation and the Rock of her refuge will she have faith to stand firm, look to him, listen to him, and wait upon him—her 'crown of glory' and 'strength to those who turn back the battle at the gate'.

Today, as the church comes under siege and the battle rages at her gate, she too—like Samaria and Jerusalem before her—has two options: to walk as the world walks, treating God as irrelevant, exalting and trusting in humanity and the work of its hands, or to walk differently, by faith, honouring God as holy, trusting him and exalting him as our crowning glory.

If the church exalts humanity and all that the world glorifies, then she will, in defiance and arrogance, stand in her own self-sufficient strength and wisdom—and fall, clinging to that which God will sweep away as false.

If, however, the church will but remember the God of her salvation and the Rock of her refuge, then she will have faith to stand firm, look to him, listen to him, and wait upon him—her crown of glory and strength to those who *turn back the battle at the gate*.

Questions for Discussion and Reflection

1. What evidence of Culture Change have you witnessed in your community or nation in your lifetime?

2. In the light of Deuteronomy 8:11–20, do you think that the 'Christian West' might have forgotten the Lord? Explain your answer.

3. What impact is this having on religious liberty and security around the world?

4. In the absence of radical social transformation, what will be the result—in the West and in the world?

5. What are you doing to combat 'forgetfulness' and to perpetuate the knowledge and memory of the Lord?

6. With 'Christian'/Western culture crumbling and the Church's enemies advancing throughout the world, what must we do to ensure the battle is turned back at the gate? (Isaiah 28:5–6)

   Discuss what this means in practice.

Prayer

That the Lord might not be forgotten.

My God and Father,
I worship you as the awesome and amazing Creator.

Forgive me Lord, for the times I have received generous blessings
from your hand yet not been thankful—as if they were my right;
as if I could take your grace for granted.

Forgive me Lord, for the times I have received your blessings and
your aid and then taken the credit, netting the glory for myself.

Though the world regards you as irrelevant, I know that you most
certainly are not.
I know that you fill the universe (Ephesians 1:23).
I know you hold all things together (Colossians 1:17).
I know you have a plan and purpose that cannot be thwarted (Job
42:2).
I know that you are present, powerful and purposeful
at every moment, in every place, and behind every blessing,
whether humanity acknowledges that fact or not.

I commit to actively remembering your great deeds, your great
power, your great love and your great faithfulness.
I commit to giving thanks in all circumstances (1 Thessalonians 5:18
& Ephesians 5:20).

I commit from this day forth, to actively perpetuating the knowledge
and memory of God:
through courageous witness and sensitive sharing;
through words and through deeds.
I will not let God's grace and mercy be forgotten!

Revive me O Lord.
May my heart burn with zeal for the honour of your glorious holy
name.
May I treasure you as priceless and be proud to lift you up, even
before a hostile world.

Revive your Church O Lord!
For only when you are our treasure and glory,
    only when you are exalted and the object of our hope,
    only when you are the precious crown of your remnant
    is there hope for the Church and hope for the world.
We simply cannot afford to forget you!
For in you and you alone, O Lord of hosts,
    is truth, justice and strength to turn back the battle.

Revive us Lord,
that the battle might be turned back at the gate in our own day.

Amen.

CHAPTER 6

Yesterday's faith is not sufficient for today

Isaiah 22:8–11 & 38–39

We are in Jerusalem.

It is 701 BC

War is imminent.

Where is Hezekiah, king of Judah?

King Hezekiah is out inspecting Jerusalem's water supply. Jerusalem does not have a natural water source inside its city walls. In the days of King Ahaz, water was brought into the city from the Gihon Spring via an aqueduct. During times of war, however, an aqueduct is a military target. So to secure the water supply King Hezekiah has had a tunnel cut through the bedrock, through which the waters of the Gihon Spring can flow, securely and out of sight, into a reservoir inside the city walls.

The 533-metre (1,750-foot) tunnel was cut through solid rock by two teams of labourers working from opposite directions. An engineering marvel in its day, the Siloam Tunnel diverted the waters of the Gihon Spring which was east of the city, to a reservoir—the Pool of Siloam/Shiloah—in the Tyropoeon Valley in the south-east corner of the city.

King Hezekiah has forged a coalition of western states to resist Assyrian imperialism. King Padi of Ekron, was resistant, but his people were not. Ousting Padi in a coup, they handed him over to Hezekiah who imprisoned him in Jerusalem. After securing guarantees of military support from a revived Egypt, the allied states threw down the gauntlet and rebelled, withholding tribute, testing the resolve of Assyria's new king, Sennacherib.

Refusing to be defied, Sennacherib has launched a reprisal. The mighty Assyrian army has stormed into the Levant to re-establish Assyrian hegemony. Sennacherib's forces have been ordered to fight their way southwards down the Mediterranean Coast, crushing all rebellion in their path en route to Jerusalem.

In anticipation of the impending invasion, King Hezekiah has been feverishly building up Jerusalem's defences. He has inspected the weapons in the House of the Forest.[1] He has inspected the walls of the city, checking for weaknesses. He has surveyed the houses to see which ones can be demolished to provide materials for repairing the wall's breaches and filling in its casemates.[2] He has inspected the water supply and infrastructure because, in a worst-case scenario, Jerusalem could come under siege.

Yet according to Isaiah—for whom this scenario was all too familiar—something, or to be more precise, someone, had been forgotten. For despite all the frenetic activity—all the military, political, strategic and defensive preparations—the LORD, the covenant king and suzerain over the City of David, had not been sought.

[8]He [God] has taken away the covering of Judah.

In that day you looked to the weapons of the House of the Forest, [9]and you saw that the breaches of the city of David were many. You collected the waters of the lower pool, [10]and you counted the houses of Jerusalem, and you broke down the houses to fortify the wall. [11]You made a reservoir between the two walls for the water of the old pool. But you did not look to him who did it, or see him who planned it long ago (22:8–11).

---

1 The House of the Forest 'was the building erected by Solomon out of wood from Lebanon (see 1 Kings 7:2), and used to store shields (1 Kings 10:17,21)', Harman, p. 157.

2 'In the Solomonic era (tenth century B.C.E.), the solid walls [of the city] were replaced with casemates … Casemates (strictly speaking, the casemates are the rectangular chambers, not the entire wall) consisted of two parallel walls, separated by five or six feet and joined at intervals by walls at right angles, creating a series of rectangular compartments. By filling the space between the outer (and thicker) and the inner wall with rubble, the casemates could be strengthened' (Phillip J. King, *Amos, Hosea, Micah: an Archaeological Commentary*, Westminster Press, Philadelphia PA, 1988, p. 72).

In preparing for war, Hezekiah had done everything the world might think the king of a threatened people should do: he had looked to the weapons, looked to the city walls and looked to the water security. Overlooked however, was the eternal, sovereign and providential 'he' (v. 8) or 'him' (v. 11b)—the one who holds Jerusalem in his hands. King Hezekiah had looked everywhere but to the God of his salvation, the Rock of his refuge, the Redeemer of Israel, the God of the covenant and true King of Zion. He worked and worked and worked for the security of Jerusalem, 'but' he 'did not look to its Maker, nor have regard for the One who designed it long ago'.[1]

This reference to the Lord God of Hosts as the 'Maker' and the designer and planner of the City of David is significant. For as Oswalt comments, gods made by people are created; they do not create, and thus

> have no plan for life and no effective purpose in their handling of affairs. By contrast, the One who made all things does have such a plan and the person who does not take him into account is being very foolish (32:26; 40:21, 28; 41:21–29).[2]

How ironic it is, that the citizens of the 'valley of vision'[3] (Jerusalem) should be so short-sighted. But before we get all self-righteous and judgemental, maybe we should examine ourselves, for the 21st-century church can be equally visionless. In our day it is not uncommon to find the church—established and built by its head, Jesus Christ[4]—responding to threat with the same frenetic 'practical atheism' that characterised the Judean response.

By investing all his energy and all his hope in human wisdom and human strength, the faithful King Hezekiah was exercising the same self-sufficient independence that faithless King Ahaz exercised when his life and liberty were on the line and the security of Jerusalem was threatened some 34 years earlier. Both kings reasoned that what Jerusalem needed was more human strength, more military hardware, more boots-on-the-ground, superior engineering, advanced technology and powerful allies!

Once again the Judeans had forgotten their God and were facing

---

1 Isaiah 22:11b, trans. Gileadi.
2 Oswalt, p. 413.
3 Isaiah 22:1.
4 Matthew 16:18.

125

existential threat without the memory that energises faith. Consequently, when their lives and liberty were on the line they 'did not look to him', they did not inquire of the Lord of Hosts.[1] As Motyer notes, there was 'a poison at work within the people of God—a reliance on human works that can only end in destruction (Ephraim, 17:7–11)'.[2] As the Assyrians advanced, the Judeans prepared themselves for battle—only without discernment, without repentance and without their covenant King.

Proclaiming 'We can do it!', some championed activism and got busy organising weapons, fortifying walls, securing water and negotiating alliances. There was much work to do: construction, organisation, administration, shuttle diplomacy, work, work and more frenetic work.

Others, however, adopted a more fatalistic attitude, believing 'We're all gonna die!' In order to avoid despair they embraced denial and busied themselves in escapism: feasting, drinking and partying—sucking up all the pleasures the city could offer before it reached its use-by date. But 'this mind-set', notes Motyer, 'denies the spiritual dimension, for their behaviours proclaimed that if their own endeavours (their weapons [8], costly defences [10], and engineering marvels [11]) could not save them, nothing could.'[3]

So everyone was busy, only not in the activity God was calling for. They were not busy in repentance.

> In that day the Lord GOD of hosts
> called for weeping and mourning,
> for baldness and wearing sackcloth;
> and behold, joy and gladness,
> killing oxen and slaughtering sheep,
> eating flesh and drinking wine.
> 'Let us eat and drink, for tomorrow we die' (22:12–13).

According to Oswalt,

> 'for tomorrow we die' expresses the ultimate rationale for a
> life of acquisition and indulgence. If indeed there is nothing

---

1 Isaiah 9:13.
2 Motyer, p. 133.
3 Ibid., p. 185.

beyond the grave, then self-sacrifice, commitment, and self-denying discipline are foolish (28:15, 18; 1 Corinthians 15:32).[1]

'To put this experience in modern terms,' writes Oswalt,

> we may imagine the situation in our own country in the wake of a nuclear attack. Those who remain alive, expecting to die in a further attack or of radiation poisoning, could turn to repentance and faith or they could engage in one last orgy of looting, indulgence, and passion. Which course we would choose would say volumes about the true nature of our commitments (cf. Lamentations 3:40–42).[2]

Just like their brothers, the Ephraimites, the Judeans had grown faithless. Just like their fathers, who suffered God's wrath and were barred from entering the Promised Land,[3] they had become 'a stubborn and rebellious generation, a generation whose heart was not steadfast, whose spirit was not faithful to God'.[4] For instead of repenting and returning to the Lord in humility, dependence and faith, the Judeans responded to the looming threat with self-sufficient activism and self-absorbed fatalism.

However, the Lord Almighty will not abide such 'practical atheism' in his people. And so Isaiah is required to deliver a shattering word of wrath—a damning judgement, the Lord's sworn oath—that this sin of unbelief will not be forgiven.

> The LORD of hosts has revealed himself in my ears:
> 'Surely [or 'I swear'[5]] this iniquity will not be atoned for you
> until you die,' says the Lord GOD of hosts (22:14).

Considering Hezekiah was one of the most godly and successful kings ever to reign in Jerusalem—how on earth did it come to this?

Hezekiah, the godly king

> And Ahaz slept with his fathers, and they buried him in the city, in Jerusalem, for they did not bring him into the tombs of

---

1 Oswalt, p. 414.
2 Ibid., p. 414.
3 Hebrews 3:16–19.
4 Psalm 78:8.
5 Harman, p. 158.

the kings of Israel. And Hezekiah his son reigned in his place (2 Chronicles 28:27).

Hezekiah began to reign when he was twenty-five years old, and he reigned twenty-nine years in Jerusalem. His mother's name was Abijah the daughter of Zechariah. And he did what was right in the eyes of the Lord, according to all that David his father had done.

In the first year of his reign, in the first month, he opened the doors of the house of the Lord and repaired them (2 Chronicles 29:1–3).

The first thing King Hezekiah did upon assuming the kingship, was reopen and cleanse the Temple (2 Chronicles 29:3–19) and restore the worship of the Lord (vv. 20–36). The 2 Chronicles 29 account is very moving—as moving (I believe) as Solomon's dedication of the Temple in 2 Chronicles 6–7, and Nehemiah's dedication of the new walls in Nehemiah 12:27–43. Let us take some time to contemplate the scene.

Imagine your city coming under the rule of a godless dictator who closed—actually sealed up—all the churches. For many years Christians are banned from entering their church. Of course, mice, cockroaches and ants have no qualms about exploiting the situation; they gleefully take up residence. A stone is thrown and a window is broken—now sparrows, pigeons and owls may also make themselves at home. All the while grasses, weeds and wild blackberries overgrow the neglected garden. Gradually the precious site comes to be wrapped in a shroud of dust, dirt, dung, death and decay, an image that symbolises—as far as the regime is concerned—the death of antiquated superstition.

Then, upon the death of that dictator, a godly leader is promoted and permission is given for the churches to be reopened. Imagine the joy! The doors of your church are unsealed and flung wide. Priests, pastors, elders, deacons and members all move in to clean out and restore the worship centre. You reconnect the electricity and turn on the lights and electric appliances. You get rid of the bats, pigeons, sparrows, rats, mice, cockroaches and ants along with their nests, feathers, hair, droppings and carcasses. You wipe away the deep layers of dust covering every surface. As you wash the windows, the sunlight starts to filter in for the first time in years. Eventually the windows are cleaned and the auditorium is floodlit with sunshine. You steam clean the carpets and all the upholstery, discarding everything that is beyond repair, replacing it with new. You polish the timber and the silverware. You clean, repair and tune the musical instruments. You clean out the kitchen, washing every dish and utensil, cleaning off the tarnish, mould, dust and droppings. While holding your nose you empty the fridge and wash it out with vanilla. You pull up the weeds; feed, water and mulch the soil; and re-plant the gardens. With the whole fellowship cooperating, it takes three weeks of full-time work. (It took the Levites 16 working days to purify the Temple.[1]) Then, when the work is done, you consecrate it all to the Lord. The church is ready for worship once again! Imagine it!

Then along come ministers of the new government. They are bearing gifts, but there is no quid pro quo, for these are gifts for the Lord from the heart. The musicians play. Voices are raised in praise and worship. There is repentance with tears. There are so many worshippers, so many penitents and so many converts, that there are not enough church officials to attend to everyone. The most upright, godly and dedicated of laypeople are hastily recruited into ministry. Clearly God had prepared the hearts of the people in advance. It is a revival of phenomenal proportions. Imagine it! Read 2 Chronicles 29 and let your heart be thrilled. Hezekiah was an awesome king and an awesome, faithful servant of the Lord.

Next on the King Hezekiah's royal agenda was national reconciliation. Extending the hand of reconciliation to Ephraim, Hezekiah invited the Israelites to join the Judeans in Jerusalem to celebrate the re-instituted Passover feast (2 Chronicles 30). To this end, King Hezekiah issued a proclamation throughout all the land: from Beersheba on the southern edge of the Judean desert, to Dan in the northern-most reaches of Israel/the Northern Kingdom. It was an invitation to repentance, reconciliation and reunification.

> So couriers went throughout all Israel and Judah with letters from the king and his princes, as the king had commanded, saying, 'O people of Israel, return to the LORD, the God of Abraham, Isaac, and Israel, that he may turn again to the remnant of you who have escaped from the hand of the kings of Assyria. Do not be like your fathers and your brothers, who were faithless to the LORD God of their fathers, so that he made them a desolation, as you see. Do not now be stiff-necked as

1 2 Chronicles 29:17.

your fathers were, but yield yourselves to the LORD and come to his sanctuary, which he has consecrated forever, and serve the LORD your God, that his fierce anger may turn away from you. For if you return to the LORD, your brothers and your children will find compassion with their captors and return to this land. For the LORD your God is gracious and merciful and will not turn away his face from you, if you return to him' (2 Chronicles 30:6–9).

While most in Ephraim, Manasseh and Zebulun (tribes of the Northern Kingdom) 'laughed them to scorn and mocked them', some 'humbled themselves and came to Jerusalem'. Meanwhile, all of Judah was united behind the king's efforts (vv. 10–12).

During the Passover, a dispute threatened to reignite division, but the wise and sensitive Hezekiah exercised godly leadership and interceded on behalf of the people.

For a majority of the people, many of them from Ephraim, Manasseh, Issachar, and Zebulun, had not cleansed themselves, yet they ate the Passover otherwise than as prescribed. For Hezekiah had prayed for them, saying, 'May the good LORD pardon everyone who sets his heart to seek God, the LORD, the God of his fathers, even though not according to the sanctuary's rules of cleanness.' And the LORD heard Hezekiah and healed the people (2 Chs 30:18–20).

Furthermore,

Hezekiah spoke encouragingly to all the Levites who showed good skill in the service of the LORD. So they ate the food of the festival for seven days, sacrificing peace offerings and giving thanks to the LORD, the God of their fathers (2 Chronicles 30:22).

So there was great joy in Jerusalem, for since the time of Solomon the son of David king of Israel there had been nothing like this in Jerusalem (2 Chronicles 30:26).

As is the case with true, genuine, Holy Spirit-inspired revival (as distinct from a revival engineered by people), the revival's impact went far beyond human emotions—it was transformative. The altars of idolatry were removed and there was deep repentance, most notably amongst the religious leadership.

Now when all this was finished, all Israel who were present
went out to the cities of Judah and broke in pieces the pillars
and cut down the Asherim and broke down the high places
and the altars throughout all Judah and Benjamin, and in
Ephraim and Manasseh, until they had destroyed them all.
Then all the people of Israel returned to their cities, every man
to his possession (2 Chronicles 31:1).

As soon as the Passover celebrations were over, Hezekiah set about
organising the priests to ensure the continuance of ministry.

And Hezekiah appointed the divisions of the priests and of the
Levites, division by division, each according to his service, the
priests and the Levites, for burnt offerings and peace offerings,
to minister in the gates of the camp of the LORD and to give
thanks and praise (2 Chronicles 31:2).

Not only did King Hezekiah provide the priests and Levites with
financial support from his own means, he exhorted the people who
lived in Jerusalem to do likewise. And in the spirit of revival, the
people freely responded with such generosity that storehouses had
to be built to hold the surplus, and priests had to be appointed to
administer it all.

And he [Hezekiah] commanded the people who lived in
Jerusalem to give the portion due to the priests and the Levites,
that they might give themselves to the Law of the LORD. As
soon as the command was spread abroad, the people of Israel
gave in abundance the firstfruits of grain, wine, oil, honey, and
of all the produce of the field. And they brought in abundantly
the tithe of everything … When Hezekiah and the princes
came and saw the heaps, they blessed the LORD and his people
Israel. And Hezekiah questioned the priests and the Levites
about the heaps. Azariah the chief priest, who was of the
house of Zadok, answered him, 'Since they began to bring the
contributions into the house of the LORD, we have eaten and
had enough and have plenty left, for the LORD has blessed his
people, so that we have this large amount left' (2 Chronicles
31:4–5, 8–10).

Then Hezekiah commanded them to prepare chambers in
the house of the LORD, and they prepared them. And they

faithfully brought in the contributions, the tithes, and the dedicated things (2 Chronicles 31:11–12).

Thus Hezekiah did throughout all Judah, and he did what was good and right and faithful before the LORD his God (2 Chronicles 31:20).

Hezekiah's pride

In those days Hezekiah became sick and was at the point of death, and he prayed to the LORD, and he answered him and gave him a sign (2 Chronicles 32:24).

To read the details of King Hezekiah's illness and healing, we need to turn to 2 Kings 20 and Isaiah 38.[1]

One day, as Hezekiah was lying on his bed, struck down and close to death, Isaiah came to him and advised him to put his house in order because he would not recover and would soon die. Confronted with the news that his death was imminent, Hezekiah, who was still young, turned his face to the wall, prayed and wept bitterly (38:1–3).

When the Lord heard Hezekiah's prayer and saw his tears, he relented and promised Hezekiah that he would heal him and add fifteen years to his life. He promised Hezekiah that by the third day he would be able to go up again to the house of the Lord. Further, God promised: 'I will deliver you and this city out of the hand of the king of Assyria, and will defend this city' (38:6) 'for my own sake, and for my servant David's sake' (2 Kings 20:6).

God was also pleased to give Hezekiah a sign to fortify his faith.

And Hezekiah said to Isaiah: 'What shall be the sign that the LORD will heal me, and that I shall go up to the house of the LORD on the third day?' And Isaiah said, 'This shall be the sign to you from the LORD, that the LORD will do the thing that he has promised: shall the shadow go forward ten steps, or go back ten steps?' And Hezekiah answered, 'It is an easy thing for the shadow to lengthen ten steps. Rather let the shadow go back ten steps.' And Isaiah the prophet called to the LORD, and he brought the shadow back ten steps, by which it had gone down on the steps of Ahaz (2 Kings 20:8–11).

---

1 Isaiah's account includes Hezekiah's psalm—Isaiah 38:10–20.

And so the great King Hezekiah was miraculously healed—mercifully delivered from the jaws of death by divine intervention in answer to prayer.

By this time King Hezekiah's religious reforms, immense prosperity and great achievements had already made him famous throughout the region. His recovery from death's doorstep and the miraculous cosmic sign that accompanied his healing only served to further enlarge his fame.

Hezekiah was indeed a most remarkable king. Yet at some point he stopped receiving God's gracious blessings with a thankful and humble heart. Rather, it seems Hezekiah succumbed to that which high achieving, successful leaders are most vulnerable: pride.

Consider Hezekiah's prayer of distress (38:3). While it is a prayer of faith in that it acknowledges God's sovereignty, it is also the prayer of a proud man seeking favour from God on the basis of his own good works. 'Please O Lord,' prayed Hezekiah, 'remember how I have walked before you in faithfulness and with a whole heart, and have done what is good in your sight.' Compare this with the heart of Daniel, who concludes his prayer with the words: 'For we do not present our pleas before you because of our righteousness, but because of your great mercy' (Daniel 9:18).

In healing Hezekiah, God graciously overlooked the works-based pride in Hezekiah's feeble prayer, and responded in pure love and compassion, having been moved by his tears (38:5). But because Hezekiah saw himself as deserving of his healing, he failed to give thanks or let God's mercy impact his life.

> But Hezekiah did not make return according to the benefit done to him, for his heart was proud. Therefore wrath came upon him and Judah and Jerusalem (2 Chronicles 32:25).

Pride goes before a fall

As the English Puritan Henry Smith observed: 'When the devil cannot stay us from a good work, then he laboureth by all means to make us proud of it.' [1]

Smith regarded pride as the most wicked of all sins.

---

1 I. D. E. Thomas (ed.), *Golden Treasury of Puritan Quotations*, Moody Press, 1975. p. 225.

For the wrathful man, the prodigal man, the lascivious man, the surfeiting man, the slothful man, is rather an enemy to himself than to God; the envious man, the covetous man, the deceitful man, the ungrateful man, is rather an enemy to men than to God; but the proud man sets himself against God (because he doth against his laws), he maketh himself equal to God (because he doth all without God and craves no help of Him); he exalteth himself above God (because he will have his own will).[1]

As Puritan Richard Greenham likewise noted:

The more godly a man is, and the more graces and blessing are upon him, the more need he hath to pray, because Satan is busiest against him, and because he is readiest to be puffed up with a conceited holiness.[2]

The great King Hezekiah had indeed become 'puffed up': inflated with blinding self-righteousness and swollen with toxic self-sufficiency:

And so in the matter of the envoys of the princes of Babylon, who had been sent to him to inquire about the sign that had been done in the land, God left him to himself, in order to test him and to know all that was in his heart (2 Chronicles 32:31).

The visit of the Babylonian envoys

At that time Merodach-baladan the son of Baladan, king of Babylon, sent envoys with letters and a present to Hezekiah, for he heard that he had been sick and had recovered (39:1).

There is little doubt that an interest in Hezekiah's health and even curiosity over the cosmic sign that had occurred were merely pretexts for a visit that had a decidedly more political agenda.

Merodach-baladan had long been a thorn in Assyria's side. Ruling Babylon since 722 BC, he was always crying 'liberty', refusing to bend the knee and submit to Assyrian suzerainty. Eventually, in 710 BC, King Sargon II of Assyria, ousted Merodach-baladan, forcing him to flee for refuge into neigbouring Elam.

The death of Sargon II in 704 BC[3] was like fuel to the fire of Merodach-

1 Ibid. pp 223–224
2 Ibid. p 223
3 Bright, p. 284.

baladan's nationalistic zeal. In 703 BC, Merodach-baladan 'marched into central Babylon, gathered fresh allies amongst the Aramean tribes along the Tigris, and defeated the Assyrians at Kish'.[1] Reestablishing his sovereignty was one thing, retaining it in the face of Assyrian aggression was quite another. Merodach-baladan knew that unless Assyrian imperialism was defeated then there would never be peace, and his life, and Babylon's independence, would always be at risk. Surely this was the real reason why Merodach-baladan sent envoys to Jerusalem.

Instead of handling the visitation of the Babylonian envoys with the suspicion and caution it warranted and the wisdom and discernment it certainly required, Hezekiah threw caution to the wind and 'welcomed them gladly' (39:2). Clearly flattered to be visited by envoys from as far away as Babylon, Hezekiah rejoiced over the visitors, showing them all his treasures: the silver and gold, the precious spices and oils, and the whole armoury.

Once the envoys had departed, Isaiah confronted Hezekiah, firing two probing questions: 'What did those men say? And from where did they come to you?'

Hezekiah, however, chose to only answer one: 'They have come to me from a far country, from Babylon' (v. 3), indicating that as far as he was concerned, what the envoys said mattered far less than from how far they had come.

Unimpressed, Isaiah continued to probe the king. 'What have they seen in your house?' he asks. To which Hezekiah defiantly responds: 'They have seen all that is in my house. There is nothing in my storehouses that I did not show them' (39:4).

At that point Isaiah realises the terrible truth. He has long known that Jerusalem will be punished for her faithlessness, only not by Assyria, for the Lord has promised deliverance from the hand of Assyria. Now he sees—the instrument of judgement will be Babylon!

> Then Isaiah said to Hezekiah, 'Hear the word of the LORD of hosts: Behold, the days are coming, when all that is in your house, and that which your fathers have stored up till this day, shall be carried to Babylon. Nothing shall be left, says the LORD. And some of your own sons, who will come from you,

---

1 Motyer, p. 296.

whom you will father, shall be taken away, and they shall be eunuchs in the palace of the king of Babylon' (39:5–7).

As if the prophecy was not shocking enough, Hezekiah's response was worse.

> Then said Hezekiah to Isaiah, 'The word of the LORD that you have spoken is good.' For he thought, 'There will be peace and security in my days' (39:8).

Hezekiah has only recently experienced a miraculous healing from the hand of his compassionate, gracious, sovereign God in response to a feeble, vain and even pathetic prayer! Yet he is unable to translate yesterday's experience of divine mercy and deliverance into a message of hope for tomorrow. His thoughts are only for himself! 'At least I'll be ok! At least my legacy is secure.'

Now the very thing that Hezekiah has exalted, glorified and sought—far-away Babylon—will come to him, only bringing death and destruction, just as did the very thing Ahaz exalted, glorified and sought—superpower Assyria. To both the godless Ahaz and the godly Hezekiah, God essentially said: 'What you want, you shall have. The object of your hope will come to you—only it will come to scourge you, not save you!' God not only has a great sense of irony, he is perfectly just.

Doubtless the Babylonian envoys were delighted to find the great King Hezekiah so bloated with pride, for pride disables a person's defenses. That is the rationale for using flattery as strategy.

Hezekiah was doubtless reasoning along these lines: 'I am so great and my fame is so phenomenal that envoys should be sent from so far away as Babylon just to bask for a moment in my glory. They wouldn't ask for my support unless they believed I was absolutely worthy and able to deliver.'

But it is impossible to make an intelligent strategic assessment and analysis without reference to the possible motives and reasoning of the 'other'? So what might the reality have been from the Babylonian perspective?

As a fiery, rebel king committed to independence, Merodach-baladan may have been reasoning along these lines:

King Sennacherib of Assyria will doubtless launch a full-scale counter offensive to wrest Kish from Babylonian control. There will be invasion, occupation, purges and deportations. Along with punishment and subjugation, Sennacharib's intention will doubtless be regime change in Babylon, meaning my life and liberty are on the line.

Babylon could improve her odds by bringing the western states into play once again. Like us, they are reeling under the burden of Assyrian imperialism and hankering for independence. If we can foment rebellion in the west that will pre-empt or coincide with an Assyrian surge, then Sennacharib will be forced to fight on two fronts. In that event, our odds would be greatly improved.

King Hezekiah of Judah is a strong nationalist. He has popular support at home because the Judeans are a strongly nationalistic people with a solid attachment to their unique religion, which he has revived throughout the land. I'll send envoys under the pretext of inquiring about his health and the cosmic sign reported there. They will do the foundational public relations work, gather intelligence and survey what Hezekiah might have to offer. We'll test how pliable he might be, whether he'd be prepared to take his little country to war against the superpower. While Hezekiah doesn't stand a chance against Assyria, it would be of great benefit to us to have him play along!

Hezekiah had been contemplating a nationalistic rebellion against Assyrian suzerainty in coalition with other western states, and so he would have welcomed the Babylonian overtures. Furthermore, that Hezekiah should rejoice over the Babylonian envoys was, notes Oswalt, 'completely understandable from a human point of view. For little Judah to be favored by the attention of Babylon was an opportunity which did not come every day.'[1]

And so Hezekiah, puffed with pride and blinded by flattery, shows the Babylonian envoys all his treasures. 'Here was a ready-made opportunity for Hezekiah to glorify God before the pagan Babylonians,' writes Oswalt,

> to tell of his greatness and of his grace. Instead he succumbed
> to the temptation to glorify himself and to prove to the

---

1 Oswalt, p. 694.

Chaldeans that he was a worthy partner for any sort of coalition they might have in mind.

There is no indication that they [the Babylonians] were interested in such an alliance, however. Much more likely they simply wished to encourage someone whom they viewed as a petty kinglet without making any commitment on their part. An unsavory picture comes to mind of Hezekiah scuttling about showing off his tawdry wealth before the politely approving gaze of Babylonians, who have in fact seen wealth many times the value of the Judean's little horde in their own homeland. Trust in God and his riches will deliver us from the need to make fools of ourselves in the presence of human glory.[1]

—⁓—

A scene repeated today

It is equally unsavory when Christian leaders negotiating with powerful dictators make fools of themselves by declaring with an air of self-importance that they represent millions of believers, the implication being that they are hugely influential, deserving of respect and worth taking seriously. Such Christian leaders might say they represent millions, but in reality, they have no disposable treasury so they can not bribe or apply economic leverage; they have no standing army so they cannot fight or threaten; and they have no real authority for they cannot actually force anyone to do anything. They are essentially (in worldly terms) absolutely powerless. And the hungrier these leaders are for worldly praise, the more vulnerable they are to having their defences disabled through flattery, leaving them open to manipulation and exploitation by unscrupulous elements. And worldly praise is cheap and easy—for it does not even have to be true, only effective.

As Hezekiah's story demonstrates, it is not only the godless and faithless who act faithlessly. Godly, faithful believers and devoted, successful servants of the Lord are all vulnerable to the sin of pride. And when successful Christian leaders fall prey to pride they hurt more than just themselves. Whole churches and peoples are led into disaster when

---

1 Ibid.

their leaders are seduced through pride into folly and sin.

In 735 BC, King Ahaz rejected the Lord, turning instead to Assyria for help against the Syro-Ephramite threat, opening the floodgates for the Assyrian occupation and annexation of northern Palestine. In 701 BC, when the godly King Hezekiah arrogantly provoked the Assyrians by conspiring with the Babylonians and withholding tribute, Assyrian wrath surged and aggressive Assyrian imperialism overflowed its banks and swept on into Judah, bringing death and destruction to Immanuel's land.[1]

If the great King Hezekiah could thus fall, then so can anyone. Only the most arrogant Christians would imagine themselves impervious to or beyond temptation. 'Pride goes before destruction, and a haughty spirit before a fall' (Proverbs 16:18).

From revival to revolt

Finally, how could a people who had been transformed by revival sink so quickly back into practical atheism and faithlessness?

As already noted in this book,[2] unless peace and prosperity are recognised as blessings from the Lord's gracious hand and received with grateful, thankful, humble hearts, then peace and prosperity will only seduce a people into arrogant self-sufficiency, self-obsession and nonchalance concerning spiritual matters. In other words, in the absence of humility and thankfulness, the blessings and fruits of revival may eventually become the source of a people's downfall.

It does not matter that that faith may have emerged from great revivals and great awakenings. Yesterday's faith is not enough. God's people must have humility and faith to look to him today.

> Search me, O God, and know my heart!
> Try me and know my thoughts!
> And see if there be any grievous way in me,
> and lead me in the way everlasting! (Psalm 139:23–24).

---

1 As prophesied in Isaiah 8:8.
2 See Chapter 5 and Deuteronomy 8:11–20.

Questions for Discussion and Reflection

1. Why is it imperative that we look to God before we confront suffering, persecution or threat?

   How does pride work to prevent us from doing so?

2. What potentially can make our strengths and successes dangerous and limiting? (Consider: Proverbs 16:18)

   Discuss how this works.

3. What potentially can make our weaknesses and failings a source of strength and empowerment? (Consider: 2 Corinthians 12:9–10) Explain how this works.

4. Pride might start out like an insignificant victimless flaw, but it grows quietly like a deadly cancer which we usually don't realise has thoroughly infected us until serious damage has been done. But there is a remedy! What is the remedy for dangerous pride?

5. How do we 'take' this remedy? What should we be doing to nurture the dependent humility that empowers, while countering the arrogant pride that limits and destroys?

Prayer

Keep me from dangerous pride.

O Lord, my God and Father,
   you alone are worthy of worship and worthy of praise.

Forgive me for the times I have gloried in my success instead of
   honouring you, stealing your glory and giving dangerous pride a
   foothold in my life.
Forgive me Lord for the suffering I have brought upon others
   because I let dangerous pride infect my thinking,
   and in arrogant independence did not seek your perspective, will
   or empowerment.
O Lord, help me make things right.

Refine your Church, O Lord.
By means of redemptive discipline, reality corrections
   and tough-love born of divine wisdom and grace,
   purge from us the dangerous pride that poisons and deforms,
   and the arrogant independence that limits and destroys.
Help us maintain a realistic view of humanity and particularly of
   ourselves.
May we thoroughly appreciate how utterly dependent upon you we
   are.
Raise up Christian leaders that are humble—
   willing to be led by you and open to being empowered by you—
   for multitudes are affected by the decisions they make.

Lord, I commit to living a Spirit-empowered life by means of humble
   dependence.
I will not fear the frailty of humanity—nor my own frailty.
For while I am limited—you are not!
While I am bound by the laws of nature—you are free!
While I am mortal flesh—you are eternal Spirit!
And while I am fallen—you are perfect in all your attributes.
May I always remember that your strength is made perfect in my
   weakness. (2 Corinthians 12:9–10)

For the sake of the Church and for the glory of the Lord,
    may I rest only in your glorious pastures,
    and never in my past glories.

'Search me, O God, and know my heart! Try me and know my
    thoughts!
And see if there be any grievous way in me,
    and lead me in the way everlasting!' (Psalm 139:23–24)

Amen.

CHAPTER 7

Christian security: not in 'Man'

Isaiah 22:15–25

Jerusalem is buzzing

Only it is not the buzz of industry.

It is the buzz of panic.

Judah, in coalition with Assyria's other Palestinian vassal states, and with backing from Egypt, has overtly rebelled against Assyrian suzerainty by withholding tribute.

King Sennacherib of Assyria has been provoked. Reprisals are in order. As the indomitable Assyrian war machine advances, the heat rises across Judah, fanned by the frenetic activity in Jerusalem.

Those who believe that Judah and her allies are up to the task are abuzz with political and military activity. Meanwhile, fatalists who see no hope are escaping into revelry and drunkenness.

King Hezekiah is preparing his city for a military confrontation. He is arming his forces, shoring up defences, and securing supplies. Missing amidst the frenetic activity however, were the only actions that God was calling for: repentance and returning, and faith (22:12).

Isaiah had long forewarned the Judeans that their lack of faith would lead them into disaster and judgement. According to the prophet, God was going to 'winnow' or 'sift' his faithless, rebellious people and what God was seeking—what would characterise the gleaned remnant—was repentance and faith. The trouble was the Judeans had grown so worldly, arrogant and self-sufficient that they were simply not interested. They heard but did not understand. They saw but did not perceive. Their hearts were dull, their ears were heavy and their eyes were blind. They refused to turn and be healed. And now disaster (the consequence of their folly) and divine judgement (the consequence of their sin) were upon them.[1]

Once again God generously and graciously provided his people with a sign that would verify Isaiah's message and help the Judeans believe the word and repent. The sign—a prophecy that would be fulfilled in the short term—concerned two Jerusalemites of high office, Shebna and Eliakim, whose reversal of fortunes would be played out in the public sphere.

But apart from its value as an interim fulfillment establishing the veracity of Isaiah's words, the story of Shebna and Eliakim is significant in its own right, for the historic drama personifies the principle that no person can be sufficient—not for themselves, nor for others. This drama, which would be played out before the watching eyes of the Judeans—particularly the citizens of Jerusalem—should have given fresh impetus to words they had already heard: 'Stop regarding man in whose nostrils is breath, for of what account is he?' (2:22).

Shebna and Eliakim

Shebna the exalted

Everyone in Judah knew who Shebna was, for he was an official of exceedingly high office, perhaps only second to the king. In the prophecy he is identified as the one who is 'over the household' (22:15), that is, responsible for the administration of all the affairs of the royal palace. Shebna's role was probably akin to that of a prime minister serving in a monarchical or presidential system.[2]

While Shebna was an exalted figure with great responsibilities, he was blighted by personal ambition and an obsession with status and appearance. And so as war loomed and matters of State acquired a sense of gravity and urgency, Shebna the Prime Minister took time out to attend to a personal project: the construction of his own memorial crypt.

So proud was Shebna of his attainments that he believed himself

---

1 Isaiah 6:9–13.
2 Oswalt, p. 418.

worthy of a grand tomb, cut into the rock on the heights overlooking Jerusalem. It would be a memorial that Judeans could look up to (literally) long after his passing, the sort of memorial that might even become a tourist attraction where his fame and glory could be immortalised.

Outwardly Shebna was impressive: successful, powerful, wealthy, glamorous and exalted. Yet inwardly he was arrogant, indulgent, irresponsible and self–obsessed. His heart yearned not for God, but for status, image, possessions and personal glory; he hankered to be seen, recognised, admired, even idolised. Had he been born into our media age he doubtless would have been a celebrity politician and a real 'media tart'.

Because Shebna walked as the world walks—as if God were irrelevant— he failed to realise that his high office was a gift from God for which he would have to give an account of his stewardship. More interested in feathering his own nest while he had the opportunity, Shebna was determined to create a legacy and immortalise his fame. He no doubt found time for manicures, waxes, facials, expensive hair treatments, shopping for designer gear, admiring his glorious chariots, upgrading his office, writing his memoir and constructing his memorial, but seemingly little time to attend to the urgent needs of God's threatened and imperilled people.

How scandalous that such a self–obsessed, self–promoting, self–serving man should be entrusted with affairs of state and the care of God's people. In reality however, Shebna was not very different from many modern politicians, even some contemporary Christian leaders.

Leaders who devote their time and energy to peripheral issues, trivialities and self–interest while existential threat looms over God's people are either blind to reality, living in denial, or simply totally detached from those they claim to represent and serve. It is possible that Shebna's mindset was so geared towards triumphalism that in order to maintain his grip on unreality in the face of impending calamity, he had to live in a state of denial. Are God's people destined to be plagued by leaders of this ilk? It is certainly not uncommon today to find triumphalist Christians doing everything they can to deny the reality of escalating persecution and deteriorating security. This does not necessarily mean they deny that persecution exists, although many like to keep this inconvenient and embarrassing subject off the radar.

Many triumphalists view persecution as just another matter that they will triumph over in their own magnificent strength.

However, not everyone is impressed by status and image. 'The LORD sees not as man sees: man looks on the outward appearance, but the LORD looks on the heart' (1 Samuel 16:7). And so God sends Isaiah to confront the arrogant, self-sufficient Shebna.

Enter Isaiah

> Thus says the Lord God of hosts, 'Come, go to this steward, to Shebna, who is over the household, and say to him: What have you to do here, and whom have you here, that you have cut out here a tomb for yourself, you who cut out a tomb on the height and carve a dwelling for yourself in the rock?' (22:15–16).

Isaiah's challenge is double-barrelled. Firstly: 'What are you doing *here*?' That is: what are you, Shebna the Prime Minister who is meant to be in charge of the palace, doing out here working on a personal project—of self glorification no less—while there is urgent, critical business of state to attend to? Your king is making preparations for war. Desperate and despairing Jerusalemites, their morale unravelling, are increasingly escaping into drunkenness and debauchery. You, Shebna, are a high official with great responsibilities. So what are you doing here?'

Secondly: 'What are *you* doing here?' That is: who do you think you are that you should be constructing a crypt in the rock on the heights to memorialise your name forever? You ride around in your flashy chariots, of which you are so proud, wearing your flashy clothes so everyone can see what you have made of yourself. But do not be deceived. Do you really think you are so great that even in death your bones should be honoured with a monumental landmark?'

Oswalt writes:

> Probably Shebna had come to work on his memorial. He may have been feeling particularly expansive and pleased with himself. If so, these biting words must have been especially humiliating. This kind of experience was typical of the prophets: when they were least wanted, in moments of fear or pride or self-sufficiency, that was the moment they appeared

(7:3, 4; 1 Samuel 13:10; 1 Kings 13:1–6; 18:16–17). But this is typical of God.[1]

Then the uninvited, unwelcomed and offensive prophet—undeterred by Shebna's contemptuous glare and clenched jaw—unleashes God's damning judgement:

> Behold, the Lord will hurl you away violently, O you strong man. He will seize firm hold on you and whirl you around and around, and throw you like a ball into a wide land. There you shall die, and there shall be your glorious chariots, you shame of your master's house. I will thrust you from your office, and you will be pulled down from your station (22:17–19).

God is going to pull the exalted Shebna down from his high station and strip him of his privilege and honour. Then he will roll up the 'strong man' (22:17) into a wad and hurl him away into a broad, faraway land—presumably the broad and faraway Nineveh plains—along with Assyria's countless other captives. And so Shebna, who is here attending to personal projects when he should be elsewhere attending to urgent matters of state, will perish elsewhere in disgrace and ignominy and not here in glory and honour. Furthermore, his beloved 'glorious chariots' (22:18) will go with him into exile—only as the booty of his captors.

> Many are the plans in the mind of a man, but it is the purpose of the LORD that will stand (Proverbs 19:21).

> 'Fool! This night your soul is required of you, and the things you have prepared, whose will they be?' So is the one who lays up treasure for himself and is not rich toward God (Luke 12:20–21).

> From everyone who has been given much, much will be demanded (Luke 12:48, NIV).

> Whoever exalts himself will be humbled, and whoever humbles himself will be exalted (Matthew 23:12).

> Therefore let anyone who thinks that he stands take heed lest he fall (1 Corinthians 10:12).

---

1 Oswalt, p. 419.

Eliakim the humble

The other individual in the prophecy is Eliakim, the son of Hilkiah, whom God affectionately describes as 'my servant' (22:20). According to the prophecy, after Shebna is pulled down from his station—doubtless for neglecting his duties at a time of national crisis—the reliable and trustworthy Eliakim will be exalted in his place. Such a high-level reshuffle would doubtless have been huge news in Jerusalem and right across Judah.

> In that day I will call my servant Eliakim the son of Hilkiah, and I will clothe him with your robe, and will bind your sash on him, and will commit your authority to his hand. And he shall be a father to the inhabitants of Jerusalem and to the house of Judah. And I will place on his shoulder the key of the house of David. He shall open, and none shall shut; and he shall shut, and none shall open. And I will fasten him like a peg in a secure place, and he will become a throne of honour to his father's house (22:20–23).

Imagine that scene! The deposed and scandalised Shebna is a spectator in a grand palace ceremony wherein Eliakim is sworn in and presented with the official robe and sash of office.

Unlike the proud, arrogant and self-obsessed Shebna, Eliakim will be a genuinely caring father figure to all who live in Jerusalem and Judah. He will be given the 'key of the house of David' (22:22), and along with it, the authority to 'open' and 'shut' definitively. This might indicate that Eliakim would be authorised 'to admit people to or exclude them from the king's presence,'[1] that is, he would be entrusted with the power to determine who might have the ear of the king; and/or he might have legislative power—the authority to make binding decisions.[2]

According to the prophecy, Eliakim will be like a peg fastened firmly in a secure place, able to withstand much pressure and bear much weight. Through all this Eliakim will bring great honour to his father's house.

By the time of the Assyrian invasion (701 BC), this element of the prophecy had already come true and thus stood as an interim

---

1 Oswalt, p. 422.
2 Motyer, p. 188.

fulfilment to Isaiah's greater prophecy concerning Jerusalem (22:1–14), which was foreshadowed by the Assyrian invasion of 701 BC, but fulfilled by the Babylonian conquest of 597 BC. Thus we read:

> In the fourteenth year of King Hezekiah, Sennacherib king of Assyria came up against all the fortified cities of Judah and took them … And the king of Assyria sent the Tartan, the Rab-saris, and the Rabshakeh with a great army from Lachish to King Hezekiah at Jerusalem. And they went up and came to Jerusalem. When they arrived, they came and stood by the conduit of the upper pool, which is on the highway to the Washer's Field. And when they called for the king, there came out to them Eliakim the son of Hilkiah, who was over the household, and Shebnah the secretary, and Joah the son of Asaph, the recorder (2 Kings 18:13, 17–18; see also Isaiah 36:1–3).

But just as Isaiah foresees beyond Shebna's demotion to his eventual death in exile, he also foresees beyond Eliakim's promotion and exaltation to his eventual collapse and humiliation. At some point, things are going fall apart for Eliakim too and, consequently, for the Judeans who had invested their hopes in him.

> And they will hang on him the whole honour of his father's house, the offspring and issue, every small vessel, from the cups to all the flagons. In that day, declares the LORD of hosts, the peg that was fastened in a secure place will give way, and it will be cut down and fall, and the load that was on it will be cut off, for the LORD has spoken (22:24–25).

Everything, from the biggest to the most trivial of matters, will be 'hung' on this efficient and reliable father–figure leader. While clearly he can bear much, eventually he will become overloaded, collapse under the weight of it all and have to be relieved of his responsibilities. Once again the good times will have proved to be transitory.

While the Bible provides no further details concerning this tragedy, we should take some time to contemplate Eliakim's fall. How could such a great and godly leader crash so spectacularly? How do great leaders fail themselves? How do we fail them?

Was Eliakim corrupted by his rise? Did he fail to delegate because he had grown proud and self–sufficient? Did he think, 'I can do it' (i.e.

carry the weight of the whole nation), when clearly, as a singular mere mortal, he could not?

Did Eliakim 'spread himself too thin' (so to speak), accepting excessive and divergent responsibilities? This is a trap for many busy and gifted people. The more successful a person is, the more requests will come their way. The temptation is to always be obliging, always saying 'yes', when really what is required is discernment and delegation. For the thinner a person is spread, the more fragile they become, no matter how much ground they cover.

Did Eliakim feel obligated? Did he reason, 'Well this is my job, I had better do it'? Was he too soft hearted for his own good? Could he simply not bear to let anyone down by refusing their request? While this sense of obligation might arise out a compassionate heart filled with noble intentions, to allow oneself to be destroyed by it is sheer weakness, short-sightedness and folly.

As the burdens accumulated and the weight compounded, was Eliakim blind to his limitations? Or had he grown proud, so that he genuinely believed he did not have any?

And as for the Judeans: had they elevated the efficient, reliable, father-like Eliakim to god-like status? Were they investing all their hopes in him—a mere mortal? Were they genuinely surprised and even shocked to discover that Eliakim could not carry the weight of the world on his shoulders?

The Bible does not answer any of these questions, and so we must conclude that the reasons why Eliakim fell are not as important as the fact that he did. The fact illuminates the principle that no man or woman is sufficient—not for themselves and not for others.

Eliakim's story mirrors Hezekiah's (to a degree). For both men were righteous and faithful servants, exalted by God, blessed and enormously successful. As such, both men became the objects of the hopes of many. Yet both men eventually stumbled. While we know that Hezekiah grew proud, we do not know whether Eliakim came to believe the popular narrative—that he was Jerusalem's hope—or was a victim of it. The answer, however, is irrelevant. For Eliakim's collapse and fall simply proved that he was not all-sufficient; but rather was merely human.

Similarly, Shebna's story mirrors Ahaz' (to a degree). For like Ahaz,

Shebna craved status and success in this world while living as if God were irrelevant or even non-existent. Investing all his energies in himself, Shebna climbed the ladder of success, gathered flashy status symbols, and was making preparations to immortalise his fame when God stepped in to reveal that his perspective was totally different.

—◇◇◇—

What about us?

Do we live our lives as did Shebna—independently, as if God is irrelevant or non-existent? Are we pursuing our own agenda, chasing success, fame, glory, status and legacy as if God's perspective and will were inconsequential?

Do we live our lives as did Eliakim—godly, faithful, dutiful and reliable, but carrying far more load than we should? Do we put ourselves, our families and our ministries at risk because we fail to delegate? Why do we fail to delegate? Do we really believe that God cannot use anyone but us? Do we actually believe that we are sufficient for these things? Do we, in pride and arrogance, think we can do it alone and do not need God or anyone else for that matter? Do we neglect to pray for guidance and wisdom because we are confident with our own solutions? Do we neglect to pray for help, for relief, for strength, for more workers, because we are confident we can do it alone, or because we want to do it alone so that we do not have to share the glory? Do we think we should not bother God with our struggles? Do we actually think that God is not interested in politics or other 'worldly' matters? Are we in denial about the fact that we are not actually in control?

Or are we like the Judeans? Are we investing all our hopes in a spouse, a friend, a pastor, a leader—that is, in someone who is, despite all illusions to the contrary, a fragile, limited mortal? Do we heap upon them burden upon burden upon burden until they—surprise, surprise—collapse under the weight of it all?

The reality is that the church is full of Shebnas, Eliakims and Judeans. In fact we if are honest, we all express elements of each at various times.

This lesson—that mortal humans are not sufficient—can be applied in a wide range of situations from personal relationships and Christian family to mission strategies as well as local and international ministry. But the lesson that Christian security is not found in humanity is especially critical in these days of escalating struggle, trial, affliction, persecution and threat. When so much is at stake, these lessons take on new urgency. For when the church is beset with tribulation and persecution—especially when the church is imminently imperilled, besieged and existentially threatened—it is absolutely imperative that we know the limits of humanity.

So despite our anxieties, and even because of them, we must be vigilant in maintaining a right view of humanity. We are:

- *fragile*: like 'jars of clay'; breakable and limited in terms of our holding capacity (2 Corinthians 4:7)

- *fallen*: with a heart that cannot be trusted (Jeremiah 17:9).

- *mortal*: a 'mist that appears for a little time and then vanishes' (James 4:14).

Those who invest their faith in fragile, limited, fallen, corrupted, mortal humans inevitably reap only disappointment and despair.

And so God cries to his besieged church: 'Stop regarding man in whose nostrils is breath, for of what account is he?' (2:22).

Christian security is not found in 'man'.

Questions for Discussion and Reflection

1. It is not hard to find leaders behaving just as arrogantly as Shebna.

   (a) What was Shebna's view of himself?

   (b) What was God's perspective?

It is also not hard to find leaders who are just as godly and dutiful as Eliakim.

   (a) How did the people respond to this godly, dutiful leader?

   (b) What was the result?

3. Consider one such godly, dutiful leader that you know of—maybe even yourself—someone who you fear could be pressured or seduced into bearing too many burdens or being stretch too thin, ultimately putting their ministry and personal wellbeing at risk. What are you going to do to help ensure they don't suffer Eliakim's fate?

4. What simple but critical, eternal and universal principle—based on the foundational exhortation of Isaiah 2:22—underpins and is confirmed through this prophesy?

Prayer

God alone is able.

O Lord my God,
You, and you alone, have shoulders broad enough to bear the
    burdens of this world,
        wings vast enough to shelter us (Psalm 57:1),
        hands deep enough to hold us (John 10:28–29),
        and arms everlasting to catch us (Deuteronomy 33:27).
Mere mortals are not able!
In you, and you alone, is salvation (Acts 4:12),
        power for radical transformation (Isaiah 2:2–4),
        and strength to turn back the battle (Isaiah 28:5–6).

You have called me, O Lord, to be your obedient servant and humble
    companion; (Micah 6:8)
        ambassador and messenger of your gospel;
        light—illuminating truth and highlighting right paths;
        salt—enhancing society and preserving that which is good;
        and yeast—influencing cities and communities from within.
You have called me to be a voice for the voiceless,
        to speak righteousness and justice;
        reflecting your glory, and yours alone.

Forgive me Lord, for the times I lost sight of my calling, and behaved
    arrogantly or foolishly as if everything depended on me.
How I praise you and thank you O Lord, that I do not have to carry
    that burden!
Forgive me for the times I have faithlessly or foolishly put my trust in
    'princes' or other mortals who cannot save. (Psalm 118 and 146)
How I praise you and thank you that my life
        is not in the hands of limited, fallen, fragile mortals,
        but in the hands of the almighty and glorious God, my faithful
        Saviour.

I will depend solely upon the Lord,
        in my God whom I serve
        and who alone is able.

Amen.

CHAPTER 8

Christian security:
not in the 'City of Man'[1]

Isaiah 24–27

'The Bible,' asserts Old Testament Professor Walter Brueggemann,

> starts out with a liturgy of abundance. Genesis 1 is a song
> of praise for God's generosity ... In an orgy of fruitfulness,
> everything in its kind is to multiply the overflowing goodness
> that pours from God's creator spirit.[2]

'So God created man in his own image, in the image of God he
created him; male and female he created them' (Genesis 1:27). And
God placed humankind in a garden where food was abundant, self-
perpetuating and free. And while we frequently forget it—accustomed
as we sophisticated, urbanised 21st-century humans are to markets,
monopolies and exploitation—food, unlike money, still does 'grow on
trees'. Such is the economy of God.

Discounting God's grace, goodness and abundant generosity,
humankind chose to believe the devil's lie that God cannot be trusted;
that God does not rule in our interests; that we would be better off
determining our own path. So we rebelled against God, introducing
sin into the world. Sin enslaved us, condemning all creation to the
curse of sin: frustration, decay and death, just as God said it would.[3]

---

1 I must state from the outset that I am indebted to the seminal work of
  Jacques Ellul, *The Meaning of the City*, Eerdmans, Grand Rapids MI, 1993. A
  history professor, Ellul specialised in the history of institutions.
2 Walter Brueggemann, *Deep Memory, Exuberant Hope: Contested Truth in a
  Post-Christian World*, Fortress Press, Minneapolis MN, 2000, p. 69.
3 Genesis 3; Romans 8:18–25.

Nothing would be easy now. But while our situation had changed, God had not. He was, and still is, the generous God of fruitfulness and abundance.

Cain and the world's first city

> Now Adam knew Eve his wife, and she conceived and bore Cain, saying, 'I have gotten a man with the help of the LORD.' And again, she bore his brother Abel ... And when they were in the field, Cain rose up against his brother Abel and killed him (Genesis 4:1–2a, 8).

In a fit of jealous rage, Cain murdered his brother, Abel, who died leaving no descendants. The Lord confronted Cain and cursed him. From now on, Cain's work would be futile. He was condemned to live as a wanderer, fugitive, nomad, vagabond (Genesis 4:12).

Driven from his land, Cain feared for his life. He cried to the Lord: 'whoever finds me will kill me' (Genesis 4:14).

'Not so!' replied the Lord, who put a mark on Cain so that, should anyone dare attack him, his death would be avenged sevenfold (Genesis 4:15).

Instead of repenting and humbling himself before the Lord, Cain—who was already in open revolt against God—turned and departed from the presence of the Lord (Genesis 4:16a). Rejecting the curse, instead of wandering, he settled (Genesis 4:16b). Refusing God's solution, instead of trusting God for his security, he erected walls and built his own (Genesis 4:17).

The world's first city was built by a rebellious murderer who had rejected God's word and departed from his presence. It was nothing other than an act of defiant independence, for Cain built his city so he could manage his own destiny and security without reference to God. 'The city,' writes history professor Jacques Ellul, 'is the direct consequence of Cain's murderous act and of his refusal to accept God's protection.'[1]

---

1 Ellul, p. 5.

Nimrod and the world's first empire

The next city-builder in the Bible is Nimrod, son of Cush, son of Ham, son of Noah (Genesis 10:1–12). As a consequence of Ham's sin against his father, Ham's descendants were cursed and condemned to live as slaves (Genesis 9:20–27).

> Once again the city is to follow upon a curse as the act by which man tries to escape the curse … From the very fact that he is condemned to slavery, he will become powerful, and his power will assert itself in building cities. Once again man's response to God's curse. And it is absolutely accurate to say that man's power is first of all the result of hardening his heart against God: man affirms that he is strong, conquers the world, and builds cities until God comes to judge the world.[1]

Ellul observes:

> When man is faced with a curse he answers, 'I'll take care of my own problems alone.' And he puts everything to work to become powerful, to keep the curse from having its effects. He creates the arts and sciences, he raises and army, he constructs chariots, he builds cities. The spirit of might is a response to the divine curse …[2]

Nimrod went further than Cain. He did not merely build himself a city in which to settle. Nimrod used his city as a launching pad for further conquest. With each conquest he built a new city which memorialised and secured that conquest, while serving as a launching pad for yet further conquest. Eventually Nimrod built an empire (Genesis 10:10–11).

'The city is now a centre from which war is waged,' writes Ellul.

> Urban civilization is warring civilization. Conqueror and builder are no longer distinct. Both are included in one man, both are an expression of that desire for might which is revolt against the Lord.

And as Ellul notes:

> What world could better demonstrate the parallel between urban civilization and warring civilization that our own, a

---

1 Ibid., p. 10.
2 Ibid., p. 11.

157

world where the city and war have become two of the poles around which the entire economic, social and political life of our time move. [1]

Babel and the world's first 'project'

At the centre of Nimrod's empire was Babel, in the land of Shinar[2] (Genesis 11:2). In Babel the people set out to make a name—a new identity—for themselves. Tired of being defined by tribalism, conflict and chaos, they determined to forge social cohesion by means of a project. They came together to build 'a city and a tower with its top in the heavens'—a tower that would stand as a monument to their success (Genesis 11:3–4).

No matter how noble their intentions and irrespective of all the good will in the mix, the project was established on a foundation of spiritual rebellion. The citizens of Babel were, in arrogant independence, walking as if God were irrelevant. They were thinking only politically— not spiritually—and pursuing social transformation without spiritual transformation. Success would only have served to validate their independence and consolidate their separation from God.

But as Ellul notes, separation from God is death.

> And if God can no longer call man by his own name, then man
> is dead. And if all relations between man and God are broken
> off (really broken, not just broken in the imagination or the
> sentiments or the pretentions of man), then man dies. But
> because God wants his creature to live, he keeps the break from
> happening.[3]

Motivated by love for his creation, God intervened to prevent the project's success.

> And the LORD said, 'Behold, they are one people, and they
> have all one language, and this is only the beginning of what
> they will do. And nothing that they propose to do will now be
> impossible for them. Come, let us go down and there confuse
> their language, so that they may not understand one another's

---

1 Ibid., p. 13.
2 Elsewhere in Scripture the name Shinar is used of Babylon to represents a land of chaos, sin, fury, thievery and plunder. See Daniel 1:2; Zechariah 5:11
3 Ellul, p. 17.

speech.' So the LORD dispersed them from there over the face of all the earth, and they left off building the city. Therefore its name was called Babel, because there the LORD confused the language of all the earth. And from there the LORD dispersed them over the face of all the earth (Genesis 11:6–9).

God did not destroy the Tower of Babel because of a physical problem with the tower. The people had a spiritual problem of which the tower (the project) was merely a symbol. And so God confused their language, leaving them unable to understand or comprehend one another.[1] Now the project must end, for its purpose—peace independent of God, social transformation without spiritual transformation—was no longer achievable. 'By the confusion of tongues, God keeps man from forming a truth valid for all men. Henceforth, man's truth will only be partial and contested.'[2]

And as the Apostle Paul explained to the Athenians, this is for our good:

And he [God] made from one man every nation of mankind to live on all the face of the earth, having determined allotted periods and the boundaries of their dwelling place, that they should seek God, and perhaps feel their way toward him and find him. Yet he is actually not far from each one of us … (Acts 17:26–27).

Despite our failings and frustrations, fallen humanity remains committed to independence: constantly seeking to prove—mostly through cooperation on political and economic projects—that we can make a new name for ourselves and live harmoniously and successfully independent of God.

Modern humanity's 'Tower of Babel' solutions

Similarly, those who today seek to make a new name for themselves by manufacturing peace and social cohesion through projects of political and economic cooperation rather than through genuine spiritual renewal and revival, are implementing 'Tower of Babel' solutions.

Some warring couples decide to have a baby in the belief that the mutual investment required for child creation plus the cooperative

---

1 Incomprehensibility is always regarded as a curse in Scripture.
2 Ellul, p. 19.

effort required for child raising will make peace not only a necessity, but an inevitability. But we all know, this does not work. This too is a 'Tower of Babel' solution.

It is not the end (peace and social cohesion) that is the problem. Obviously peace and social cohesion are noble, even biblical goals. It is the means that is the problem. Tower of Babel solutions invest faith in humanity and depend on works independent of God.

Because Tower of Babel solutions are a means that the world can embrace, they are frequently offered up by Christian peacemakers desperate to win support from the world. The trouble is, no matter how noble the ideals and no matter how much good will there is in the mix, to choose wrong means is to choose disaster.

The UN and the EU are projects through which men and women—many of them Christians—hope to achieve social transformation without spiritual transformation. 'We can do it,' they declare. 'Come, let us build ...' And while some peacemakers are drawn to Tower of Babel solutions on account of overt spiritual rebellion and faithlessness, others propose these solutions out of ignorance or because their theology is corrupted and works-orientated.

As Christian author Vishal Mangalwadi notes,

> Devote Roman Catholics who hate secular nationalism but do not appreciate biblical nationalism have fueled the recent reaction against nationalism and the yearning for a united continent in Europe ... The Reformation broke up the Holy Roman Empire into modern nation-states, often defined by language. Beginning with Genesis 11, the Bible teaches that nations are an invention of the sovereign God. Although all human beings came from one set of parents, they were separated into different linguistic communities as a result of human sinfulness. Living in a particular nation can be hellish, but sovereign nation-states serve as a barrier to global totalitarianism.[1]

Now consider the European Parliament. Built in Strasburg, France, it is modelled—provocatively, I would say—on the famous painting by Pieter Brueghel *The Tower of Babel*. With construction of the Tower

---

1 Vishal Mangalwadi, *The Book That Made Your World: How the Bible Created the Soul of Western Civilisation*, Thomas Nelson, Nashville TN, 2011, p. 171.

of Babel as its symbol; with 'Europe: many tongues, one voice' as its slogan; and with a constitution that refuses to even acknowledge Christianity's role in the formation and foundations of European culture, the EU is a project through which European men and women hope to establish a name—that is, a new identity—for themselves through the construction of a united, harmonious, progressive society on a continent devastated by two World Wars.

Such hope can only exist if we believe the falsehood that the behaviour of men and women can be transformed (as in 2:4b) without those men and women first coming to the Lord for spiritual transformation (as in 2:2–4a). But this is vain. Yes, it might be possible to convince men and women that it is in their interests to beat their swords into plowshares, but unless greed, selfishness and hatred—that is, the problems of sinful human nature—are dealt with, there is no guarantee that they will not use their plowshare to kill each other in a fight for power and profits.

Regardless of the fact that the EU, the UN, and all similar projects were established with the best of intentions and volumes of good will, and regardless of the fact that they are constructed of noble, even biblical, ideals and often championed by well-meaning Christians, they are still Tower of Babel solutions: projects doomed to confusion and failure.

The City of Man

In his seminal work, *The Meaning of the City*, Jacques Ellul presents the reader with a comprehensive theology of the city. Commencing with Cain in Genesis 4 and working through to the New Jerusalem of Revelation, Ellul's thesis is that the city is not merely a collection of houses, walls and ramparts, 'but it is also a spiritual power.' This does not imply that the city is a being, but that the city has a spiritual influence.

> It is capable of directing and changing man's life, all his life …
> But how can this be possible in something purely material?

Cain put all his revolt into it. Man puts all his power into it and other powers come backing up man's efforts.[1]

Ellul describes the city as a human-eating parasite that exists for its own sake, surviving on that which is brought in from the outside. Furthermore, despite our noble intentions and good will, the city remains a centre for idolatry and a place where our sins are concentrated. For the city is a seductress, writes Ellul. She lures men, women and kings, drawing them in. But once they are in her arms and under her spell, a metamorphosis takes place and those who came to her in search of merchandise, security and meaning end up becoming her slaves. Though she uses them up and spits them out, men and women just keep pouring in on an endless conveyer belt of human sacrifice.[2]

The City of Man—*Babylon*—a counter-creation in which humanity assumes control of its own destiny—entraps men and women in a life of slavery and death which is diametrically opposed to that which God in his grace, goodness and generosity ever intended.

Compelled by love for his creation, God intervened in history through the incarnation. Yet Emmanuel—'God with us'—did not entrust himself or his plan of salvation to the City of Man. As Ellul notes:

> The phrase *City of Man* comes from St Augustine. In *The City of God* he distinguishes between the eternal City of God and the temporal City of Man: two rival cities with different origins, shaped by opposing views of life and working towards different ends.

What a beautiful field of action Jesus could have had in Jerusalem—in his capital, near the authorities whom he could have influenced, near the high priest whom he could have converted, in his country's religious nerve centre, at the Temple where he could have preached to the theologians. What an opportunity, to be in the great city, where he had the multitude within reach and all the proletariat he should have sought![3]

Rather, as Ellul observes, Jesus chose against the city. Taking on the totality of the human condition, he refused to accept what people use

---

1 Ibid., p. 11.
2 Ellul, pp. 53–5.
3 Ibid., p. 123.

to escape their condition. He was even crucified outside the city gates, thereby conquering the power of the city 'from the outside'.[1]

Now through Christ, and only through Christ, can men and women live in the city and not be enslaved and devoured by it, for the spirit of the city has no hold over those who are free in Christ. That does not mean that the city has been redeemed. No, the City of Man is still the City of Man. Only now, on account of Christ and by means of the Holy Spirit, the spiritual power of the city might be resisted. The cross of Christ deprives the city of her power to ruin and enslave those who set their faith in Christ.[2] Yes the one who is free in Christ is free indeed.[3]

'Jesus,' writes Ellul,

> in his very person and in his entire life, shows himself to be a stranger to the world of the city. In no way does he participate in this work of man, he who in all other aspects participated fully in man's life. And it is precisely because he took on himself the fullness of human life that he refused this false remedy, this false source of help, this false greatness. And it is because he was establishing the Kingdom of Heaven in the midst of the world that he totally rejected man's counter-creation.[4]

And so, Ellul concludes, Christ shows us that we cannot evangelise the city only by the Word. Rather, the only way to speak to her, to get through to her, is by miracle (divine intervention) or by martyrdom.[5]

While God's righteous ones may live in the city, they are to live there as light and salt and yeast. And while they are to seek the welfare of the city,[6] they must understand that it is a welfare that the city rejects. Because God's faithful are not 'of the world', but have been 'chosen out of the world', the world hates them, just as it hated Christ.[7] When Christ came into the world, the world did not receive him. It was not inconsequential that Jesus was born in a stable in the smallest most insignificant little town in Judah, or that his death took place outside

---

1 Ibid., p. 124.
2 Ibid., p. 132.
3 John 8:31–36.
4 Ellul, p. 124.
5 Ibid.
6 Jeremiah 29:4–7.
7 John 15:18–19.

the city gates—for the City of Man simply could not, and cannot, abide Christ. And we are not greater than Christ. We should remember what he said: 'A servant is not greater than his master. If they persecuted me, they will also persecute you. If they kept my word, they will also keep yours.'[1]

And so we must conclude, as Ellul does so powerfully:

If you see the powers of the world so well disposed, when you see the state, money, cities accepting your word, it is because your word, whether you are only a man of good will or an evangelist, has become false. For it is only to the extent that you are a traitor that the world can put up with you.[2]

Committed as it is to human autonomy, dependent as it is on human enslavement, the City of Man must resist those who are free in Christ, for their presence in freedom and their testimony of liberation are a threat to the city's domination and hegemony. For if men and women were to put their faith in God, the City of Man would lose its very reason for existence.

And so, to the extent that God's children are righteous and faithful, they will be persecuted.[3] 'Indeed, all who desire to live a godly life in Christ Jesus will be persecuted' (2 Timothy 3:12).

A city under judgement

Far too many Christians invest far too much faith in the City of Man and its seemingly noble projects. But Christian security can not be found in the City of Man, for the spirit of this city stands in opposition to Jesus Christ. Despite this, many persecuted Christians and religious liberty advocates crave nothing more than access to the City's institutions and projects, convinced that rescue is found therein. Yet these institutions and projects are nothing more than humanity's attempts at making a name—a new identity—for itself: united, peaceful, noble, successful and independent.

Gathered around the exalted principle of 'universal human rights', men and women invest their faith and hope in the fundamental goodness of human beings. The failure that is ever before us is too painful and

---

1 John 15:20.
2 Ellul, p. 37.
3 See E. Kendal, 'Persecution, whatever that is', RLM, 28 April 2010.

too challenging to accept, so we embrace denial and press on.

But God will neither entertain nor bless such spiritual rebellion and folly. It was on account of spiritual rebellion that Babel's seemingly noble project was condemned. In wrath and mercy God cursed Babel's project with confusion, condemning it to futility, so that its defiant, humanistic aim of social transformation without spiritual transformation, of unity, harmony and 'success' without God—an outcome that would only serve to consolidate humankind's separation from God—could not be realised.

Our contemporary towers of Babel are likewise under judgement. These projects are, even now, cursed with confusion and failure. Eventually they, like Babel's tower, will be abandoned. And while this scenario seems horrific—reeking as it does of failure and hopelessness—it is not. For endings frequently precede new beginnings.

If Christian security is not found in the City of Man or its projects, then where can the besieged church turn? As hardship escalates, as religious liberty fades, as hostility mounts and security becomes tenuous, where can the church go to find refuge and deliverance?

Where?

The City of God

> We have a strong city; he sets up salvation
> as walls and bulwarks.
> Open the gates, that the righteous nation
> that keeps faith may enter in (26:1b–2).

Isaiah 24–27 juxtaposes the City of Man with the City of God. The City of God exists as a spiritual entity within the City of Man. These two cities have diametrically opposed destinies, each involving a reversal of fortunes. A different song is sung in each. In the City of Man, songs of revelry are silenced by judgement, while in the City of God the silence of suffering is displaced by songs of salvation rising from the ashes.

Raymond Ortlund writes:

> What is our world really all about? It's a massive social
> construct, often beautiful and even heroic, rendering plausible
> life without God at the centre. The human race is deeply united
> in building its own world on its own terms. That construction

of reality is passing away. But there is another city, and it can never fall. It wasn't built by human hands; it can't be destroyed by human hands. It's the city of God. And God is inviting us to pick up and move, leave our old lives behind, and build new lives in his city.[1]

The destiny of the City of Man is destruction. God will render it empty and desolate (24:1–4). The earth is defiled on account of humanity (24:5). 'Therefore a curse devours the earth, and its inhabitants suffer for their guilt …' (24:6). Eventually the wine runs out, the music is shut off and the revelry ends. The song of the City of Man falls silent. 'No more do they drink wine with singing' (24:7–9). The City of Man is shut up due to insecurity (24:10). Alcohol shortages lead to riots. Desolation reigns and 'all joy has grown dark' (24:11–12). But 'in the midst of the earth among the nations' there is a remnant (24:13). 'They lift up their voices, they sing for joy … From the ends of the earth we hear songs of praise, of glory to the Righteous One' (24:14–16).

Meanwhile, there is betrayal and terror, catastrophe and death. The earth is broken; the earth is shaken. 'Its transgression lies heavy upon it, and it falls and will not rise again' (24:16b–20). 'On that day' the Lord will dispense justice and the Lord alone will be exalted (24:21–23). He will make the fortified city—the City of Man—a ruin, never to be rebuilt (25:2). The Lord will be exalted and glorified as the defender of the weak, as the faithful one, while 'the song of the ruthless is put down' (25:3–5).

The Lord will prepare a feast for his people—a fine and luxurious feast that makes manifest his gracious generosity and fruitful abundance (25:6). And the shroud (burial sheet) that has covered the nations will be removed (25:7).

> He will swallow up death forever;
> and the Lord God will wipe away tears from all faces,
> and the reproach of his people he will take away from all the
> earth, for the Lord has spoken (25:8).

'On that day', the remnant will be glad that they waited for the Lord (25:9). For the Lord will preserve his remnant in security while enacting his judgements on the earth, bringing down the pretentious fortifications of the City of Man (25:10–12).

---

1 Ortlund, p. 141.

'And in that day' (26:1), as the Babels of the world, along with all their vain rebellious projects, are judged and cast to the ground, God's righteous remnant will sing:

> We have a strong city;
>   he sets up salvation
>   as walls and bulwarks.
> Open the gates,
>   that the righteous nation that keeps faith may enter in.
> You keep him in perfect peace
>   whose mind is stayed on you,
>   because he trusts in you.
> Trust in the LORD forever,
>   for the LORD GOD is an everlasting rock.
> For he has humbled
>   the inhabitants of the height,
>   the lofty city.
> He lays it low, lays it low to the ground,
>   casts it to the dust.
> The foot tramples it,
>   the feet of the poor,
>   the steps of the needy (26:1b–6).

Christian security

The City of Man stands condemned. In judgement, the City and its projects will be humbled and cast down. Christian security cannot be found in the City of Man. Christian security may only be found in the City of God.

And inside the City of God—which is a spiritual not a geographical entity—those who stay their mind on God, because they trust in him, have a real and genuine 'perfect peace' that comes from and is sustained by the Lord (26:3). And so the call comes: 'Trust in the LORD forever, for the LORD GOD is an everlasting rock' (26:4). God is an everlasting *rock*, after the manner of the rock at Horeb in Exodus 17, from which the Lord brought forth life-saving waters in the middle of the desert.

The City of God is the place of sanctuary (as in 8:14a)—that is, *miqdāš*, the place where God dwells in all his holiness.

Remember the paradigm for threatened Christians from Isaiah 8:11–14a?[1]

Do not *walk* the way the world walks (as if God were irrelevant) (v. 11).

Do not *think* as the world thinks (only politically and materially) (v. 12a).

Do not *fear* what the world fears (pain, poverty, persecution, etc.) (v. 12b).

Think differently (spiritually, honouring the Lord as holy.) (v. 13a).

Fear differently (fear only the Lord,) (v. 13b,c).

Walk differently (by faith not by sight, trusting him), knowing the Lord is with you (v. 14a).

Remember the promise of 8:14a, that to those who live by this paradigm, God will be a sanctuary, a *miqdāš*?

When believers enter by faith the City of God, they are entering the presence of the Lord, regardless of their circumstances. The City of God is a place where Christians walk, think and fear differently—and the key to this difference is radical faith. Without faith it is impossible to please God.[2]

Unfortunately, far too many threatened, persecuted Christians, religious liberty advocates and Christian leaders are investing all their energies and hopes in Babylon (the City of Man) and in worldly Tower of Babel solutions as if the spiritual rebellion at their core was inconsequential.

When Isaiah approached the political powers in Jerusalem, he always did so as Yahweh's ambassador, as Yahweh's prophet, and never in the manner of a union representative. Isaiah presented Jerusalem's political powerbrokers with the clear and simple word of God. He invested no faith in kings or political players per se. Neither did he invest faith in the power of weapons or funds or influence or projects that these political powerbrokers had at their disposal. His faith was in the Lord alone.

---

1 See Chapter 3.
2 Hebrews 11:6.

Christian security is not found in the City of Man.
Christian security is only found in the City of God.

Of course, the security found in the City of God is different to that sought in the City of Man. The security that may be obtained in the City of Man is only ever limited and temporal. Furthermore, it is usually deceptive, illusory and costly. However, the security that is guaranteed in the City of God is spiritual and eternal, divine, glorious and free. Sometimes God vanquishes worldly foes. Sometimes, as the testimony of countless martyrs shows, he does not. But regardless of circumstances, God's promise is: that to those who faithfully honour, fear and trust him, he will be to them a sanctuary[1] and a strong city where they might rest in perfect peace, knowing their salvation is totally secure.

———

The Lord makes level the way of the righteous (26:7). As God works out his purposes and enacts his judgements in the earth, the righteous wait, their souls yearning for their Lord. They wait as he delivers justice. They wait as he reveals his glory. They wait as he teaches the world righteousness (26:8–9). The futility of appeasement is confirmed: 'If favor is shown to the wicked, he does not learn righteousness...' (26:10a). For the wicked are so blind that they simply do not discern the majesty of the Lord or his uplifted hand (26:10–11).

The destiny of the City of God is peace, enlargement and resurrection. This is all the Lord's doing—he ordains it and he performs it (26:12–15). Jesus Christ will build his church and the gates of hell shall not prevail against it![2]

Meanwhile, those suffering tribulation and distress whisper prayers to God. They acknowledge that their advocacy and activism in the City of Man has achieved little. They have worked and struggled like a woman in childbirth, pushing through the agony in anticipation of a delivery—and yet they have achieved nothing and have given birth only to wind (26:17–18a).

> We have accomplished no deliverance in the earth,
> and the inhabitants of the world have not fallen (26:18b).

---

1 Isaiah 8:14a.
2 Matthew 16:18.

Yet the Lord's dead shall live; their bodies shall rise, awake and sing for joy! (26:19).

And so the Lord calls:

> Come, my people, enter your chambers,
>   and shut your doors behind you;
> hide yourselves for a little while
>   until the fury has passed by.
> For behold, the LORD is coming out from his place
>   to punish the inhabitants of the earth for their iniquity,
> and the earth will disclose the blood shed on it,
>   and will no more cover its slain (26:20–21).

Yes, 'Leviathan the fleeing serpent, Leviathan the twisting serpent', the dragon Satan shall be slain (27:1). As Ortlund notes:

> God has not only restrained evil, he has not only made it serve his good purposes, he will also annihilate evil at the end of time … No compromise. No mercy. It will be good versus evil, simple as that, and evil will be destroyed fully and forever.[1]

This battle, explains Ortlund, was won at the cross.

> At his cross, Christ triumphed over demonic powers (Colossians 2:15). That's when the devil lost his power to manipulate us with fear (Hebrews 2:14,15). He has no more claim on us, no advantage over us. We are no longer the devil's victims … And at Christ's second coming he will obliterate all his enemies with finality.[2]

The times in which we live—these days between the cross and the culmination of history—are days of intensifying spiritual conflict. For while the powers of evil have been conquered, they have not as yet been eliminated. They still have their power to act, and are, in fact, resisting the inevitable with all the energy they can muster. 'These defeated powers', writes Jacques Ellul,

> are acting, with what we might call the energy of despair. They gather all their means, put all their possibilities to work, no longer acting by trickery and with restraint, but violently and unrestrained.[3]

---

1 Ortlund, p.148.
2 Ibid.
3 Ellul, p. 164 .

Ellul, who fought with the French resistance in the Second World War, notes that the bloodiest struggles against the resistance movement came after 1943, after the war's decisive battles—Stalingrad and El Alamein—had been fought. The general staffs of both sides knew that the war had already been decided. Yet the Germans, in a last-ditch effort to resist the inevitable, issued orders in haste and panic. They launched mass exterminations in the concentration camps and mass deportations of workers to Germany (to replace deployed Germans). 'Thus from an individual standpoint the last year of the war was undeniably the most dangerous and most threatening.' The defeated powers were still able to execute tactical manoeuvres and even score minor victories despite the fact that 'from an overall strategic point of view, the war had already been won'. According to Ellul, after the Allies' victories at Stalingrad and El Alamein, 'All that was left was a massive clean-up operation and the enemy's recognition of their defeat.'[1]

In the great battle between God and evil, the decisive battle has already been fought and won by Jesus Christ on the cross of Calvary. And so the Lord exhorts his faithful: 'Sing!'—sing of that pleasant vineyard, the Lord is its keeper. He cares for his beloved vineyard. He sustains and defends it while appealing to the rebels: 'lay hold of my protection ... make peace with me' (27:2–5). Yes those who place their trust in God will find grace and mercy.

Meanwhile, those in the City of Man will find only terror, for it will be made desolate, a habitation deserted and forsaken, like the wilderness (27:7–11). There will be no security in the City of Man for anyone.

Through it all, the people of God will be 'threshed out of the grain'. They will be 'gleaned one by one' (27:12), gathered from across the earth, to worship the Lord together on his 'holy mountain at Jerusalem' (27:13).[2]

—–⟋⟍⟍—–

It is urgent that Christians—especially persecuted Christians, religious liberty advocates and Christian leaders—come to terms with the fact that Christian security is not found in the City of Man.

---

1 Ibid., pp. 164–5.
2 Cf. Matthew 13:11–12.

Despite humanity's fine intentions and regardless of the abundant good will invested therein, Babel and its projects are built on a foundation of spiritual rebellion. The City of Man along with its vain projects, are thus doomed—they cannot save us. The only role we can have vis-à-vis the City of Man and its vain and futile projects is that of ambassador or witness for Christ: as an evangelist (one who cries: 'Come to the Lord, for you are a sinner and judgement is at hand'), or as a prophet (one who cries: 'You are a sinner and judgement is at hand, so come to the Lord').

Even as I write, Babel's facade is crumbling and her proud, arrogant projects—blighted as they are with confusion—are failing. Men and women—mostly secular humanists—angered by their failure to secure harmony independent of God, proceed to blame God for all their distress. Today the spirit of Babel is no longer content to just subvert the church with projects of false hope. Today the spirit of Babel has become an openly hostile and aggressive enemy.

Using the language of human rights, the spirit of Babel targets the church, accusing her of 'racist' Islamophobia, 'intolerant' homohyphobia, arrogant exclusivism and laughable backwardness. She is accused of being unable to meet even minimum 'human rights' standards. Furthermore, the spirit of Babel condemns the church's witness as destabilising, offensive and divisive—while maintaining that religious expression be strictly controlled or even banned in order to uphold international human rights obligations and maintain social cohesion and a harmonious society. And so the truth is exposed—'the Emperor has no clothes.'

The expression 'the Emperor has no clothes' comes from Hans Christian Anderson's fable, *The Emperor's New Suit* (1837). Swindlers had convinced everyone, including the emperor, that the emperor was magnificently dressed, when in reality he was totally naked. The proclamation, 'But he has nothing on at all', marked the moment when denial was shattered and the horrifying reality was embraced (at least at that point the emperor could cover himself!).

For many this truth is just too shocking to bear. But fear not! The gates of the City of God are open to us (26:2) and the king of that city is calling for us to 'come' (26:20).

Let the criticism begin

In June 2011, the World Council of Churches, the Pontifical Council for Interreligious Dialogue and the World Evangelical Alliance released a document titled 'Christian Witness in a Multi-Religious World. Recommendations for Conduct'. This document is little more than an attempt to reduce persecution by means of appeasement and accommodation, made at the expense of the Great Commission and in denial of the reality of the world's inherent hatred of Christ. As a denial of reality, this attack on mission and betrayal of the persecuted can only fail.[1]

Of course, we will never enter the City of God until we are prepared to leave the City of Man. And that will not happen until we are prepared to end denial and face reality: the church is under siege and Christian security will not be found in the City of Man.

The Western church especially finds it difficult to accept that her position has changed from that of guardian of culture (a safe, authoritative voice in a Judeo-Christian culture) to that of cultural critic (a risky, prophetic voice in a post-Christian culture). But it most certainly has! And so it has become essential that we end denial, grieve our loss and—instead of trying to appease and accommodate the world—let the criticism begin.

In his incredible book, *The Prophetic Imagination*, Walter Brueggemann notes: 'Criticism is not carping and denouncing. It is asserting that false claims to authority and power cannot keep their promises ...'[2]

'Criticism begins', writes Brueggemann,

in the capacity to grieve because that is the most visceral announcement that things are not right. Only in the empire are we pressed and urged and invited to pretend that things are all right—either in the dean's office or in our marriage or in the hospital room. And as long as the empire can keep the pretense alive that things are all right, there will be no real grieving and no serious criticism.[3]

---

1 For my response, see E. Kendal, 'Christian Missions and Persecution', RLM, 6 July 2011.
2 Walter Brueggemann, *The Prophetic Imagination*, 2nd edn, Augsburg Fortress, Minneapolis MN, 2001, p. 11.
3 Ibid.

Brueggemann notes that for the enslaved descendents of Jacob in Egypt, their 'narrative of liberation begins with the grieving complaint' found in Exodus 2:23–25. The cry, he remarks, is not merely a cry of misery and self-pity. It is 'the official filing of a legal complaint', with the mournful one as the plaintiff.[1] It is not the voice of resignation, but the voice of expectation.

> 'and the people of Israel groaned because of their slavery and cried out for help. Their cry for rescue from slavery came up to God. And God heard their groaning, and God remembered his covenant...'
>
> Exodus 2:23–25

'Thus,' writes Brueggemann,

> the history of Israel begins on the day when its people no longer address the Egyptian gods who will not listen and cannot answer. The life of freedom and justice comes when they risk the freedom of the free grace of God against the regime.[2]

The grieving of God's enslaved people leads to complaint but not to resignation, and this marks the beginning of that criticism which has the power to expose the myths and dismantle the unacceptable status quo. Things are definitely not as they should be. 'Bringing hurt to public expression is an important first step in the dismantling criticism that permits a new reality, theological and social, to emerge.'[3]

As the plagues ravaged Egypt, the people, desperate for relief, cried to Pharaoh yet again (Exodus 5:8, 15). But, notes Brueggemann:

> By the middle of the plague cycle Israel has disengaged from the empire, cries no more to it, expects nothing of it, acknowledges it in no way, knows it cannot keep its promises, and knows that nothing is owed or expected of it. That is the ultimate criticism which leads to dismantling.[4]

The church likewise needs to disengage from the City of Man and from its vain and futile projects. This sounds like I am advocating retreat and inaction. But I am not—far from it. I strongly advocate cultural

---

1 Brueggemann, p. 11.
2 Ibid., p. 12.
3 Ibid.,
4 Ibid., pp. 12–13.

174

criticism and Christian witness. For while Christian witness might be the trigger for most persecution, it must be acknowledged that Christian witness is the only solution to the problem of persecution.

> '*But all these things they will do to you* [they will persecute you] *on account of my name, because they do not know him who sent me*'
> John 15:21

While it might be difficult to disengage from the City of Man and give up on its seemingly noble projects, we simply must do it. We cannot start out on a new journey—a journey to the Promised Land where the promises of God are fulfilled—

> '*And they will do these things* [persecute you] *because they have not known the Father, nor me*'
> John 16:3

until we end our denial, give up on Pharaoh, let go of Egypt and step out in faith, trusting the Lord.

———

Christian security is *not* found in the City of Man.

So let us sing a lament and grieve our loss.

Let us stop crying to useless Pharaoh.

Let us hold a funeral and light a pyre for all the vain and futile projects of rebellious humanity.

Let us risk the free grace of our generous sovereign God.

For Christian security is *only* found in the City of God.

And the Lord is calling: 'Come, my people …' (26:20).

Questions for Discussion and Reflection

1. If humanity's cities and 'Tower of Babel' projects are rooted in rebellion, cursed with confusion and devoted to destruction, should we be investing our trust and hopes in them or witnessing and speaking prophetically to them?

   What does this mean in practice?

2. Might it help to re-classify advocacy as prophetic witness rather than as political activism? Why?

3. In what ways is the prophet Isaiah a perfect example of speaking prophetically into power while never investing trust and hope there?

4. How did Isaiah's acceptance of his role as prophetic witness—as distinct from political activist—safeguard his advocacy ministry against corruption and deception?

5. Our move from the condemned 'City of Man' to the secure 'City of God' is essentially one of re-orientation; but what does this move involve in practice?

How does the concept of the 'City of God' fit in with

   (a) the reality expressed in John 15:19; 17:14?

   (b) the promises found in Isaiah 8:14a and John 16:33?

Prayer

Moving into the City of God.

Lord, you are my Saviour and Redeemer,
    I praise and thank you for your great love and faithfulness.
For you have brought me out of darkness into your marvelous light,
    out of this failing world into your unshakable kingdom.
Now O Lord, help me to live in this reality.

Forgive me Lord, for the times I have faithlessly or foolishly put my
        faith in the political, economic and military power of cities
    that are rooted in rebellion and destined for destruction—
    rather than in you, my Saviour.
Lord, open my eyes that I might see the 'City of Man' as you see it:
    not as a testament to human power and glory,
    but as a mission field in desperate need
    of Gospel witness and radical transformation.

Forgive me Lord, for the times I have faithlessly or foolishly put my
        faith
    in spiritually rebellious humanistic projects
    that are founded on faithlessness and cursed with confusion—
    rather than in you, my Lord.
Lord, open my eyes that I might see these projects for what they are:
    desperate, arrogant, humanistic efforts at self-salvation,
    designed to consolidate and legitimise human independence—
    a path that leads to eternal death.

May the Church understand that these cities and projects cannot
        save her.
Rather, they are in desperate need of the transformative truth and
        power of Jesus Christ, whose ambassadors we are and whose
        Good News we bear.

And so I commit, Lord, from this day forth, to practically living out
        my reality as a citizen of the City of God
    and ambassador for my king.
I acknowledge that this may well lead to rejection, scorn, persecution
        and even death—
    'and if I perish, I perish.' (Esther 4:16)

Yet, for the sake of your Church and this world and that the Lord
  might be exalted and glorified,
I commit to stepping out in faith to risk the free grace of God.

How wonderful it is, that my security rests with the God of all grace;
God, who is my sanctuary (Isaiah 8:14a) and everlasting rock.
  (Isaiah 26:4)
The Lord is my fortress, deliverer, shield, and stronghold:
strength and refuge are found in him. (Psalm 18:2)

Amen.

CHAPTER 9

Christian security:
not in a 'covenant with death'

Isaiah 28:9–22

In 704 BC the ruthlessly imperialistic Assyrian king, Sargon II, was killed in battle, and the conquered peoples, long hungry for independence, wondered if a window of opportunity may have opened. As Sargon's son, the untested Sennacherib, ascended to the throne, conspiracies simmered in Babylon to the south and throughout Palestine to the west as dreams of liberation and national independence dared find voice once again.

Challenging the status quo: rebellions and reprisals

King Merodach-baladan of Babylon fomented revolt in the south while King Hezekiah of Judah mustered an anti–Assyrian coalition in the west and brokered a security treaty with Egypt, the ascendant regional power. Ultimately, in an act of provocative, defiant rebellion King Hezekiah withheld tribute (2 Kings 18:7).

Most Judeans regarded the security treaty with Egypt as a diplomatic coup. Long weak and divided, Egypt had been a useless ally to the Palestinian states throughout the middle and late 8th century BC. As historian Bright notes, 'This was the situation when Samaria fell and Egyptian help proved so worthless.'[1] 'But,' explains Bright,

> ca. 716/15 the Ethiopian king, Piankhi, having made himself
> master of Upper Egypt, overran the entire land, ending the
> Twenty–third Dynasty and allowing Bocchoris, the last king

---

1 Bright, p. 281.

of the Twenty–fourth, to rule as his vassal. Piankhi founded the Twenty–fifth (Ethiopian) Dynasty; at least by 710/9 all Egypt was united under its control. In view of these signs of resurgence, Assyrian vassals in Palestine might dare once more to look to Egypt for help.[1]

Back in Nineveh, meanwhile, King Sennacherib, enraged by Babylon's rebellion and Jerusalem's provocations, was preparing devastating reprisals.

Fully cognisant of the looming threat, Jerusalem was abuzz with activity. Those investing faith and hope in political and military processes celebrated diplomatic successes, in particular the covenant (treaty) with Egypt, drinking themselves blind. Those believing that nothing could save them opted for escape, exploiting life before death, drinking themselves blind (22:8–14; 28:7–8). Eventually all the tables were 'full of filthy vomit, with no space left' (28:8).

Enter Isaiah

Meanwhile, Isaiah was preaching the same old message, the same old timeless word of God: walk in the light of the Lord and stop regarding and exalting human beings. Do not walk the way the world walks: as if God were irrelevant. Do not think as the world thinks: only politically and materially. Do not fear what the world fears: anger, pain, people. Think differently: spiritually, honouring the Lord as holy. Fear differently: fear only the Lord. Walk differently: by faith not by sight. Remember the faithful God of your salvation and the Rock of your refuge. Remember and return!

It was (and is) a very simple and timeless message. And while it undoubtedly was (and is) a very difficult word to implement, such radical faith had been exemplified by Noah, Abraham, David and others. Yet the Judeans would not receive it. The fruits of revival had been carelessly consumed rather than diligently preserved and propagated. Pride had set in, displacing faith. God had been forgotten yet again.

And so the Judeans rejected God's word and scoffed at God's prophet, belittling his message as unsophisticated, simplistic, repetitious babble fit only for the ears of infants (28:9–10).

---

1 Ibid.

No way were these Judeans going to trust God. They were far too sophisticated for that. They had 'moved on' from the days of revival and were proud of their ability to engage politically with great (albeit earthly) powers. As far as they were concerned, they did not need God anymore; they were quite above that.

'We have secured an alliance with power,' they boasted. 'We have a treaty with strength; a covenant with life! Egypt, the ascendant regional power, has promised to protect us and deliver us from our enemies.'

'You already have a covenant,' roared Isaiah, 'with God! Remember him—your Saviour and Rock? He is the *supreme* superpower, and he has promised to protect you. All you have to do is trust him.'

But they did not want to listen, and so they scoffed: 'Get lost, Isaiah, you nagging, repetitive pain. Keep your simplistic message for the simple minded and unsophisticated. We'll play politics thank you. We're in the big league now!'

—⁓⁓—

Example: Lebanon

Lebanon's Christians: from majority to minority (1970–2000)

During the latter part of the 20th century, Lebanon underwent a radical demographic metamorphosis. In 1970, Lebanon was around 62 percent Christian and supposedly a showcase of Christian–Muslim co-existence. Actually, Lebanon was an experiment in Christian–Muslim co-existence.

In September 1970, Palestinian militants in Jordan fought unsuccessfully to overthrow Jordan's King Hussein. In response to 'Black September', King Hussein expelled many thousands of Palestinian Liberation Organization militants, who subsequently re-established themselves in southern Lebanon. Ultimately this only served to make Jordan's problem Lebanon's problem. Palestinian militants flooded into Lebanon through the 1970s, creating the situation which led to the sectarian and civil war that wracked the state through the 1980s. When Lebanon refused to reign in Palestinian Liberation Organization militants—who were now focused on committing terror against Israel—Israel invaded and occupied southern Lebanon to do the job itself. Lebanon subsequently erupted in an orgy of sectarian killing.

During this period, developments in Afghanistan were exerting an influence throughout the Muslim world. The Afghan jihad was essentially a Cold War proxy battle wherein the US supported the Afghan mujahedeen in their fight against Soviet occupation. The jihad attracted fighters from all over the Muslim world, who received ideological and military training. In February 1989, when the last Soviet troops departed Afghanistan, nine years of jihad came to an end and the mujahedeen dispersed, taking their jihadist ideology and fighting skills with them. As a result the 1990s saw a dramatic escalation in global Islamic fundamentalism and militancy.

As intolerant Islamic fundamentalism escalated in Lebanon through the 1990s, many Christians took flight, seeking a safer, more peaceable, equitable and secure existence in the West.

Further, rather than helping Lebanon's beleaguered Christians, 'democracy' (reduced to sheer *majoritarianism*) only served to advance their marginalisation as electoral gerrymandering, political assassinations and violent intimidation became the order of the day.[1] By the year 2000, Christians comprised only 32 percent of majority-Muslim (23 percent Sunni and 36 percent Shi'ite) Sunni-dominated Lebanon.

> *Majoritarianism* is what happens when Western democracy is separated from the Judeo-Christian values that underpin it, it is reduced to an electoral process and a majority rule vulnerable to human forces of greed, self-interest, sectarianism and raw tribalism.

Shi'ite ascendency (2003–2010)

Sunnis and Shi'ites have been avowed enemies ever since the 7th century AD. While Shi'ites have historically been settled peoples, content to wait for the return of the Mahdi (the Shi'ite messiah), Sunnis have historically been traders, nomads, warriors and imperialists. Consequently, Sunni Islam has spread far and wide, and today around 85 percent of the world's Muslims are Sunni. In the Middle East, however, the Sunni-Shi'ite ratio is around 50:50.

---

1 See E. Kendal, 'Lebanon: elections will entrench Christian marginalisation', RLM, 20 May 2005.

The 1979 Iranian Shi'ite Revolution emboldened the region's Shi'ites so that Shi'ite psychology (generally speaking) underwent a seismic shift: from quietist to revolutionary. This, and the subsequent failed Sunni Wahhabist coup in Mecca in November 1979,[1] left the region's US-allied Sunni Arab dictatorships seriously rattled.

To counter the threat posed by revolutionary Shi'ite forces, the region's Sunni Arab dictators, along with their Western allies, supported Iraq's Ba'athist dictator, Saddam Hussein, in his eight-year war against Iran. To counter an additional threat posed by Sunni fundamentalist jihadists, they supported the jihad against the Soviets in Afghanistan, happily sponsoring their own local jihadists to go and fight jihad far, far away (anywhere but at home).

With the revolutionary Shi'ites bogged down in the Iran-Iraq war (September 1980 to August 1988), and the international Sunni jihadists tied up in Afghanistan (December 1979 to February 1989), the Middle East's Sunni Arab dictators were able to perpetuate their regional dominance through the 1980s virtually unchallenged.

They maintained the status quo through the 1990s by repressing returned jihadists, exiling or incarcerating any that threatened trouble at home—all with US support.

In November 1979, an international Sunni radical jihadist group led by Juhayman al Uteybi, laid siege to Islam's holiest shrine, the Grand Mosque in Mecca. Hundreds died in this failed Wahhabist coup aimed at removing the Saudi royal family and effecting a fundamentalist Sunni revolution. The House of Saud only survived thanks to US support and the involvement of French Special Forces.

Founded by an Arab Christian, the Ba'ath Party aimed to unite Arabs of all sects on a platform of secular, socialist Arab nationalism: i.e. national unity and social equality. Ba'athism was pan-Arabist, anti-imperialist and anti-Islamist. Ba'athist dictatorships have generally respected religious freedom while ruthlessly crushing political opposition, especially that of political Islam (the most threatening opposition of all).

1 See Yaroslav Trofimov, *The Siege of Mecca: The 1979 Uprising at Islam's Holiest Shrine*, Anchor Books, New York, 2007, siegeofmecca.com.

However, the 2003 US-led invasion of Iraq—along with the short-sighted policies that resulted in a power vacuum and sectarian-civil war—saw Iraq's long-repressed Shi'ite majority liberated and empowered. This radically altered the Sunni-Shi'ite balance of power, enabling a Shi'ite ascendency not only in Iraq, but regionally. Suddenly Iran, Iraq's Shi'ite neighbour, was strategically significant as never before.[1] As Iranian power and influence rose, so too did that of its proxies, in particular Hezballah (the army of Allah) in highly strategic, sectarian, volatile Lebanon.

Free Patriotic Movement brokers treaty with Hezballah

Lebanese elections have long been sectarian affairs, with Sunnis voting for Sunnis, Shi'ites voting for Shi'ites, and Druze voting for Druze. Lebanon's Christians, however, are politically diverse and profoundly divided. At the time of the 2005 elections, around seventy percent of Lebanon's Christians supported the Free Patriotic Movement of retired General Michel Aoun (a Maronite Christian).

On 6 February 2006, the highly ambitious Aoun signed a 'Memorandum of Understanding' with Hezballah leader Hassan Nasrallah in a ceremony in Mar Mikhail Church, located a few blocks from Hezballah's headquarters in Beirut's southern suburbs. This was nothing other than a pragmatic alliance for political gain. While Hezballah was betting it could secure political power by bringing the largest Christian party into its alliance, Aoun was betting he could ride into the presidential office (reserved for a Christian) on the back of an ascendant Hezballah. Meanwhile, the Free Patriotic Movement's Christian supporters were hoping they could advance Christian security by political means, through an alliance, or covenant, with the ascendant power: the Iranian proxy and terrorist paramilitary, Hezballah.

Meanwhile, it had become clear to the US that there would be no dignified exit from the Iraqi war theatre unless Iraq could be stabilised. It had also become clear to the US that Iran wielded considerable influence over Iraq's Shi'ite militias, for most of Iraq's Shi'ite militias originated in Iran during the Saddam years and maintained strong roots there. Thus Iran could facilitate stability in Iraq by reigning in

---

1 See E. Kendal, 'Religious Liberty Trend: Shi'ite ascendency', RLM, 5 February 2007.

Iraq's Shi'ite militias and disrupting the dangerous cycle of sectarian violence.

While no one could rein in al-Qaeda and its affiliates, Iran could rein in the Shi'ite groups and thus break the cycle of sectarian conflict. In late 2007, years of sectarian war ended because, despite continued Sunni militant and al-Qaeda terrorism, the Shi'ites no longer responded. They would wait for the US withdrawal.

And so this is how it came to be, that in the space of a few short years, the US had gone from being the Middle East's regional hegemon, to being increasingly dependent on ascendant Iran—for both supply in Afghanistan (as Pakistan's Khyber Pass became increasingly insecure) and stability in Iraq (essential for a dignified US exit).

To this end, writes terrorism analyst Yossef Bodansky, US President G. W. Bush brokered a deal with the Iranians in November 2007 whereby the US would not challenge Iranian hegemony in Iraq or the wider region, in exchange for Iran's guarantee that the US could have an honourable exit from Iraq (one resembling 'achievement').[1]

From that pivotal moment—which was marked by a US policy U-turn on Iran's nuclear program—Iran's rise to that of regional hegemon was meteoritic.[2]

By the end of 2007, after years of Sunni versus Shi'ite sectarian war, not only was Iraq totally polarised along religious lines, but the balance of power in the wider Middle East had radically shifted. Centuries of Sunni domination were giving way to a regional Sunni-Shi'ite struggle.

Hezballah's blitzkrieg

On 6 May 2008, Lebanon's pro-West, US-backed, Sunni-led government passed a resolution decreeing that Hezballah's extensive and independent parallel telecommunications network be integrated into the government's national network. The government also ruled that the illegal surveillance system on Runway 17 of Beirut airport—installed by the chief of airport security, Wafiq Shuqayr, at Hezballah's

---

1 Yossef Bodansky, 'Washington's deal with Iran: an early US withdrawal from Iraq, but at the peril of long-term Western interests and stability in the Middle East', *Defense & Foreign Affairs Strategic Policy*, vol 36, issue 1, 2008.
2 See E. Kendal, 'Religious Liberty Trends 2007–2008', RLM, 15 February 2008. (under the subheading 'A word on the Middle East).

request—be dismantled, and that Shuqayr (a Shi'ite with known ties to Hezballah) be removed from his position.

Hezballah's response was swift and devastating. After blockading all the roads to the airport, Hezballah seized Sunni West Beruit, shutting down all Sunni-owned pro-government media. After two days of fighting in the Sunni areas of Beirut, Hezballah moved its fight to the Druze areas of Mount Lebanon. Eventually, with the state on the brink of civil war, and with their homes under siege, both Sunni leader Saad Hariri and his then-ally Druze leader Walid Jumblatt capitulated to Hezballah's terms. It was a most impressive blitzkrieg—one which the Lebanese army, under the direction of General Suleiman (who had been appointed to the post with Syrian approval in 1998), did not resist.

While the Lebanese Army did not resist Hezballah, it doggedly fought and profoundly defeated al-Qaeda-inspired Fatah al-Islam (Sunni) in north Lebanon over three months in the summer of 2007.

The subsequent 21 May 2008 'peace' deal brokered in Qatar—which is, according to analyst Barry Rubin, 'an integral part of the Iran-Syria-Hezballah axis'[1]—gave the Shi'ite-dominated, Iran-backed, Hezballah-led opposition veto power over the elected Sunni-dominated, US-backed, pro-West government. The West's inability and/or unwillingness to defend its allies, along with its impotence vis-à-vis the Shi'ite ascendency, were exposed for the whole world to see.

If Hezballah's terrorism, belligerence, violent anti-Semitic rhetoric and Iranian roots had not been enough to alert Lebanese Christians to its treacherous nature, you might think that its violent May 2008 blitzkrieg, wherein it took up arms against Lebanese citizens, might have. But no!

Covenant with death

While I was unable to see an alliance with Hezballah as anything other than a 'covenant with death'—that is, as an alliance with one who either will not or cannot save you—senior Lebanese evangelicals were hailing the Christian-Hezballah alliance as a covenant with life; a means to political power whereby the problems of Christian

---

1 Barry Rubin, 'The Fall of Lebanon', The Global Research in International Affairs Center 24 May 2008, www.globalpolitician.com/24855-lebanon.

marginalisation and insecurity could be solved.

Now some might think—indeed I have been told—that there is no right or wrong in these matters; that this is an area of Christian liberty and the desired end—Christian security—is all that matters: that is, the end will justify the means.

But as Isaiah preached, and as the history of Judah demonstrates: means matter. Wrong means invite disaster (the consequence of folly) and judgement (the consequence of sin, spiritual rebellion and covenantal betrayal). The issue is trust. When considering means, will we trust God enough to seek his perspective and then obey his revealed word?

Judah brokers covenant with Egypt

When the Judeans rejected the clear and simple word of God, and traded the Lordship of their true covenant king, Yahweh, for an alliance with ascendant military might, God vowed in his wrath to deliver them over to foreign occupiers whose words, being in the Assyrian language, they would not understand (28:11): incomprehensibility is always a curse in Scripture.

God was offering his people 'rest'—that is, the rest and perfect peace that may be found in his sanctuary and under his loving kingship—but they were not interested.

This is rest;
    give rest to the weary;
and this is repose';
    yet they would not hear it (28:12).

Isaiah warned that those who reject God's simple word would inevitably 'fall backward, and be broken, and snared, and taken' (28:13d). This is exactly what he had prophesied more than three decades earlier when he warned that those who reject God will consequently 'stumble' over him; they 'shall fall and be broken; they shall be snared and taken' (8:15). The message is the same for it is a truth for all times.

Meanwhile, God has a word for the scoffers (28:14–22).

Therefore hear the word of the LORD, you scoffers,
  who rule this people in Jerusalem!
Because you have said, 'We have made a covenant with death,
  and with Sheol we have an agreement,
when the overwhelming whip passes through
  it will not come to us,
for we have made lies our refuge,
  and in falsehood we have taken shelter' … (28:14–15).

Isaiah's sarcastic representation of the attitude of Jerusalem's ruling elites is potent. They truly believed their covenant with ascendant power (Egypt) would save them; that when the 'overwhelming whip [the Assyrian Army] passes through', it would not touch them because the ascendant power, their ally Egypt, would protect and deliver them.

It is ironic that the very same elites who saw themselves as too sophisticated to abide Isaiah's simple message would themselves employ such infantile simplicity, breathtaking naivety and fatal short-sightedness in their foreign policy. For ascendant Egypt would prove no match for the aggrieved, imperialistic, superpower Assyria.

As Gileadi notes, there can only be '"woe" (*hôy*), the pronouncement of a covenant curse … woe or malediction [for] those who seek to implant their own "schemes" or "counsel".'[1] Indeed, while Judah celebrated her agreement with Egypt as a covenant with life, God condemned it as a 'covenant with death', an 'agreement with Sheol' (28:15, 18).

'[T]herefore' (28:16), because they have made a 'covenant with death'—the consequence of which is disaster, terror and devastation—God exhorts his people to look to him: to behold their God. He is the God who chose Jerusalem and established its foundations. He is the God who has invested himself in Jerusalem and has promised to establish justice and righteousness there.

therefore thus says the Lord GOD,
'Behold, I am the one who has laid as a foundation in Zion,
  a stone, a tested stone,
a precious cornerstone, of a sure foundation:
  'Whoever believes will not be in haste.'

---

1 Gileadi, p. 215.

And I will make justice the line,
and righteousness the plumb line ... (28:16–17a).

God's promise is that 'Whoever believes will not be in haste'—that is, whoever will put their faith in God will not be hurried, agitated, shaken, reactionary. Rather they will find 'rest' for their souls. Oswalt explains: "The sense is clear: for the person who puts his or her trust in God, there can be a serenity and a calm deliberateness which is not possible otherwise (26:3, 4; 30:15–17). To refuse to entrust my ways to God is to open myself up to a hectic and feverish existence in which I rush here and there with decreasing

> 'Come to me, all who labour and are heavy laden, and I will give you rest. Take my yoke upon you, and learn from me, for I am gentle and lowly in heart, and you will find rest for your souls. For my yoke is easy, and my burden is light.'
> Matthew 11:28–30

success to control the disparate parts of my life. To commit my ways to him may not increase my success but it will grant peace through the realization that my times are in his hands.'[1]

God then declares that the covenant brokered with Egypt will not stand, but will be swept away as the overwhelming flood—the Assyrian military—sweeps through the land.

'... and hail will sweep away the refuge of lies,
and waters will overwhelm the shelter.
Then your covenant with death will be annulled,
and your agreement with Sheol will not stand;
when the overwhelming scourge passes through,
you will be beaten down by it.
As often as it passes through it will take you;
for morning by morning it will pass through,
by day and by night;
and it will be sheer terror to understand the message.'
(28:17b–19).

For as the prophet had forewarned, the 'waters of the River' (the Euphrates)—the 'mighty and many' armed forces of King Sennacherib of Assyria—were on their way. And this surging Assyrian river of soldiers 'will rise over all its channels and go over all its banks, and it will sweep on into Judah, overflowing, passing on, reaching even to

1 Oswalt, p. 519.

189

the neck. Its 'outspread wings' will fill the breadth of Immanuel's land.[1]

And when the mighty Assyrian river floods into Judah, then, despite the fact that the Assyrians speak in an unintelligible tongue, their message will be unmistakeably clear: 'Assyria is here to stay!' The Judeans will be overcome with terror as they are forced to confront their new reality. For no matter how impressive ascendant Egypt appeared, no matter what deliverance she promised, Egyptian aid will prove insufficient. 'For the bed is too short to stretch oneself on, and the covering too narrow to wrap oneself in' (28:20).

In other words: God's people, who have arrogantly pursued their own security as if God were irrelevant, who thought they would be able to rest and repose under the covering blanket of Egypt, will discover, to their absolute terror, that security built upon their own efforts is invariably inadequate and unreliable. Though they lie down under the covering blanket of Egypt, they will not be able to rest. For no matter which way God's people turn, they will remain uncomfortable and exposed. Their covenant with Egypt will afford them no rest, no repose. Such is the absolute folly of seeking security in a *covenant with death*.

―∿∿―

Lebanon 2009–2010: 'the traitor betrays ...'

Lebanon went to the polls again on 7 June 2009. Although the Sunni-dominated, Saudi and US-backed, pro-West 'March 14 Alliance' won the elections with 70 seats to 58, the Shi'ite-dominated, Syria and Iran-backed, Hezballah-led opposition—the 'March 8 Alliance'—actually won the popular vote with 55 percent of the ballot.[2]

Moreover, because Hezballah had already established its hegemony as the strongest military force in the state, it was able to dictate terms. Eventually, after months of political paralysis, the 'March 14 Alliance' consented to appease Hezballah and form a government of national unity. Hezballah thus secured, through terror, the right not only to veto

---

1 Isaiah 8:7–8.
2 E. Kendal, 'Lebanon: pivotal elections spotlight Christians', RLPB 007, 3 June 2009; 'Hizbullah boasts victory in the popular vote of the Lebanese elections', AHN, 11 June 2009, www.allheadlinenews.com/articles/7015462027.

parliament, but to control the foreign affairs, health, communications, energy and industry portfolios. Free Patriotic Movement head Michel Aoun secured the communications portfolio for his son-in-law, Gebran Bassil, despite the fact that Bassil had just lost his seat in parliament.[1] With communications under their control, Hezballah's Christian allies could make sure Hezballah's illegal, parallel telecommunications network would not be challenged again.

It did appear, however, that a significant number of Christians deserted the Free Patriotic Movement in the weeks prior to the election. On 11 May 2009, *The Lebanon Daily Times* reported:

> Aoun's troubles were made worse by an uproar over Hizbullah's presence in Kesrouan, a staunchly nationalist district in the Christian heartland. Hizbullah has triggered insular Christians' suspicions by placing outposts in the area, which lies north of Beirut, and failing to explain how such activity fits with its external fight against Israel. Aoun may have swept Kesrouan in 2005, but his allies' actions have moved the district back into play.[2]

Ah yes; Hezballah *loves* Christians—as vote-cattle and human-shields! After Hezballah's war against Israel in 2006, Shi'ites in southern Beirut criticised Hezballah for the heavy price they paid as human shields. Clearly, launching missiles from Christian residential areas would be preferable, as it would draw the Israeli response into those districts, producing Christian rather than Shi'ite casualties, and doubtless generating a Western backlash against Israel.

During the latter part of 2010, as Prime Minister Saad Hariri wilted under Hezballah pressure, leading Maronite Christian Sami Gemayel protested against Hezballah's dominance over Lebanese affairs. Sami Gemayel is the son of former president Amin Gemayel, the brother of assassinated Member of Parliament Pierre Gemayel, and the nephew of assassinated former president-elect Bachir Gemayel. (Such is Lebanese politics!)

---

1 H. Varulkar, 'The March 14 forces after the formation of the new Lebanese government: from electoral victory to political defeat and disintegration within five months', Middle East Media Research Institute, 22 November, 2009, www.memri.org/report/en/0/0/0/0/259/0/3804.htm.
2 Anthony Elghossain, 'Rival Lebanese Christian factions now hold political cards in Levant', *The Daily Star*, Lebanon, 11 May 2009.

As a strong Lebanese nationalist and staunch, courageous critic of Hezballah, Sami Gemayel objected vehemently to Prime Minister Saad Hariri's U-turn on the Special Tribunal for Lebanon, an international tribunal set up by the UN at the request of the Lebanese government to investigate the 2005 assassination of Saad Hariri's father, former Prime Minister Rafik Hariri.[1] Gemayel accused Hezballah of collaborating against Lebanon's interests.

Hezballah leader Hassan Nasrallah responded by posting a grim threat on Hezballah's website (Islamic Resistance Forum) in which he denounced the Christian leader as an Israeli spy and called for his 'crucifixion on a pole in the Pride and Dignity Square in Beirut'.[2]

By September 2010, Hezballah had reportedly deployed some 3,500 armed militiamen along the Mediterranean coast and throughout the Christian regions north of Beirut. Having taken up residence in chalets and apartments purchased with the assistance of their Christian allies in the Free Patriotic Movement, these 3,500 Hezballah militants were positioned such that, should Hezballah decide to stage another policy-reversing blitzkrieg, they could besiege the homes of their last remaining opponents—Dr. Samir Geagea, head of the Christian Lebanese Forces Party, and Amin Gemayel, head of the Kataeb Christian Party—and subdue the Christian regions by force.

Should that happen, analysts summised, Hezballah would doubtless withdraw, leaving their Christian allies with the task of fighting their Christian opponents.[3]

It is not hard to determine who would gain from such a self-destructive inter-Christian conflagration: Hezballah of course!—'the traitor betrays and the destroyer destroys' (21:2).

---

1 See www.stl-tsl.org/.
2 Deutsche Presse Agentur, 'Lebanese parliamentarian to sue Hezbollah over crucifixion threat' Haaretz, 12 September 2010, www.haaretz.com/news/international/lebanese-parliamentarian-to-sue-hezbollah-over-crucifixion-threat-1.313385.
3 See E. Kendal, 'Hezballah's Christian allies': a "covenant with death" if ever there was one', RLM, 25 September 2010; 'Hizbullah agents taking up positions in Lebanon's Christian areas' World Tribune, 21 September 2010, www.worldtribune.com/worldtribune/WTARC/2010/me_lebanon0921_09_21.asp; Elias Youssef Beijjani, 'An imminent coup by Hezballah in Lebanon', International Analyst Networ, 18 September, 2010, www.analyst-network.com/article.php?art_id=3584.

A covenant with death indeed!

—⁓—

Covenants with death abound

The Free Patriotic Movement's alliance with Hezballah is but one of a multitude of cases that could be offered as an example of a modern day 'covenant with death'—that is, a covenant or alliance with one who in the end will not or cannot save you. It is but one of a multitude of contemporary cases where Christian peoples, their leaders, representatives or advocates have or are pursuing Christian security through alliances with ascendant worldly power, undeterred by the fact that the power in which they are investing their hope is in fact a power that routinely fails, betrays or even devours Christians and is fundamentally set against God.

Philippines 2008

In 2008, when leading evangelicals in the Philippines helped mediate a land-for-peace deal between the government of Gloria Macapagal-Arroyo and the Moro Islamic Liberation Front (MILF), they were brokering a covenant with death.

The Philippine government was acting against the advice of its own Department of Justice that had warned only months earlier that some provisions of the draft Memorandum of Agreement on Ancestral Domain were unconstitutional and threatened the sovereignty of the Philippines by essentially establishing an Islamic state on the island of Mindanao, within the Philippine state. To be incorporated into this Islamic entity, which would be under MILF control, were hundreds of predominantly Christian villages.

MILF is a breakaway, more radicalised faction of the Moro National Liberation Front. In 1987 the Moro National Liberation Front signed a peace agreement with the Philippine government, accepting semi-autonomy in a disputed portion of the southern Philippine island of Mindanao. MILF rejected the agreement and declared jihad.

193

The government was also ignoring the warnings coming from Mindanao, that if the Memorandum was signed, 'There will be chaos and it will be bloody.'[1]

Fortunately, two of Mindanao's Christian governors—North Cotabato Governor Jesus Sacdalan and Vice Governor Emmanuel Pinol—petitioned the Supreme Court, which voted unanimously to issue the Philippine government with a temporary restraining order to stop it from trading the liberty of Mindanao's Christians for a 'peace' agreement with MILF.[2]

Why did some of the state's most senior evangelicals advocate for this? They described this as Muslim-Christian rapprochement and Christian peacemaking in action!

However, no sooner was the Memorandum scuttled (the day before it was due to be signed) and MILF fighters, already in position, were rampaging through Christian villages in Mindanao. Dozens of Christian locals were killed; more than 160,000 civilians—some 16,650 mostly Catholic farming families—were displaced, unable to return on account of land mines and booby traps.[3]

Should MILF be trusted with Christian security?

A covenant with death indeed!

Sudan 2010

In April 2010, when the South Sudan-based Sudan People's Liberation Movement pulled out of the National Consensus—an oppositional alliance, withdrew their presidential candidate Yasar Arman, and agreed to support the presidency of the racist, Islamist President Omar el-Bashir in exchange for promises of a peaceful referendum on Southern self-determination, it was a profound strategic blunder: a covenant with death.[4]

President Omar el-Bashir—a known liar and master of the 'divide and conquer' strategy—had successfully, with mere words, removed

---

1 E. Kendal, 'Philippines: government to sign deal with MILF', RLM, 31 July 2008.
2 Ibid.
3 E. Kendal, 'Philippines: update on Gov-MILF peace deal', RLM, 14 August 2008.
4 E. Kendal, 'SPLM-NCP alliance: a "covenant with death"', RLM, 14 May 2010.

the only presidential candidate who actually posed a threat, while shattering the opposition.

El-Bashir had spent six years resisting the implementation of the Comprehensive Peace Agreement; he was never going to let South Sudan just walk away with eighty percent of the country's oil reserves. War loomed inevitable. Only now, there would be no unity amongst Sudan's long-suffering, war-ravaged and marginalised peoples; and a declaration of Southern independence would leave all Christians in the North, especially those in the resource-rich 'new south'—Abyei, South Kordofan and Blue Nile (the region immediately north of the new international border)—at risk of genocide.[1]

A covenant with death indeed!

Vietnam 2010

In April 2010, the Vatican capitulated to Hanoi and retired the heroic and faithful Archbishop of Hanoi, Msgr Joseph Ngo Quang Kiet, for the sake of 'quiet diplomacy' and guarantees (mere words) from the belligerent and duplicitous Communist Party of Vietnam.[2]

For years Archbishop Kiet had stood firm in the face of the Communist regime's threats and vilification, courageously championing religious liberty and leading a most phenomenal, sustained and historic prayer movement—one that had the ruling Communists seriously rattled.[3]

As soon as Kiet was removed to Rome and 'retired', the Communists replaced him with a Communist Party-appointed puppet—to the absolute horror and despair of Hanoi's Catholics.[4]

And to what end? Persecution has only escalated.[5]

A covenant with death indeed!

---

1 E. Kendal, 'Sudan: referendum soon and war looms', RLPB 084, 1 December 2010. For updates see RLPB. See also RLM, labels 'Sudan' & 'Nuba Genocide Resumes', 24 June 2011; E. Kendal, 'War spreads across "new south" into Blue Nile', RLM, 13 September 2011.
2 E. Kendal, 'Sacrificed on the altar of "quiet diplomacy"?', RLM, 17 May 2010.
3 See E. Kendal, 'Vietnam: prayer vigils push government to breaking point', RLM, 16 September 2008; E. Kendal, 'Vietnam: Govt belligerence escalates against Hanoi Catholics', RLM, 26 September 2008.
4 E. Kendal, 'Sacrificed on the altar of "quiet diplomacy"?', fn. 33.
5 See label 'Vietnam' in RLPB & RLM. In particular, see E. Kendal, 'Vietnam: state repressing Christians violently', RLPB 121, 17 August 2011.

Means matter

Church history is replete with such horror stories of how covenants with death have failed Christian individuals and the church and brought tragedy to multitudes. Church history is replete with shameful and embarrassing stories of Christian leaders seditiously conspiring with, or naively allying themselves to, or desperately investing their hopes in, dedicated persecutors of the church. Some have done so out of self-interest: in pursuit of protection and promotion. Others, meanwhile, have been motivated by the best of noble intentions and the passionate hope that they might be able to broker favourable deals with megalomaniacs, liars, traitors, terrorists, dictators, persecutors and Christ-haters—deals they imagine will be blessed by God and of benefit his church.

Despite the fact that church history is replete with such stories of strategic failure, they are rarely if ever talked about, debated or studied. Of course, after bubbling with excitement over deals brokered in the halls of power; after boasting of lofty promises procured from powerful men; after taking credit for 'successes' in high-level 'quiet diplomacy' and international peace-making; after photos have been taken, press releases have been issued, reports and articles have been published and congratulations and even international awards have been received, religious liberty advocates are loath to admit that they were used, duped, exploited, lied to and betrayed; and that years of 'quiet diplomacy' and accommodation have not only failed to help the church but may have actually made things worse.

These failures should not surprise us. For why should we expect deals, alliances or unions that involve betrayals, morally questionable compromises, and a profound yoking of the unequal, to be of any benefit to the church? Consider Paul's challenge to the Corinthian church:

> 'Do not be unequally yoked with unbelievers. For what
> partnership has righteousness with lawlessness? Or what
> fellowship has light with darkness? What accord has Christ
> with Belial? Or what portion does a believer share with an
> unbeliever? What agreement has the temple of God with idols?
> For we are the temple of the living God; as God said,

> "I will make my dwelling among them and walk among them,
>   and I will be their God,

and they shall be my people.
Therefore go out from their midst,
and be separate from them, says the Lord,
and touch no unclean thing;
then I will welcome you,
and I will be a father to you,
and you shall be sons and daughters to me,
says the Lord Almighty"' (2 Corinthians 6:14–18).

And even if our spiritually rebellious, faithless or simply misguided policies seem to succeed (as did King Ahaz's), we must realise that the end—no matter how sweet—will never justify faithless means. For one thing, we most certainly learn from Isaiah is that means matter, and that without faith it is impossible to please God.

The church must talk about her strategic policy failures; contemplate them, debate them, study them and repent of them so that the mistakes that have been made can at least be redeemed as lessons learned. Without that, what hope is there that we will ever stop repeating our highly destructive and deadly errors?

―◦◦◦―

Yahweh to rise up as he did on Mount Perazim

As if Isaiah's prophecy of impending Assyrian invasion and the obliteration of allies was not shocking enough (28:17–20), Isaiah had words that were even more shocking still. In a word that must have caused the hearts of God's people to melt with fear, Isaiah declared that Judah's security pact with Egypt would be swept away and 'annulled' (28:17–18) because (28:21) the Lord will rise up as he did on Mount Perazim and in the Valley of Gibeon when he fought with David's forces and gave them victory over the Philistines, only this time God will be rising up in a totally strange way to do a completely alien work. Instead of rising up with his covenant people to deliver them from their enemies, he would be rising up with the enemy (Assyria) to deliver judgement to his own people (28:21), for they had become just as intoxicated with themselves and the world of money, status, power and politics as their brothers and sisters in Israel, whose demise and catastrophic fall they seemed to have forgotten.

The battles at Mount Perazim and in the Valley of Gibeon provide us with two of the most magnificent examples of God honouring the radical faith of a godly Hebrew king.

The story is told in 2 Samuel 5:17–25 of how, after David had been anointed king over Israel, the Philistines came up in search of him, spreading out in the Valley of Rephaim. When David heard of it, he went immediately to the stronghold to inquire of the Lord.

> And David inquired of the LORD, 'Shall I go up against the Philistines? Will you give them into my hand?' And the LORD said to David, 'Go up, for I will certainly give the Philistines into your hand' (2 Samuel 5:19).

After seeking God's perspective and will on the matter, David confidently and faithfully obeyed, fighting the Philistines in the Valley of Rephaim. Upon victory, David claimed no credit for himself, for he knew that God had delivered the Philistines into his hand. Rather, he glorified God, declaring: 'The LORD has burst through my enemies before me like a bursting flood' (2 Samuel 5:20).

In honour of the Lord, and so that the Lord's mighty act of deliverance might be remembered, David called that place *Baal-perazim* (2 Samuel 5:20), which means 'the Lord of bursting through' (ESV reference notes) or 'the Lord of the breakthrough' (KJV reference notes).

What a wonderful passage for teaching on right responses to insecurity and existential threat. David was a realist. He was watchful and alert. He was not taken by surprise because his intelligence was good and the lines of communication were open. He did not react to the news of the Philistine threat with 'haste' and panic (as in 28:16) or despair. Rather, he immediately sought the Lord and inquired of him. He then obeyed the Lord, in faith, despite the confronting scene before him of a valley filled with hostile, armed Philistines. Upon victory, David resisted the temptation to attribute glory to himself. Rather he gave thanks and glorified the Lord, who rose up and 'burst through' his enemies 'like a bursting flood'.

Not content with one crushing defeat, the Philistines came up against David again, spreading out in the Valley of Rephaim as before (2 Samuel 5:22).

Again, the first thing David did was inquire of the Lord (2 Samuel 5:23). And again, the next thing David did was obey the Lord in faith

(2 Samuel 5:24).

It must be noted that despite the fact that the problem was the same—
King David's life was threatened by a valley full of hostile armed
Philistines—David did not presume that God's will or means would
be the same. Despite his sense of déjà-vu, David, in deference to
God's absolute freedom, sought God's will on the matter. And God
in absolute freedom, despite the fact that the circumstances were the
same, did not recommend the same means.

> And when David inquired of the LORD, he [God] said, 'You
> shall not go up; go around to their rear, and come against
> them opposite the balsam trees. And when you hear the
> sound of marching in the tops of the balsam trees, then rouse
> yourself, for then the LORD has gone out before you to strike
> down the army of the Philistines.' And David did as the LORD
> commanded him, and struck down the Philistines from Geba
> [Gibeon, 1 Chronicles 14:16] to Gezer (2 Samuel 5:23–25),

This is why God's imminent work in Isaiah 28:21 is described as
strange and alien. God was going to rise up in power just as he did at
Mount Perazim, just as he did in the Valley of Gibeon, only not in a
bursting flood that would burst through and sweep away the enemy.
Rather, God would be rising up in the Assyrian flood that would burst
through and sweep away the Egyptian rescue party before flooding
into Judah in judgement. How strange and alien indeed!

Ortlund comments:

> The question is, who is God fighting for? Anyone who trusts
> him, according to the gospel. And who is God fighting against?
> Anyone who refuses him, including his own covenant people.
> No one owns God. And yesterday's faith belongs to yesterday.
> If God doesn't find in us a real faith for today, he's prepared to
> do something strange. He is prepared to leave his own people
> out of the loop and move on to those who will listen (Acts
> 28:23–28).[1]

'Now therefore do not scoff lest your bonds be made strong,' warns
Isaiah (28:22). In other words: stop scoffing or you will only make
your judgement worse.

---

1 Ortlund, p. 158.

Destruction is coming, 'destruction from the Lord God of hosts against the whole land' (28:22)—destruction in the form of an Assyrian flood (military invasion) that will 'overwhelm the shelter' (Egypt) (28:17), eventually 'reaching even to the neck' (Jerusalem) (8:8).

If God's people will only rest in him they will find he can be trusted to become to them a sanctuary. But to those who reject him, 'our God is a consuming fire' (Hebrews 12:29).

—∿∿—

The central principle of Isaiah 28:14–22, is this: means matter.

It is tragic in the extreme that multitudes of vulnerable, threatened and persecuted Christians—believers in need of strong spiritual leadership; sheep in need of wise and faithful shepherds—are victims of their leaders' and advocates' covenants with death.

We do not need *covenants with death.*

Christian security is not found in covenants with death.

Praise God, for he who has promised to be with us through the storms of life has provided us with an anchor—Jesus Christ. Jesus Christ, the son of David, our eternal covenant king, can be trusted. He should always be the object of our hope. Jesus Christ has gone 'within the veil', into the sanctuary of God. He has gone there for us, as our forerunner. Our souls are anchored there securely through our union with him (Hebrews 6:17–20).[1]

It is my most fervent prayer that those who, like Peter (the Lord's disciple), have on account of pride or fear taken their eyes off Christ only to find themselves overwhelmed and sinking in deep and troubled waters, might yet return and reach out to our Lord, just as did Peter.

---

1 See Arthur W. Pink, *An Exposition of Hebrews*, Baker Book House, Grand Rapids MI, 2006, p. 354. Pink quotes Bagster's interlinear translation: 'The winds may roar and the waves lash the ship, but it rides them steadily, being held fast by something outside itself. Surely the figure is plain. The "anchor" is Christ Himself', sustaining His people down here in this world, in the midst of the wicked, who are likened unto "the troubled sea" when it cannot rest' (Isaiah 57:20) ... Certainly there is nothing in us "both sure and steadfast": it is the love (John 13:1), power (Mattthew 28:18, 20), and faithfulness (Hebrews 7:25) of Christ which is in view.'

Do not bother trying to broker a deal with the sharks. In the end they will not save you!

> But when he saw the wind, he [Peter] was afraid, and beginning to sink he cried out, 'Lord, save me.' Jesus immediately [as soon as he heard Peter's cry] reached out his hand and took hold of him ...' (Matthew 14:30–31a).

May God, by his Holy Spirit, enlighten our hearts and minds to the great reality of the Christian life: that our living God and covenant king is sovereign, present, faithful, just and compelled always by everlasting love (*hesed*). He calls us simply to *come* and walk in his light; to *rest* in him, *trust* in him and *wait* for him. For to those who trust him, he promises to become a sanctuary and strength to turn back the battle at the gate.

He is *Baal Perazim*, the Lord of bursting through; the Lord of the breakthrough.

He simply asks us to trust him.

Why do we not do it?

Why?

Questions for Discussion and Reflection

1. Can a noble end justify any means? **or** Do means matter?

   Why?

2. Can a noble end (i.e. a harmonious society) ever be achieved by wrong, immoral and faithless means (i.e. repression or ethnic cleansing)?

   or

   Do wrong, immoral and faithless means guarantee a corrupted end (i.e. fake harmony with empowered dictators)?

   Explain your answer and how this principle might apply to the pursuit of Christian security / religious liberty.

3. What drives threatened Christians to broker 'covenants with death'?

   What enables Christians to stand firm so that God is glorified?

4. Detail—step by step—how King David responded when he was threatened by hostile armed Philistine forces at Perazim and Gibeon (2 Samuel 5:17–25).

5. What qualities did David display?

   What was the result?

6. The image of the Lord as *Baal Perazim*: the Lord of bursting through / the Lord of the breakthrough is immensely powerful and inspiring. Do you know of situations where God's people are this day in desperate need of a breakthrough? Pray for them now.

Prayer

Our God is Baal Perazim!

My Lord and God,
    you are *Baal Perazim*: the Lord of bursting through / the Lord of
    the breakthrough. (2 Samuel 5:20)

Forgive me Lord, for the times I have let misplaced fear dictate my
    responses and even drive me into the arms of false saviours.
May I always remember, O Lord, that you are a truth-speaking and
    covenant-keeping God!
Those who resist you and break faith with you should fear;
    while those who trust you and are faithful will see your salvation.

Forgive me Lord, for all the times I have been so focused on and
    passionate about the noble ends I am pursuing, that I have either
    arrogantly or foolishly failed to trust you with the means.
May I always remember that without faith it is impossible to please
    you. (Hebrews 11:6)

And so, dear Lord, I commit to actively remembering David and the
    battles of Perazim and Gibeon. (2 Samuel 2:17–25)
Like David, I will look to, trust in and wait upon the exciting and
    awesome *Baal Perazim*: the Lord of bursting through, the Lord of
    the breakthrough.

'I will remember the deeds of the Lord;
    yes, I will remember your wonders of old.
    I will ponder all your work, and meditate on your mighty deeds.
    Your way, O God, is holy.
    What god is great like our God?' (Psalm 77:11–13)

That the Church might know your salvation;
    that your spectacular grace and power might be seen in the
    heavens and on the earth;
    that your holy name might be honoured and lifted high;

In God I will trust!

Amen.

203

CHAPTER 10

Christian security:
not in practical atheism

Isaiah 30–31

Terror in Pakistan

Crack! Crack! The activity at Murree Christian School, Rawalpindi District, Punjab Province, Pakistan is interrupted not by the chiming of school bells, but by the air–splitting, spine–chilling crack of Kalashnikovs.

On 5 August 2002, a team of four Islamic militants invaded Murree Christian School, intent on sending a deadly message. Built as it was, into a huge deconstructed 19th-century British garrison church, Murree Christian School stands as a visual symbol of a Christian history, a Christian presence, and a Christian witness that Islamic hardliners would prefer erased. But more importantly, Murree Christian School was home to over 100 children of expatriate Christians working across South and Central Asia. As such, Murree Christian School was a perfect target for Islamic terrorists wanting to send a message to America and her Western allies, who had been waging Operation Enduring Freedom in Afghanistan from bases inside Pakistan since 7 October 2001.

This was not the first time Christians in Pakistan had been targeted for terror since the launch of Operation Enduring Freedom. On Sunday 28 October 2001, six Islamic militants descended upon St Dominic's Church in Bahawalpur, Eastern Punjab province, during morning worship. After murdering the Muslim security guard, they invaded the church, spraying automatic weapon fire through the congregation. Of

205

the 16 Pakistani Christians who died (one quarter of the congregation), seven were children.

Then on Sunday 17 March 2002, five Christians died and 46 were injured (six critically), when Islamic suicide bombers invaded the Protestant International Church in Pakistan's capital city, Islamabad. The terrorists shot at worshippers and hurled grenades before self–detonating, sending shrapnel flying and splattering flesh and blood throughout the interior of the church. The dead and injured

The US launched Operation Enduring Freedom on 7 October 2001, to destroy al-Qaeda bases and Taliban power in Afghanistan after the 11 September 2001 terrorist attacks on New York and Washington DC that took nearly 3,000 lives. The fact that this alleged war against Muslims was being launched from bases in Muslim Pakistan outraged the region's Muslim masses.

Christians were from Pakistan, Afghanistan, Iran, Iraq, Ethiopia, the US, Canada, Germany, Great Britain, Switzerland and Australia. Although the US Embassy was only 300 metres away, it was the church at worship, and not the US Embassy, that the terrorists had in their sights.

A six-year-old child who had been in the church with his expatriate parents throughout the horrific attack subsequently recounted an amazing experience. The child told his parents that while the attack was unfolding, he had been watching angels, and that some were protecting people while others were taking people to heaven.[1]

It seems God mercifully opened this child's eyes to see spiritual reality. I have read and heard many accounts of children who, when in similar terrifying, life–threatening circumstances, were transfixed and pacified by similar experiences in which their eyes where opened to see the angels shielding and defending them. Pastors too have told me that it is not uncommon for dying Christian children to be likewise comforted and calmed in their dying moments by visions of angels.

Transfixed into stillness and mesmerised into silence by this vision of ministering spirits, this young child was spared the panic that would have doubtless resulted

Are not all angels ministering spirits sent to serve those who will inherit salvation?
Hebrews 1:14, NIV

1 Testimony gleaned from personal correspondence.

in him—and probably his parents—being shot. Doubtless he was also spared massive, crippling, life–scarring trauma. God opened this child's eyes that he might see the spiritual reality that we who are spiritually mature should know by faith to be true, even though our eyes see it not.

Pakistan's church was under siege. One faithful Pakistani evangelist commented to me concerning the perilous times: 'This is the time the Christian community must look up to the heavenly security system. There is one who never sleeps nor slumbers.[1] He is our refuge.'[2]

> I lift up my eyes to the hills.
>   From where does my help come?
> My help comes from the Lord,
>   who made heaven and earth (Psalm 121:1–2).

A prayer request was issued for Pakistan's besieged church.[3]

On 5 August 2002, as the sound of Kalashnikovs shattered the peace at Murree Christian School, the teaching staff hurriedly gathered up the children in their care. Fortunately a light shower of rain had driven all classes bar one inside just prior to the attack. Consequently, only that one class had to be gathered from the playground. Once everyone was inside, the large wooden doors were bolted shut.

The school Director Russell Morton describes the event:

> The attackers moved carefully and purposefully through the campus. They took few risks. They knew where they were going. They knew where our guards were. They knew, or thought they knew, that many people would be in the dining room of the boarding hostel for a coffee break, but their plans were confused and they were 15 minutes late.

As Mr. Morton discovered, the militants had been quietly living nearby and planning the attack for the past two months.[4]

---

1 Psalm 121:4.
2 From personal correspondence.
3 E. Kendal, 'Pakistan: Christians targeted in terror attack', Religious Liberty Prayer List, no. 160, 20 March 2002, www.ea.org.au/ea-family/Religious-Liberty/PAKISTAN--CHRISTIANS-TARGETED-IN-TERROR-ATTACK.aspx.
4 Sue Morton (ed.), *Angels in the Rafters. Reflections from the MCS community following the attack on Monday 5 August 2002*, Murree Christian School, Chiang Mai, 2002, p. 7.

The terrorists smashed windows, fired their weapons and furiously kicked at the large wooden doors in their efforts to infiltrate the main building. Meanwhile, the students inside the high school facility huddled together with their teachers in upstairs classrooms beneath Muree Christian School's towering cathedral ceiling. They had discussed lock-down situations but never experienced the terror of one. Sitting quietly and out of sight, never before had they been in a situation of siege where their lives were so profoundly and imminently imperiled.

Standing strong against all the efforts of the terrorists, the school's large wooden doors refused to budge. For reasons unknown, the terrorists did not enter through a window. For reason unknown, they did not use their grenades to blow out the doors. Eventually, frustrated by their lack of success, and aware that alarms had been raised and the police were on their way, the terrorists opted for flight.

In all, five locals who were employed by Murree Christian School—in the office, on the grounds and in security—were shot and killed, as was one passer-by caught at the front gate. The mother of one student was injured, shot through the hand. It was an appalling tragedy for the whole community—but things could have been so much worse.

Russell Morton writes: 'Police told us they [the terrorists] were equipped for a suicide mission, and that it was probably their intention to enter the hostel and detonate explosives.'

He concludes:

> God's hand in protection was evident in this tragic event, despite the evil perpetrated and the immense cost to the community. There were many miracles, large and small, which combined to limit the injury and loss ... Some students who spent a very long hour hiding in rooms on the upper floors during the attack heard singing coming from above them. 'There must have been angels in the rafters', one said. There were.[1]

One young student named Becca (Grade 8) testified:

> Sitting in the hall, waiting to die, was the worst time of my life. Then I heard singing. It was faint at first, then it became clearer. It was while the shooting was still going on and I

---

1 Ibid., p. 9.

thought somebody had put a tape or CD on to calm us down. It was really nice choir music coming from the rafters. When the day was over, I told my friends and they said they had heard it too. That's why I know there were angels in the rafters.[1]

Terror in Ivory Coast

On 19 September 2002, only six weeks after the terrorist attack on Murree Christian School, gun battles erupted right over the top of the International Christian Academy in Bouaké, Ivory Coast (Côte d'Ivoire), endangering the lives of the student body, which included more than 100 children of expatriate Christians working throughout West and North Africa.

The International Christian Academy in Bouaké had become 'ground zero' in an attempted coup (described by Western media as an attempted mutiny). While the students were all eventually rescued and evacuated unharmed, the traditionally hospitable, free and prosperous nation of Ivory Coast descended into civil war.

Ivory Coast sits atop Africa's great ethnic–religious 'faultline' that runs (more or less) along the eight degree north parallel: through northern Liberia in the west and every state running east—including central Ivory Coast, central Nigeria, northern Cameroon, southern Chad and Southern Sudan—before veering northeast towards Asmara, Eritrea on the Red Sea.

At this faultline, southward–migrating, traditionally nomadic Muslim tribes from the north meet settled, indigenous African non-Muslim and predominantly Christian tribes. Long a relatively friendly affair, the latter part of the 20th century saw this 'meeting' become increasingly poisoned by the confluence of several strategic trends. In particular, rapid population growth and urbanisation—a trend accelerated along the faultline by drought—have seen social tensions escalate as increasing numbers of more diverse peoples compete for limited resources, jobs, land and power. The 1990s saw the trend of Islamic radicalisation added to the already volatile mix, raising the stakes phenomenally.

Tensions along the ethnic–religious faultline perpetually simmer until

---

1 Ibid., p. 19.

something—usually something quite minor—sets off an explosion. While religion is usually a secondary element, it tends to rise up through the centre like a mushroom cloud, quickly becoming the conflict's overwhelming expression.[1]

When Ivory Coast's civil war erupted in 2002, Ivory Coast was officially 31.8 percent Christian and 38.6 percent Muslim, with the remainder mostly practicing traditional African religions.[2] However, while decades of mass immigration (1960–1993) from the neighbouring Muslim countries of Burkina Faso, Mali and Guinea might have been great for the economy, it also served to accelerate Ivory Coast's ethnic–religious faultline crisis. While Ivory Coast was straining under the effects of economic downturn, the immigrant community (40% of the total population) was demanding more rights, including land rights and citizenship.

While the Western media portrayed Ivory Coast's civil war as a struggle for 'justice', 'democracy' and 'human rights' in the face of Southern 'xenophobia' and 'Islamophobia', it was in reality a war between those who wanted all of Ivory Coast's Muslim immigrants naturalised—making Ivory Coast a Muslim majority state overnight—and those who did not.

> Islam is imperialistic in nature. Classical Islamic jurisprudence divides the world into two spheres: dar al harb (land of war) and dar al Islam (land of Islam). The purpose of war/jihad is to bring territory under the rule of Allah and his law (Sharia). When the Islamic drive to dominate or even supplant the indigenous Christian population meets with indigenous and Christian resistance, the result is immense tension between immigrants vs indigenes and Muslims vs Christians.

The naturalisation drive was led by former Prime Minister Alassane Ouattara, a northern Muslim with strong ties to neighbouring Burkina Faso and to the neo-colonial hegemon France. While Ouattara had his sights set on the presidency, France had her sights set on regime change. For while Ouattara was essentially France's ally in Ivory Coast, popularly elected President Gbagbo was a staunch African nationalist who wanted nothing more than to sever the exploitative French apron

---

1 See E. Kendal, 'Nigeria: Why is Jos such a tinderbox?', RLM, 9 March 2010.
2 Statistics from Johnstone et al., *Operation World 21ˢᵗ Century Edition.*

strings and see Ivory Coast truly independent.

With backing from Islamic States (such as neighbouring Burkina Faso and Gadhafi's Libya), Islamic fundamentalist and jihadist movements, and Ivory Coast's former colonial master, France—set to gain economically from a Ouattara presidency[1]—Ouattara made himself the champion of Ivory Coast's Muslim and immigrant communities and tossed the flaming ethnic–religious card into the already incendiary environment.

As the nation tore apart, polarising along ethnic–religious lines, Christian residents of the predominantly Muslim north—including numerous southerners there as doctors, teachers and humanitarian workers—fled for their lives through hostile territory as bands of foreign-backed Islamists incited local Muslims to cleanse the north of Christians.[2]

On 5 February 2003 I received an email that both distressed and amazed me. It was from my primary source inside Ivory Coast. According to this source, Christians who had escaped captivity in northern rebel strongholds where they had been tortured for information were reporting that the rebels were blaming their lack of success in capturing Ivory Coast on the prayers of Christians. To counter this, rebel leaders decreed it imperative that Christian leaders be eliminated.

This news merely confirmed what my contact had already seen and heard: that pastors, particularly pastors who were converts from Islam and active in mission to Muslims, were receiving death threats. My contact appealed for urgent prayer.

While this email was of course very distressing, what amazed me was the spiritual awareness of the rebels. They fully understood the spiritual nature of the warfare they were in. They believed that a mighty spiritual power was harnessed and released through the prayers of Christians, so much so, in fact, that they were convinced that for victory to be realised, the prayers of Christians must be silenced.

---

1   E. Kendal, 'Cote d'Ivoire—the foreign muscle behind the rebellion', RLM, 5 November 2002; 'Ivory Coast: where Islamic and Western interests converge', RLM, 11 April 2011.

2   E. Kendal, 'Ivory Coast: Christians facing terror', RLM, no. 191, 16 October 2002; 'Cote d'Ivoire—tearing apart', RLM, 17 October 2002; 'Ivory Coast: ceasefire, but Christians still in peril', RLM, no. 192, 21 October 2002.

I wondered: Why do West African Islamic militants have more confidence in the prayers of Christians than most Christians do?

Because my West African Christian contact is a man of radical faith, prayer—as distinct from an appeal to the US or UN—was exactly what he requested. And so an urgent Religious Liberty Prayer bulletin was issued.[1]

No pastors were killed and the rebel advance remained paralysed.

A few months later, my contact wrote to me concerning a rebel combatant who had been captured by the Ivorian Army in the north-east after his group failed in another attack. In custody, this rebel complained bitterly about the lack of rebel success. He fumed that no matter what they did, they failed. They failed despite receiving international funds, arms and logistics support. They failed despite attention to occult rituals: drinking human blood and eating human parts.[2] They failed despite 'adoring' (worshipping) the moon and its spirit.

With that my contact exclaimed: '*Yahweh Sabaoth*! The God of the Armies is fighting for us and he will certainly deliver us!'[3]

And to that I said 'AMEN!'

Spiritual in theory or in practice?

I share these stories because a key element in each is a strong awareness of spiritual realities. Christians, especially Western Christians, tend to forget—in practice if not in theory[4]—that they are in a spiritual

---

1 E. Kendal, 'Ivory Coast: decisive hour, RLM, no. 206, 12 February 2003.
2 This is confirmed by extremely disturbing and graphic footage that dates back to 2002. It shows pro–Ouattara, northern New Forces rebels at their base in Bouake. Though they had failed to capture all of Ivory Coast, they celebrate their seizure of the north with the ritual slaughter of an Ivorian constable in the presence of French troops (www.youtube.com/user/Crizafric1#p/u/6/mQ-8hbOMo3Q).
3 *Yahweh Sabaoth*, usually translated 'Lord of Hosts' or 'Lord Almighty', literally means the Lord, the Commander of all heaven's hosts/armies/forces.
4 We forget something 'in practice if not in theory' when we push what we know (theory) behind our backs so we do not have to live (practice) in its light.

battle and that the Lord—whose footprints are not seen[1]—is there for them. He is *Baal Perazim*: the Lord who bursts through.[2] He is *Yahweh Sabaoth*: the Lord of Hosts and the commander of heaven's armies. He is there with legions of heavenly hosts and forces at his disposal. But we do not pray for what we do not remember or do not believe. Real prayer is thus an expression of radical faith.

It is indicative of the sad state of the church that such radical faith is uncommon, especially in the West where theology and faith have been (generally speaking) so poisoned with Enlightenment thought that Western Christianity has essentially become a powerless syncretised faith. Western Enlightenment thought has subsequently poisoned the church in the non–West, leaving it with a Christianity that is essentially powerless in the face of the occultic forces that have historically plagued pagan and animist societies.

Generally, the church has, with great pride, accepted—in practice if not in theory[3]—the 'enlightened' and humanistic notion that human reason is brilliantly sufficient, which is why we preach and debate to win hearts and convince minds far more passionately and confidently than we pray for the Holy Spirit to open hearts and illuminate minds. We have, with great pride, accepted (in practice if not in theory) the 'enlightened' and humanistic notion that human means are wonderfully sufficient, which is why we exhaust ourselves attending to means, making ourselves dizzy with 'shuttle diplomacy' and faint with breathlessness from endless political negotiation and works upon works upon works, before we will even consider petitioning the Almighty King of Heaven that he might intervene on behalf of his own precious redeemed people.

In spite of all biblical teaching, we have accepted (in practice if not in theory) the relegation of the supernatural to superstition, which is why we wring our hands and cry 'they have more guns' more passionately than we petition heaven's courts, appealing to *Baal Perazim, Yahweh Sabaoth*. This is why we are so desperate and so fearful. This is why we cannot rest. This is why we have no peace. For what peace could we possibly have if the church is under siege and her deliverance depends

---

1 'Your way was through the sea, your path through the great waters; yet your footprints were unseen' (Psalm 77:19).

2 2 Samuel 5:20.

3 We accept something 'in practice if not in theory' when we act (practice) in a manner contrary to what we say we believe (theory).

on us and us alone?

'Our generation is overwhelmingly naturalistic', wrote Francis Schaeffer in his 1971 classic, *True Spirituality*.

> There is an almost complete commitment to the concept of the uniformity of natural causes in a closed system. This is its distinguishing mark. If we are not careful, even though we say we are biblical Christians and supernaturalists, nevertheless the naturalism of our generation tends to come in upon us. It may infiltrate our thinking without our recognizing its coming, like a fog creeping in through a window opened only half an inch. As soon as that happens, Christians begin to lose the reality of their Christian lives.[1]

As Schaeffer argues, 'All the reality of Christianity rests upon the reality of the existence of a personal God, and the reality of the supernatural view of the total universe.'[2] Furthermore, the truly Bible-believing Christian is not the one who simply knows right doctrines, but the one who lives in practice in the supernatural world. 'Being a biblical Christian means living in the supernatural now—not only theoretically, but in practice.'[3]

The very sad truth of the matter is that far too many Christians are far more spiritual in theory than in practice.

But Christian security is not found in practical atheism.

—⁓—

Pride, practical atheism and historical amnesia

Hezekiah was a godly king who knew the Lord. But, at the height of a phenomenally successful career, he let pride take root in his heart. Pride turned his eyes inwards, blinding him to the big picture: to spiritual realities. Consequently, Hezekiah stumbled. Believing that he was wise and strong and sufficient in himself, he acted independently of the Lord and brought disaster upon Judah.

---

1 Francis A. Schaeffer, *True Spirituality*, Tyndale House Publishers, 1971, 2001, p. 54.
2 Ibid., p. 56.
3 Ibid., p. 57.

As Assyrian war drums pounded in the distance, the proud, self-sufficient King Hezekiah looked to the weapons, looked to the walls, and looked to the water, but did not look to him (22:11), to the one who had chosen and established Jerusalem; the one who had covenanted with David; the one who was the true Sovereign over God's people. Though Hezekiah believed (theoretically) in God, he was acting (practically) as if he did not.

Hezekiah was not alone, for Jerusalem was filled with *practical atheists*. They all knew God (in theory)—indeed they had witnessed revival—they had just chosen to forget him (in practice) so they could live without him (in theory).

> A *practical atheist* is one who says they believe in God, but lives as if they do not. The faith of a practical atheist exists in theory, but not in practice.

Just as the faithless King Ahaz, when confronted with the Syro–Ephramite threat, sought refuge in Assyria's shadow, so too did the godly and successful King Hezekiah, when confronted with the Assyrian invasion, seek refuge in Egypt's shade. And so sin was added to sin.

But could Assyria's shadow be bigger than God's? Could Egypt's shade be broader and deeper than God's? How could such folly bring anything but disaster? How could such covenantal betrayal attract anything but judgement?

> 'Ah, stubborn children,' declares the LORD,
> 'who carry out a plan, but not mine,
> and who make an alliance, but not of my Spirit,
>   that they may add sin to sin;
> who set out to go down to Egypt,
>   without asking for my direction,
> to take refuge in the protection of Pharaoh
>   and to seek shelter in the shadow of Egypt!
> Therefore shall the protection of Pharaoh turn to your shame,
>   and the shelter in the shadow of Egypt to your humiliation.
> For though his officials are at Zoan
>   and his envoys reach Hanes,[1]

---

1 Zoan is located on the northeastern edge of the Nile Delta, while Hanes (Tahpanhes) is in Upper (southern) Egypt, south of Memphis. So from Zoan to Hanes indicates from one end of Egypt to the other (Oswalt, p. 546).

  everyone comes to shame
    through a people that cannot profit them,
  that brings neither help nor profit,
    but shame and disgrace (30:1–5).

Isaiah's focus here is not what God's people claim to believe (their theory), but what they have done and how they have acted (their practice). They have demonstrated their lack of faith by walking as the world walks, as if God were irrelevant or non-existent. Driven by misplaced fear, they have enacted a conspiracy against the Lord by brokering a covenant with Egypt in violation of their covenant with God. They are the Lord's people, yet they have not honoured the Lord as holy by seeking his perspective or will. Instead, they have sought salvation in one who cannot save them: Pharaoh, their former slavemaster. And so, while Jerusalem's envoys travel far, through many dangers, bearing tribute, it is to 'a people that cannot profit them' (30:6). 'Egypt's help is worthless and empty' (30:7).

The alliance with Egypt, warned Isaiah, was destined to fail. It was a 'covenant with death' (28:15,18) which would be swept away by the overwhelming flood (Assyria). The covenant (or 'alliance,' also translated as 'covering' or 'blanket' in 28:20)—would not provide the warm, comforting security for which Jerusalem hoped.

God's people had chosen the path of practical atheism. They had chosen to invest their hopes in political diplomacy, military might and alliances with power rather than in the God of their salvation and Rock of their refuge; in *Baal Perazim*, the Lord who bursts through; in *Yahweh Sabaoth*, the Commander of Heaven's hosts.

The Judeans were exercising historical amnesia, forgetting (in practice if not in theory) that most critical of faith–inspiring precedents: the Exodus and the words that Moses spoke to the imperilled, besieged, entrapped Israelites as they stood at the edge of the Red Sea watching Pharaoh's forces advance upon them.

  And Moses said to the people, 'Fear not, stand firm, and see
  the salvation of the LORD, which he will work for you today.
  For the Egyptians whom you see today, you shall never see
  again. The LORD will fight for you, and you have only to be
  silent.' (Exodus 14:13–14).

That day, the Lord saved Israel from the hand of the Egyptians (Exodus

14:30a) and Israel saw the great power that the Lord used (Exodus 14:31a).

The Judeans clearly did not believe that their God could or would fulfil his promises as contained in his covenant:

> When you go out to war against your enemies, and see horses and chariots and an army larger than your own, you shall not be afraid of them, for the LORD your God is with you, who brought you up out of the land of Egypt. And when you draw near to the battle, the priest shall come forward and speak to the people and shall say to them, 'Hear, O Israel, today you are drawing near for battle against your enemies: let not your heart faint. Do not fear or panic or be in dread of them, for the LORD your God is he who goes with you to fight for you against your enemies, to give you the victory' (Deuteronomy 20:1–4).

> And if you faithfully obey the voice of the LORD your God, being careful to do all his commandments that I command you today, the LORD your God will set you high above all the nations of the earth. And all these blessings shall come upon you and overtake you, if you obey the voice of the LORD your God … The LORD will cause your enemies who rise against you to be defeated before you. They shall come out against you one way and flee before you seven ways (Deuteronomy 28:1–2, 7).

> But if you will not obey the voice of the LORD your God or be careful to do all his commandments and his statutes that I command you today, then all these curses shall come upon you and overtake you … The LORD will cause you to be defeated before your enemies. You shall go out one way against them and flee seven ways before them. And you shall be a horror to all the kingdoms of the earth (Deuteronomy 28:15, 25).

Maybe they did believe that God could and would fulfil his word, but knew, deep in their hearts that they had been unfaithful and disobedient and were therefore deserving of wrath. If that was the case, then we can only assume that pure spiritual rebellion prevented their repentance. Faith is more than mere belief.[1]

God's people had forgotten (in practice if not in theory) Elisha's victory over the forces of the king of Syria.

---

1 James 2:18–20.

When the servant of the man of God rose early in the morning and went out, behold, an army with horses and chariots was all around the city. And the servant said, 'Alas, my master! What shall we do?' He [Elisha] said, 'Do not be afraid, for those who are with us are more than those who are with them.' Then Elisha prayed and said, 'O LORD, please open his eyes that he may see.' So the LORD opened the eyes of the young man, and he saw, and behold, the mountain was full of horses and chariots of fire all around Elisha (2 Kings 6:15–17).

They did not share the faith of King David, who knew, even as a youth, that 'the battle is the Lord's'.

And the Philistine said to David, 'Am I a dog, that you come to me with sticks?' And the Philistine cursed David by his gods. The Philistine said to David, 'Come to me, and I will give your flesh to the birds of the air and to the beasts of the field.' Then David said to the Philistine, 'You come to me with a sword and with a spear and with a javelin, but I come to you in the name of the LORD of hosts, the God of the armies of Israel, whom you have defied. This day the LORD will deliver you into my hand, and I will strike you down and cut off your head. And I will give the dead bodies of the host of the Philistines this day to the birds of the air and to the wild beasts of the earth, that all the earth may know that there is a God in Israel, and that all this assembly may know that the LORD saves not with sword and spear. For the battle is the LORD's, and he will give you into our hand.' (1 Samuel 17:43–47).

Some trust in chariots and some in horses,
but we trust in the name of the LORD our God (Psalm 20:7).

Despite their theological knowledge and historical experience, God's people had chosen to forget God and walk the path of practical atheism instead. Despite their faithlessness and betrayal, God graciously called his people to return and rest in him—but they would not.

They were rebellious 'children unwilling to hear the instruction of the Lord' (30:9). Rejecting the prophetic voice, they sought words that would soothe—even if they were lies (30:10)—from teachers who would say whatever it was that their itching ears wanted to hear (cf. 2 Timothy 4:3). They simply did not want to hear about 'the Holy One of Israel' (30:11). And why would they? For they had already made up their minds as to their course of action and certainly were not interested in hearing anything contrary.

'Therefore' (30:12), God's rebellious people would meet with disaster. For just as a breached wall bulges and bulges until it collapses under its own weight, eventually the weight of sin added to sin brings down a people (30:13). As the burden of sin compounds, so too does the wrath of God compound until judgement day dawns and the potter throws his defective creation to the ground, smashing it to pieces (30:14).

Yet the God of justice and steadfast love, the redeeming God who finds 'no pleasure in the death of anyone',[1] graciously calls to his people to return to him and be saved.

> For thus said the Lord GOD, the Holy One of Israel,
> 'In returning and rest you shall be saved;
> in quietness and in trust shall be your strength' (30:15a–c).

As Motyer notes:

> Isaiah's recipe for national security had remained unchanged
> since the days of Ahaz (7:4, 10–12; cf. 28:12). First there should
> be repentance/'returning', the active pathway for coming back
> to the Lord (cf. 1:27); such a return as brings them to 'rest
> down' on the Lord. Then there is quietness, the absence of
> frenzy and restless anxiety that evidences a true trust.[2]

God's people 'were in a military situation but the prophet did not recommend armaments, only the armament of faith'.[3]

We must not gloss over this; for it is a radical message. Picture it. A military invasion is imminent. As God's people contemplate the prospect of occupation, slaughter, exile and siege, they are called upon to invest their hope not in objects they can see and touch—impressive objects like fortified walls, advanced weaponry, and the impressive military might of Egypt—but in the invisible Lord God: *Baal Perazim* (the Lord of bursting through), *Yahweh Sabaoth* (the commander of heaven's hosts).

God's people, however, were unwilling (30:15d).

---

1 Ezekiel 18:32.
2 Motyer, p. 249.
3 Ibid.

They would not repent. They would not rest in God, trust in God, wait for God.

> 'No! We will flee upon horses';
>   therefore you shall flee away;
> and, 'We will ride upon swift steeds';
>   therefore your pursuers shall be swift.
> A thousand shall flee at the threat of one;
>   at the threat of five you shall flee,
> till you are left
>   like a flagstaff on the top of a mountain,
>   like a signal on a hill (30:16–17).

And then we have what must surely be one of the most invisible and neglected, yet profoundly important verses of the whole Bible:

> Therefore the LORD waits to be gracious to you,
>   and therefore he exalts himself to show mercy to you.
> For the LORD is a God of justice;
>   blessed are all those who wait for him (30:18).

The 'wait' in the first and last line of verse 18 are the same Hebrew word, *chakah*, which means 'to tarry': that is, 'remain inactive in expectation (of something)'.[1]

Motyer comments:

> A logic of God is at work. Judge and punish he must, but forsake his purposes he will not! Judgement must intervene, 'therefore' he (lit.) 'will wait in order to be gracious …'[2]

Oswalt elaborates:

> Until we are ready to exercise trust, until we are ready to wait for him, he must wait for us.[3]

> Because Judah will not wait on the Lord (26:8) but insists on rushing off on horses, the Lord must wait to show his grace until they are in a position to receive it. So to the repeated cry of 'How long, O Lord?' his answer is, 'Whenever you are ready'.[4]

---

1 Definition of 'tarry': Collins Concise Dictionary, 5th edn. HarperCollins Publishers, Glasgow, 2001
2 Motyer, p. 250.
3 Oswalt, p. 554.
4 Ibid., p. 557.

Justice demands judgement, yet after judgement there will be grace. 'It is judgement,' writes Oswalt, 'which shatters the false values and makes one attentive. It is grace which motivates the broken to believe and obey. Neither is ultimately effective without the other.'[1]

The same idea—that God is prepared to wait (tarry, or hold off)—is found in Hosea:

> I will return again to my place,
>   until they acknowledge their guilt and seek my face,
>   and in their distress earnestly seek me (Hosea 5:15).

Hosea commentator J. Andrew Dearman notes that Yahweh's place cannot be limited to geography, for even the heavens cannot contain him. And while he is removed, he is still always near his people.

> That can be good news when they acknowledge their guilt,
> but terrifying news if they do not … In his return to his place,
> YHWH awaits the return (6:1) of his people to him.[2]

Preaching on Hosea 5:15, the great American Puritan Jonathan Edwards (1703–1756) observed that God, in his providence, commonly orders that men and women be 'brought to see their miserable condition as they are in themselves, and to despair of help from themselves or from an arm of flesh, before he appears for them …'[3] In order to do this, remarked Edwards, God may withdraw himself or withhold his hand, allowing humankind's wickedness free expression. By this means, the myth of human sufficiency might be exposed and humanity's vulnerability, insufficiency, helplessness and dependency might be revealed. With options exhausted, the helpless, now dependent man or woman cries out to the Lord for mercy and deliverance.

At that point, the Lord's wait is over (30:18). At the very sound of their cry or prayer he rises to show mercy (30:19).

'It is God's manner,' concludes Edwards after an overview of Old Testament history, 'when he will bestow signal blessings in answer to

---

1 Ibid., p. 559.
2 J. Andrew Dearman, 'The book of Hosea', in *The New International Commentary on the Old Testament*, Eerdmans, Grand Rapids MI & Cambridge UK, 2010, p. 188.
3 'God makes men sensible of their misery before he reveals his mercy and love' (Hosea 5:15), sermon 2 in 'Seventeen Occasional Sermons', *The Works of Jonathan Edwards*, vol 2, Hendrickson Publishers, Peabody MA, 2004, p. 830.

prayer, to make men seek them, and pray for them with a sense of their sin and misery.'[1]

In other words, it is commonly the case that when God plans to bestow blessing, he leads the intended recipients into a position of dependence and draws them to pray the very prayer he intends to answer.

In a sermon on Psalm 65:2,[2] entitled 'The Most High A Prayer–Hearing God', Edwards declares:

> It is the will of God to bestow mercy in this way, vis. in answer
> to prayer, when he designs beforehand to bestow mercy; yea,
> when he has promised it … God has been pleased to constitute
> prayer to be antecedent to the bestowment of mercy; and
> he is pleased to bestow mercy in consequence of prayer, as
> though he were prevailed on by prayer. When the people of
> God are stirred up to prayer, it is the effect of his intention
> to show mercy; therefore he pours out the spirit of grace and
> supplication.[3]

This was also the thinking of Blaise Pascal (1623–1662), who contended: 'God has established prayer to communicate the dignity of causality to his creatures.'[4]

Until God's people arrive at that place where they *return* to him and cry out to him with humbled hearts the dependent prayer of faith; until they are prepared to *rest* in him, *trust* in him, and *wait* for him, God waits to be gracious.

Blessed are all those who wait for him.

Then, lest we forget what is at stake, Isaiah, with words and images reminiscent of Isaiah 2:1–4, re-delivers God's promise of future glory (30:19–26). In the Jerusalem of this vision, there are no more tears or false religion. Instead of giving 'the bread of adversity and the water of affliction' (30:20), the Lord will give 'rain for the seed …' and

---

1 Ibid. p 831
2 'O you who hear prayer, to you shall all flesh come' (Psalm 65:2).
3 'The Most High prayer–hearing God' (Psalm 65:2), sermon 2 in 'Seven
   Sermons on Important Subjects', *The Works of Jonathan Edwards*, vol 2, p.
   116.
4 Quoted by Jacques Ellul in *The Politics of God and the Politics of Man*,
   Eerdmans Publishing Company, Grand Rapids MI, 1977 (1972), p. 22.

'brooks running with water' (30:25)—everything that is required for fruitful abundance in the land (30:23-24). The Lord will be revealed and perceived (30:20). He will teach and lead his people. The idols of the past will be defiled and discarded. There will be provision, peace, healing and harmony in nature and amongst people. Is not this worth waiting for? Yes? So, 'Walk in the light of the Lord' (2:5), and 'Stop regarding man!' (2:22). Blessed are all those who wait for him (30:18d).

But before God's faithful can enjoy that glorious future, they must first face the immediate and live through tomorrow. So without delay, Isaiah adjusts his focus from the distant horizon to that which is near; and what he sees there is imminent deliverance from the Assyrians. In Isaiah 30:27-33 the prophet delivers God's promise that the maligned, despised and rejected Holy One of Israel—the Lord himself—will burst through in all his sovereign might and righteous zeal, with smoke and fire, anger and fury, to supernaturally deliver Judah from the Assyrian threat.

Like a river in flood, the waters of the Euphrates (the Assyrian armed forces), mighty and many, will overflow its channels and run over its banks (8:7). Rushing south down the coast, it will overwhelm the Egyptian detachment, sweeping away 'the refuge of lies' (28:17) so that Judah's 'covenant with death will be annulled' and her 'agreement with Sheol will not stand' (28:18). The Assyrians will then flood on into Judah (28:19), surging forth with terror, until they have flooded Immanuel's land right up to its neck (8:8, i.e. to the gates of Jerusalem), just as Isaiah had forecast 34 years earlier.

> Isaiah waited 34 years to see the fulfilment of his prophecy of Assyrian invasion. It would be more than 100 years before his prophecy of Babylonian conquest would come to pass. This is worth remembering in these days of 'drive-thou', 'fast' and instant everything. Modern men and women barely know the meaning of the words rest and wait any more.

Then, declares Isaiah, the 'name of the Lord' (30:27) will roll in like a storm (30:27, 30) and his breath will be 'like an overflowing stream that reaches up to the neck' (30:28). He will come with burning anger and rising smoke; with lips of fury and a tongue like devouring fire (30:27). He will 'sift the nations with the sieve of destruction' and 'place on the jaws of the peoples a bridle that leads astray' (30:28).

While the Judeans will rejoice to see God's deliverance, 'The Assyrians will be terror-stricken at the voice of the Lord when he strikes with his rod … Battling with brandished arm he will fight them' (30:31–32).

And so God promised that Jerusalem would be delivered, not by any man or woman, but by God. Just as God described Pekah and Rezin as 'smouldering stumps of firebrands'[1] (men who were no threat to Judah as their lights were already fading), he described Sennacherib as a king who, while he thinks he is coming to conquer, is in reality 'climbing into his own funeral pyre'.[2] From God's perspective, in 735 BC Pekah and Rezin were about to burn out, and in 701 BC Sennacherib was about to burn up!

According to Isaiah 30:33, this pyre for King Sennacherib of Assyria had been prepared long ago.

All it wants is the Lord's breath to kindle it into flame (cf. 31:9). So again Isaiah is counselling his people that they need not go to Egypt out of fear of Assyria. What they should do is to move even closer to the only One in the universe who truly holds Assyria's destiny in his hand.[3]

———∿∿∿———

You have God, so why settle for less?

Nothing exposes weak faith and practical atheism like affliction, tribulation and pressure, persecution and threat. The practical atheist fears as the world fears (8:12–13). But it is a misplaced fear. The practical atheist walks as the world walks, stumbling in darkness, perceiving the politics but blind to spiritual realities, looking everywhere for help but to *Baal Perazim, Yahweh Sabaoth*. Consequently, practical atheists can only ever bring catastrophe upon themselves and all who travel with them.

Woe to those who go down to Egypt for help
and rely on horses,

---

1 King Pekah of Israel, the son of Remaliah, and King Rezin of Syria (735 BC). Isaiah 7:1–9.
2 Motyer, p. 251.
3 Oswalt, p. 569.

who trust in chariots because they are many
and in horsemen because they are very strong,
but do not look to the Holy One of Israel
or consult the LORD!
And yet he is wise and brings disaster;
he does not call back his words,
but will arise against the house of the evildoers
and against the helpers of those who work iniquity.
The Egyptians are man, and not God,
and their horses are flesh, and not spirit.
When the LORD stretches out his hand,
the helper will stumble, and he who is helped will fall,
and they will all perish together (31:1–3).

The Lord, not Egypt, will save Jerusalem. Undaunted by the military might and imperialistic bluster of Assyria, the Lion of Judah will roar and 'fight on Mount Zion and on its hill' (31:4). Hovering over Jerusalem like an instinctively protective mother bird, 'he will protect and deliver it; he will spare and rescue it' (31:5).

How foolish, insufficient and limiting it is to trust mortal, fallen, limited flesh over immortal, exalted, omnipotent divinity. What a coup it is for the devil when he can blind our eyes to spiritual realities. If he can do that, he need do nothing else. He can sit back and watch as the breach progresses to its inevitable end (30:13) and the blind lead the blind into catastrophe and judgement (30:14).

After yet another appeal for repentance (31:6) made in view of the impending catastrophe (which will result in awakening, v. 7), the promise of divine deliverance is repeated:

'And the Assyrian shall fall by a sword, not of man;
and a sword, not of man, shall devour him;
and he shall flee from the sword,
and his young men shall be put to forced labour.
His rock shall pass away in terror,
and his officers desert the standard in panic,'
declares the LORD, whose fire is in Zion,
and whose furnace is in Jerusalem (31:8–9).

The concept of supernatural deliverance should not be foreign to God's people. 'It is God, not man, who delivers,' writes Oswalt.

225

This truth surfaces again and again in Scripture. It appears in the conception of Isaac, when human power was long gone. It appears at the crossing of the Red Sea and again at Jericho. It is there in the Gideon story and in the rout of the Philistines in Samuel's day. Jehoshaphat experienced it in his fight with the Edomites. It is this truth which is at the heart of Paul's contrast of flesh and spirit (Galatians 5:16–26). When people believe they can save themselves, they effectively dethrone God in their lives and doom themselves (Philippians 3:7), for it is only as the king of our lives that he can help us.[1]

Practical atheism might impress the elites of the City of Man, but it blinds eyes to spiritual realities, gives the devil a foothold and creates a bulwark against genuine spiritual warfare by limiting minds and hopes to that which can be seen. And while God's footsteps are normally unseen, faithful intercessors will testify that through faithful, expectant prayer with watchfulness, God's presence and his providence may be clearly and wonderfully perceived.

O LORD, in the morning you hear my voice;
in the morning I prepare a sacrifice for you and watch
(Psalm 5:3).

Continue steadfastly in prayer, being watchful in it with thanksgiving (Colossians 4:2).

—◦◦◦—

As I write (2011–2012), the al-Qaeda–Taliban alliance is ascendant in Afghanistan and Pakistan. Unless something dramatic and unforeseen occurs, both states are heading towards failure, implosion and disintegration.

Meanwhile, despite years of talks, Ivory Coast has remained deeply divided. The 28 November 2010 high-stakes elections, conducted despite the northern rebels' refusal to disarm, resulted in the incumbent Laurent Gbagbo and his opponent Alassane Ouattara both declaring themselves victorious. Ivory Coast was on the brink once again.

Then in March–April 2011, pro–Ouattara forces (ethnic Muslim militias), with military assistance from France, took power by force

---

1 Oswalt, p. 576.

in a bloody blitzkrieg.[1] Hundreds of Gbagbo supporters (i.e. southern and western tribes, Christians, non–Muslims) were slaughtered while hundreds of thousands were displaced.[2] As pro–Ouattara forces conducted cleaning operations, the churches filled up with refugees, some of whom bore massive injuries, including gunshot wounds. The Catholic mission in Duékoué found itself sheltering more than 27,000 refugees, survivors of pro–Ouattara militia pogroms. The churches of Abidjan and San Pedro also filled with refugees—no food, no water, no medicines, but thousands of refugees.[3] As I write, the UN is investigating a massacre by Ouattara's new army at a Baptist church in the Yopougon district of Abidjan. The church had been sheltering some 2,500 refugees.[4] By mid–April 2011, Ivory Coast had fallen to Islam.[5]

These battles are not over. Even if they were, others would emerge in their place. For each of these conflicts, like all conflicts, have sin at their core: lies, blasphemies, megalomania, greed, injustice. Sin gives the devil his foothold. Not until we live in a world without sin will we be free of tribulation and pressure. Until then, there can be no security for Christians in 'Man', in the City of Man, in the projects of the City of Man, in 'covenants with death' or in practical atheism. These can only yield disappointment and destruction.

God is shaking this world, bringing down all humanity's idols and all its pride. Hardship, affliction, tribulation and persecution are escalating. But though darkness is rolling in, God is doing something amazing in our midst—something both wonderful yet terrifying, sweet yet bitter, old yet new.

1 E. Kendal, 'Ivory Coast: where Islamic and Western interests converge', RLM, 7 April 2011.
2 E. Kendal, 'A cry from Abidjan: Christians imperiled', RLM, 14 April 2011.
3 E. Kendal, 'Ivory Coast: churches filling up—with refugees', ELM, 24 April 2011.
4 E. Kendal, 'Ivory Coast: church attacked; refugees suffering; lawyers refused; Mbeki speaks', RLM, 11 May 2011; 'UN probing reports of attack on Ivory Coast church', Reuters Africa, 6 May 2011, af.reuters.com/article/topNews/idAFJOE7450ES20110506?sp=true.
5 For full background and updates on religious liberty and persecution issues, see RLM, elizabethkendal.blogspot.com.au, and RLPB, rlprayerbulletin.blogspot.com.au.

We must *remember* him, *trust* him, and in faith, *wait* for him. 'For the Lord is a God of justice; blessed are all those who wait for him' (30:18b).

He is *Baal Perazim*: the Lord of bursting through, the Lord of the breakthrough.

He is *Yahweh Sabaoth*: the Lord of Hosts, the commander of heaven's hosts.

'He will surely be gracious to you at the sound of your cry. As soon as he hears it, he answers you' (30:19b).

And while we work this out,
while we struggle to let go of our pride
    and arrogant self–sufficiency;
while we struggle to disengage from the world
    and its vain projects;
while we wrestle with grace and struggle with faith—
the Lord waits to be gracious.

Questions for Discussion and Reflection

1. Can you remember a time when God intervened for you, when he guided, rescued, healed or aided you, in answer to prayer? (It does not have to be spectacular.)

   Write down one such case as a testimony to how God lives and loves and intervenes in answer to prayer. (If in a group: share your testimony.)

2. If we are spiritual in theory but not in practice, what does this imply about our faith? (Consider James 2:14–26). Why? What is the connection between faith and practice?

3. How does the principle expressed in Isaiah 30:18—that God waits for us to wait for him—compare with that expressed in Matthew 7:7–11?

   And with that expressed in Hebrews 11:6?

4. The image of the Lord as *Yahweh Sabaoth*—the Lord of Host; the commander of heaven's angelic armies—is powerful and inspiring. What divine attributes does *Yahweh Sabaoth* display?

5. More of God's attributes are revealed in the two illustrations from nature found in Isaiah 31:4–5.

   Read: Isaiah 31:4–5.

   How does it make you feel to know that God—*Yahweh Sabaoth, Baal Perazim*—is as possessive of you as a young lion is over his precious catch; and as protective of you as a mother bird is of her chicks?

Prayer

Our God is Yahweh Sabaoth!

O Lord my God,
You are *Baal Perazim*: the Lord of bursting through / the Lord of the
    breakthrough! (2 Samuel 5:20)
You are *Yahweh Sabaoth*: the Lord of hosts / the commander of
    heaven's angelic forces!
Almighty, majestic and awesome beyond comprehension,
    you are ready, willing and able to save
    waiting only for us to wait for you.

Forgive me Lord, for the times I put my trust in limited, mortal
'man', (Isaiah 2:22)
    rather than in you;
    and put my trust in money, weapons or status—
    limited and corrupted means—
    rather than in you.
For each time I put my trust in that which is limited
    I accepted far less than what you intended.
And each time I resisted grace
    I prolonged suffering for myself and for others.
I am sorry Lord. Please help me make things right.

That the surging tide of materialistic culture might never consume
    me again,
I will commit to establishing myself firmly
    on the exalted, solid Rock of Jesus Christ.
I will feed on your faith–energising holy word
    and drink of your faith–empowering Holy Spirit.
Help me Lord! Increase my faith! Fill me with your Holy Spirit!

When enemies advance upon me;
    when they besiege me and breath out threats against me,
    I will remember that I am not alone,
    and in remembering, I will not fear!
By faith I will know what my eyes cannot see,
    that you—the almighty and glorious *Yahweh Sabaoth*—
    are with me.
And when the Lord of hosts bursts through for me,

then no-one can stand against me.

All praises be to the glorious Lord of hosts,
    to my God, in whom I trust.

Amen.

CHAPTER 11

'In Whom Do You Now Trust?'
Faith Tested at the Upper Pool

Isaiah 36–37

In the fourteenth year of King Hezekiah, Sennacherib king of Assyria came up against all the fortified cities of Judah and took them (36:1; 2 Kings 18:13).

And Hezekiah king of Judah sent to the king of Assyria at Lachish, saying, 'I have done wrong; withdraw from me. Whatever you impose on me I will bear.' And the king of Assyria required of Hezekiah king of Judah three hundred talents of silver and thirty talents of gold. And Hezekiah gave him all the silver that was found in the house of the LORD and in the treasuries of the king's house. At that time Hezekiah stripped the gold from the doors of the temple of the LORD and from the doorposts that Hezekiah king of Judah had overlaid and gave it to the king of Assyria (2 Kings 18:14–16).

And the king of Assyria sent the Rabshakeh from Lachish to King Hezekiah at Jerusalem, with a great army. And he stood by the conduit of the upper pool on the highway to the Washer's Field. And there came out to him Eliakim the son of Hilkiah, who was over the household, and Shebna the secretary, and Joah the son of Asaph, the recorder.

And the Rabshakeh said to them, 'Say to Hezekiah, "Thus says the great king, the king of Assyria: On what do you rest this trust of yours? Do you think that mere words are strategy and power for war? In whom do you now trust …?"' (36:2–5; see also 2 Kings 18:17–20).

———

Everything falls apart

If King Merodach-baladan of Babylon's incitement of anti-Assyrian rebellion in the west had been a tactic designed to increase his own odds of victory, then it failed. For Sennacherib, having launched a devastating reprisal, was not going to be distracted. By early 702 BC, Merodach-baladan's adventure was over. His reign cut short, Merodach-baladan was forced to flee for his life yet again, and Babylon was forced to resubmit to the Assyrian yoke.

With Babylon subdued, Sennacherib turned his gaze west towards Palestine where Hezekiah and his coalition of rebel states were defiantly withholding tribute.

Isaiah had warned God's people that their security would not be found in the City of Man, not even in an exotic cosmopolitan city state such as Babylon. Furthermore, Isaiah had even prophesied the fall of Babylon: 'Fallen, fallen is Babylon; and all her carved images of her gods he has shattered to the ground' (21:9b).

As with many prophecies, the interpretation of this oracle starts at our fingertips and stretches to the far horizon with imminent, future and eschatological application. For while Sennacherib was successful in putting down Merodach-baladan's rebellion of 703 BC, the Babylonians remained restless and rebellious. Eventually, after numerous revolts and reprisals, Sennacherib laid siege to the city. When Babylon fell in 689 BC, Sennacherib showed no mercy, razing the city such that it was uninhabitable for years. Ultimately, at the end of world history, the metaphoric Babylon—representing the City of Man—will be brought down forever. 'Fallen, fallen is Babylon the great!' (Revelation 18). Security is not found in the City of Man.

In 701 BC, Sennacherib's army swarmed west, descending on Sidon[1] with vengeance. With Sidon subdued, Sennacherib's forces advanced southward down the Mediterranean coast, crushing all rebellion en route: eliminating rebellious kings, replacing them with Assyrian puppets, and extracting tribute from each and every subjugated Phoenician city.

---

1 Sidon is in modern-day Lebanon.

Next in Sennacherib's sights was the regional economic powerhouse of Tyre. This fabulously wealthy port city sat with her back against the mountains, her toes in the sea and her fingers in the great port cities of the Mediterranean. Her magnificent fleet had brought her great wealth, enabling her to rise high. Consequently, her fall was devastating. Indeed the fall of Tyre, whose king fled to Cyprus, sent shockwaves through the whole region.

Isaiah had warned of this too. In fact, Isaiah had warned God's people repeatedly that God is committed to bringing down the 'pompous pride' of humankind,[1] reducing all that humanity exalts and glories in, exposing it as folly and useless idolatry. That which is vain and temporal must be exposed as such, so that men and women might stop deceiving themselves and turn to God who alone is eternal, worthy, faithful and able to save.

> Wail, O ships of Tarshish,
>   for Tyre is laid waste, without house or harbor!
> From the land of Cyprus
>   it is revealed to them ...
> When the report comes to Egypt,
>   they will be in anguish over the report about Tyre ...
> Who has purposed this
>   against Tyre, the bestower of crowns,
> whose merchants were princes,
>   whose traders were the honoured of the earth?
> The LORD of hosts has purposed it,
>   to defile the pompous pride of all glory,
>   to dishonour all the honoured of the earth ...
> Wail, O ships of Tarshish,
>   for your stronghold is laid waste.
> In that day Tyre will be forgotten for seventy years ...
>   (23:1, 5, 8–9, 14–15a).

As with the prophecy concerning Babylon, the interpretation of the oracle concerning Tyre starts at our fingertips and stretches to the far horizon, with imminent, future and eschatological application.

In 701 BC, King Sennacherib of Assyria crushed rebellion in Tyre and restored Assyrian suzerainty over the city. Tyre, which never

---

1 Isaiah 13:11; 23:9; 25:11.

recovered its status, did not regain its independence until 630 BC.[1] Eventually, in 332 BC, Tyre fell to Alexander the Great. Every mortal dies and everything temporal is temporary. Money comes and money goes. Kingdoms rise and kingdoms fall. Only God endures forever.

According to Bright, when Tyre fell to Sennacherib in 701 BC, the western revolt began to unravel and 'kings from far and near—Byblos, Arvad, Ashdod, Moab, Edom, Ammon—hastened to Sennacherib with tribute.'[2] Only the city states of Ashkelon and Ekron, together with Judah, held out.

After putting down rebellion and effecting regime-change in Ashkelon, Sennacherib proceeded to subdue all the cities of northern Philistia, including Ekron, whose king, Padi, was incarcerated in Jerusalem.

News of Tyre's fate quickly reached Egypt (23:5), propelling the Egyptian forces into action. Gallantly they marched to the rescue, determined this time to fulfil their promise of military aid through a demonstration of superior force. Advancing northward through Philistia to assist in the defense of Ekron, the Egyptian detachment was intercepted by Assyrian forces at Eltekeh (some twenty miles west of Jerusalem at the edge of the hill country) and decisively routed. Egypt would not be coming to anyone's aid.

Isaiah had warned repeatedly that Egypt could not be relied upon for military support. For despite Egypt's resurgence under the Cushite (Ethiopian) kings of the 25th dynasty—Piankhi (751–712 BC) and then Shabako (712–701 BC)—Egypt still was not the supreme superpower the Palestinian states (or Egypt) wished it to be. More importantly, Egypt was not God! Egypt was a state like any other—a state comprised of flesh-and-blood people and flesh-and-blood horses, a state with its own limitations and its own interests.

Back in 713 BC, when King Sargon II of Assyria sent his commander-in-chief west to subdue and annex Ashdod, Egypt and its Cushite king were worse than useless. Egypt, which had incited the rebellion, had promised Ashdod military aid. It was all part of Egypt's defence strategy to create a buffer zone in Palestine as a bulwark against Assyrian expansion. But as soon as the Assyrian reprisal materialised, Egypt turned to jelly and reneged. When Ashdod fell to the Assyrians in 711 BC, King Yamani—Egypt's ally in Ashdod—fled to Egypt in

---

1 Motyer, p. 192.
2 Bright, p. 286.

search of asylum. The Egyptians, however, opted for appeasement over confrontation, and pragmatism over principle. They betrayed Yamani, who they had bound and delivered over to the Assyrians in exchange for peace.

During the three years that Ashdod was under siege—deserted by its ally Egypt and its Cushite king—Isaiah walked Jerusalem naked—that is, wearing only a loin cloth—and barefoot in obedience to the Lord's command (20:1–2).

> Then the LORD said, 'As my servant Isaiah has walked naked and barefoot for three years as a sign and a portent against Egypt and Cush, so shall the king of Assyria lead away the Egyptian captives and the Cushite exiles, both the young and the old, naked and barefoot, with buttocks uncovered, the nakedness of Egypt. Then they shall be dismayed and ashamed because of Cush their hope and of Egypt their boast. And the inhabitants of this coastland will say in that day, 'Behold, this is what has happened to those in whom we hoped and to whom we fled for help to be delivered from the king of Assyria! And we, how shall we escape?' (20:3–6).

Yes, God had already told his people that, just as Egypt did not save Ashdod, Egypt would not save Judah or anyone who put their trust in her. Rather, Egypt's promises would prove hollow. Egypt's words are just powerless talk and bluster, more likely to hurt than to help. Isaiah forewarned that when the king of Assyria subdued Egypt, then all who had hoped in her—that she might save them—would be dismayed and ashamed. In horror they would cry, 'If this has happened to Egypt, our hope, then how shall we escape?'

Surely this cry rang out across Judah in 701 BC, as reports filtered in from the battlefield at Eltekeh where Egypt's finest soldiers—the hope of Judah—lay dead on the ground. Later, in 671 BC, Assyria's King Esarhaddon would invade and conquer Egypt and deport Egyptian captives back to Assyria, providing a further fulfilment of Isaiah's prophecy.

After routing the Egyptian detachment at Eltekeh, Sennacherib's forces flooded into Judah. Along with numerous small towns and villages, 46 fortified Judean cities were razed—levelled with battering rams and siege engines—then stormed. A reported 200,150 Judeans were deported.[1]

The Assyrians then laid siege to Lachish, a Judean garrison city second in importance only to Jerusalem. Located high atop steep cliffs, Lachish was fortified by two massive city walls. Undeterred, the Assyrians built a huge siege ramp of earth and stone against the city's vulnerable south-west corner.[2] Excavations of the area have uncovered a mass grave containing some 1,500 bodies covered in pig bones—presumably the garbage of the Assyrian army.[3]

Hezekiah's misadventure had unravelled. Sennacherib, with his sights set firmly on Jerusalem, was able to boast that he had the rebellious and troublesome Hezekiah shut up 'like a bird in a cage'.[4]

In a last-ditch attempt to broker a political solution, appease Assyrian wrath and buy his way out of trouble, Hezekiah sent envoys to Sennacherib at Lachish, pleading: 'I have done wrong; withdraw from me. Whatever you impose on me I will bear.'

So exorbitant was the tribute demanded by Sennacherib, that Hezekiah was forced to empty the treasury and even strip the gold from the Temple in order to raise it (2 Kings 18:14–16).

Assyria launches propaganda campaign in pursuit of unconditional surrender

Enter Rabshakeh

After receiving all the silver and gold that Hezekiah could offer, Sennacherib dispatched a high-powered delegation to Jerusalem to extract one thing more from the king of Judah: unconditional surrender.

---

1 Details from the Taylor Prism, a six-sided baked clay document (or prism) discovered at the Assyrian capital Nineveh, in an area known today as Nebi Yunus. Recording the first eight campaigns of King Sennacherib (704–681 BC), the Taylor Prism is now housed in the British Museum (www.britishmuseum.org).
2 King, p. 44.
3 Bright, p. 286.
4 Sennacherib's boast, recorded on the Taylor Prism.

By the time the Rabshakeh[1] and his 'great army' arrived at Jerusalem, everything and everyone Hezekiah had invested his faith in had been crushed under the Assyrian fist and swept away. Babylon, Sidon, Tyre, Ashdod: all fallen. The Egyptian army—Judah's great hope: routed. Judah had been ravaged: her fortified cities razed, her peoples massacred and deported. The garrison city of Lachish was under siege. Hezekiah—the last king standing before the aggrieved and rapacious imperialistic superpower—was totally isolated. In whom could he now trust?

And so it was a supremely confident Rabshakeh who stood at the conduit of the upper pool on the highway to the Washer's Field. Refusing to dignify the Assyrian delegation with his presence, King Hezekiah sent Eliakim the son of Hilkiah, who was over the household, and Shebna the secretary, and Joah the son of Asaph, the recorder or archivist (i.e. two senior officials and a reporter) to dialogue with the Rabshakeh.

From the conduit of the upper pool on the highway to the Washer's Field, the Rabshakeh delivered two speeches. These two speeches are worthy of attention on account of the fact that the strategy and propaganda contained therein mirror much of what the world throws at the church today.[2]

While the Rabshakeh's first speech (36:4–10) is essentially diplomatic in nature and addressed to the king via his representatives, it is delivered in a loud clear voice and in Hebrew because the Rabshakeh wants to make sure that all the spectators watching and listening from the city wall both hear and understand it. If he had been living in the 21st century he would doubtless have opted for a media statement over two-party talks. For while the Rabshakeh's primary aim was to procure Hezekiah's unconditional surrender, his subplot involved undermining Judean solidarity and confidence, so that, in the event that Hezekiah did not capitulate, then his people might be incited to revolt and surrender themselves and their king in exchange for guarantees.

---

1 *Rabshakeh* (36:2) is also translated 'field commander' (NIV) or 'personal representative' (NLT). A footnote in the NKJV defines the Rabshakeh as the Chief of Staff or Governor.
2 Jacques Ellul's *The Politics of God and The Politics of Man* devotes a whole chapter to the Rabshakeh's speeches.

And so the Rabshakeh launched his attack with two audiences in mind: 'Say to Hezekiah, "Thus says the great king, the king of Assyria ..."' (36:4).

Note the disrespect! Hezekiah is addressed as a commoner, not as the king of Judah. In contrast, the message comes from 'the great king, the king of Assyria'. From the very outset the Rabshakeh displays contempt for this ant, Hezekiah, who dares to challenge the great king of superpower Assyria.

Then the Rabshakeh fires off an exposé of Hezekiah's political and strategic failings. Hezekiah, he notes, has foolishly and irresponsibly made a bid for independence without having the means to see it through. What sort of an idiot picks a fight with a superpower armed only with promises, boasts, reasons—that is, 'mere words'? Who in their right mind would back 'mere words' over a 'great army'? Military might—that is what you need! Mere words are no strategy or power for war (36:5).

With his next verbal volley the Rabshakeh mocks Hezekiah's disastrous foreign policy and military miscalculation in turning to Egypt for help, noting that Egypt never had the means to pose a serious threat to Assyria (36:6).

Then, taking aim at what he mistakenly regards as a disastrous religious policy, the Rabshakeh boldly asserts that God will not save Jerusalem now that Hezekiah has pulled down his high places (36:7). Clearly the Assyrian foreign office had been monitoring Hezekiah's religious reforms, particularly as those reforms would have indicated a rise in nationalistic zeal, along with the consolidation and centralisation of power. While Assyrian intelligence was obviously good, the analysis was flawed. The Assyrians, who were idolaters and polytheists, were clearly ignorant concerning the worship of Yahweh.

> *And he [Hezekiah] did what was right in the eyes of the Lord, according to all that David his father had done. He removed the high places and broke the pillars and cut down the Asherah. And he broke in pieces the bronze serpent that Moses had made, for until those days the people of Israel had made offerings to it (it was called Nehushtan.* 2 Kings 18:3–4; see also 2 Chronicles 31:1

According to the Rabshakeh's logic, Hezekiah had no other option than

240

to surrender or die. As an incentive towards surrender, the Rabshakeh offered a gift of two thousand horses, while taking a jibe at Judah's weakness, contemptuously scoffing that the Judeans would not even be able to put riders on them. This opened the way for the Rabshakeh to announce that which had already become perfectly obvious: Jerusalem—being so weak and helpless that she has to rely on Egypt for chariots and horsemen—cannot possibly repel the Assyrian army (36:8–9).

'Moreover,' the Rabshakeh cries as he attempts to strike a fatal blow against Judean morale, 'is it without the LORD that I have come up against this land to destroy it? The LORD said to me, Go up against this land and destroy it' (36:10).

The Assyrian foreign office was doubtless also fully aware of Isaiah's dissent and his prophecies warning of divine judgement.

> Ah, Assyria, the rod of my anger;
>   the staff in their hands is my fury!
> Against a godless nation I send him,
>   and against the people of my wrath I command him,
> to take spoil and seize plunder,
>   and to tread them down like the mire of the streets …
> As my hand has reached to the kingdoms of the idols,
>   whose carved images were greater than those of Jerusalem
>   and Samaria,
> shall I not do to Jerusalem and her idols
>   as I have done to Samaria and her images? (10:5–6, 10–11).

And so the Rabshakeh fires off what he intends to be a fatal blow designed to shatter the confidence of a people who had long resisted Isaiah and his prophecy that Assyria would be God's 'overwhelming whip'[1] and 'rod'. Indeed, he fires Isaiah's words (selectively, of course) right into the peoples' faces. 'Maybe,' he thinks, 'they might reason, "Isaiah was right after all, and the judgement he prophesied is coming to pass, in which case we are helpless indeed."'

While much of the Rabshakeh's speech is true, much is false. It is true that Hezekiah has miscalculated virtually all strategic contingencies and that Judah is militarily and economically out of her depth.

---

1 Isaiah 28:15.

However, as is generally the case amongst those who belong to the world, the Rabshakeh is confused and ignorant about Yahweh. And his ignorance, like all ignorance, leads to false assumptions and strategic blunders. The Rabshakeh's false perception of Judah's God as just another territorial and vengeful god amongst the gods, accounts for his false assumption that Judah's God must be angry with Hezekiah for pulling down his high places. This assumption is false on two grounds. Firstly, God is not territorial and embodied in idols, but universal and transcendent. Secondly, unlike all the gods ever invented by human beings, Yahweh is a God of grace. Consequently, even when his people sin, God extends grace to those who repent. But as is generally the case amongst those of the world, the Rabshakeh has little understanding of grace. Like so many others before him and since, the Rabshakeh has fashioned Yahweh after his own measure. Consequently, while the Rabshakeh's message is true as it pertains to politics, it is false as it pertains to Yahweh.

Nothing has changed, for still today this is typically the case: when the world's spokespersons speak out against the church they are often correct with regards to political matters, but incorrect with regards to matters pertaining to the Lord. The church needs to listen with humility and discernment, accepting that which is true while resisting and refusing to entertain or be deceived by that which is false.

Of course, we know that Sennacherib did have divine sanction, in as much as God did appoint Assyria to be his rod and whip against faithless Judah. But in scourging his people, God's aim was not an alteration of the geopolitical landscape. God's aim was the repentance and sanctification of his wayward people. His desire was that his people should turn from enmity and be reconciled with him, that they might be on his side once again.

God sent Assyria to scourge, not to destroy, and to serve and exalt the Lord, not itself.[1] Sennacherib, however, was not concerned with the will of Yahweh. He had his own end in mind—Assyrian expansion— and was using his own brutal means to get it. Yahweh was not even in the picture. The Rabshakeh was merely exploiting Yahweh as a tool of propaganda, with the aim of shaking the faith and crushing the spirit of those listening from the city wall.

The Rabshakeh's blow must have hit a nerve, for Eliakim, Shebna

---

1 Isaiah 10:7–8.

and Joah are compelled to interject. They appeal to the Rabshakeh that he speak to them in Aramaic, the diplomatic language of the day, rather than in Hebrew, the language of Judah (36:11). The king's representatives are keen to shield the people on the wall from such challenging propaganda.

However, like fuel on a fire, this only emboldens the Rabshakeh, who redoubles his efforts. After reminding the masses of their suffering and impressing upon them, in the most vulgar way, the terrors of siege to which Hezekiah is condemning them (36:12), he delivers a second speech which is nothing other than a barrage of pure propaganda (36:14–20). Spoken in Hebrew, it was aimed directly at the masses gathered on the city wall with the intention of inciting revolt.

The Rabshakeh starts well, taking aim at the bond between the masses and their king. Repeated volleys are aimed at the head. 'Do not let Hezekiah deceive you … Do not let Hezekiah make you trust in the Lord… Do not listen to Hezekiah… Beware lest Hezekiah mislead you…' In other words: 'Hezekiah is a stupid, lying dictator whose ultimate interest is himself. Do not trust him.'

If the Rabshakeh can separate the masses from their king, then he will have breached a psychological defence, leaving the masses vulnerable to manipulation and exploitation. Is not this too the way of the world, which strikes at the shepherd in order to scatter the sheep?

The Rabshakeh then ups the ante, tempting the masses with something they long for: something that stands in stark contrast to the inequality that has become a feature of Judah through the 8th century; something diametrically opposed to the conditions they would suffer under siege. The Rabshakeh promises the masses that if they make peace with him, if they surrender themselves to him, then each person will, in equity and justice, eat the fruit of their own vines and the fruit of their own fig trees, and drink water from of their own cistern (36:16) until he takes them away 'to a land like your own land, a land of grain and wine, a land of bread and vineyards' (36:17).

Not only is this an outright lie, it is an old and familiar one at that. 'Just follow me and you'll get what you seek: you'll be like God, and without cost', said the serpent to Eve in the Garden of Eden.[1] 'Just follow me and I'll get what you're after: the kingdoms of the word, only without

---

1 Genesis 3.

cost', said Satan to Jesus as he tempted him in the wilderness.[1] 'Just follow me and you'll get whatever your heart desires: glory, prosperity, the nations, security, and without cost', is the temptation Satan dangles before men and women everywhere.

It is amazing how many Christians will depart from God's revealed way and step out from the light of the Lord when power, fame, glory, prosperity, success and Christian security are offered them on a faithless, cross-less platter. But be warned; Satan's lies are no different to the Rabshakeh's—they are wicked deceptions, covenants with death, offering a mirage of liberty and happiness, when the reality is always going to be bondage and misery.

'Hezekiah has failed you', cries the Rabshakeh. 'You owe him nothing! Determine your own fate. Reject the terrors of siege. Reject certain military defeat. Accept the king of Assyria's generous offer.'

But then the Rabshakeh's tone changes, for by now he has gotten a little worked up. Excited and agitated, he starts to boast and blaspheme. Having made the point that Judah's king is unable to save them, the Rabshakeh confidently and emphatically asserts that neither is their God able to save them, for their God is no different to any other god, and no other god of any other nation has ever been unable to deliver any people or any land from the hands of King Sennacherib of Assyria who has, without mercy, crushed them all. Can you feel the heat rising?

With arrogant rage, the Rabshakeh throws down the gauntlet: 'You people in Jerusalem had better overthrow your loser king, forget your useless god, and surrender to the peaceful and prosperous life and an exiled captive—or you will suffer and die just like everyone else who has resisted Assyria!'

In his agitation and excitement, the Rabshakeh's sheep disguise has slipped. Now that his cold flashing eyes, angry snarl, hungry drool, and razor sharp teeth have been exposed, it becomes far more difficult for him to convince the spectators on the wall that he is a benevolent saviour. Until this point (36:18b) the propaganda had doubtless been highly effective. Now, however, it has become obvious that the Rabshakeh's previous words were exactly that: 'mere words.'

Yes, the real Rabshakeh has now stood up. Only instead of producing a collapse in Judean morale, the Rabshakeh's blasphemies against

---

1 Matthew 4:7–10.

Yahweh and his boasts of Assyrian invincibility have jolted the Jerusalemites to their senses and awakened something deep within.

Faith awakened

Just as an earthquake splits the ground exposing buried treasures, the Rabshakeh's blasphemies and boasts split open the people's hardened hearts. Memories of Yahweh surface; the remnant revives.

No! Yahweh is not like other gods: he lives, he loves, he is sovereign and he saves. And as for the Rabshakeh's boast that Assyrian forces have overpowered all the gods of all the nations they have ever conquered, well that does not sound like the guarantee of a benevolent rescuer. Doubtless the Rabshakeh undid all his excellent propaganda through this most revealing, emotional and undisciplined outburst. For while they may have been confused, while their faith may have been shaken, and while their hearts may have been heavy, the men and women of Jerusalem held their ground and maintained their silence, just as their king had commanded (36:21). The people chose to act with restraint and quiet discernment rather than with reactionary, fear-induced knee-jerking. I wonder if the largely biblically illiterate, channel-hopping, fast-food peoples of the 21st century would be capable of such thoughtful discernment and restraint. I wonder if we even have the memory required to energise such faith.

Then Eliakim the son of Hilkiah, who was over the household, and Shebna the secretary, and Joah the son of Asaph, the recorder, reported the Rabshakeh's blasphemous words to King Hezekiah.

> As soon as King Hezekiah heard it, he tore his clothes and covered himself with sackcloth and went into the house of the LORD. And he sent Eliakim, who was over the household, and Shebna the secretary, and the senior priests, covered with sackcloth, to the prophet Isaiah the son of Amoz (37:1–2).

What! That does not sound much like the response of a mighty warrior king or the commander in chief of a proud people. But what had become clear to Hezekiah was that politics had failed. As reason screamed, 'Jerusalem is doomed, her fate is sealed, strike a deal', Hezekiah remembered his Lord and sought him—finally.

When Hezekiah chose to seek the Lord, he chose not to deliver a motivational speech and rally the troops for a fight to the death. He

245

chose not to rush envoys out the back door to Egypt to see if hope might yet emerge from the south. He chose not to negotiate a quid-quo-pro 'spare us and we will do anything you ask' deal with Sennacherib. No! Of all the options before him, Hezekiah chose to send the state's most senior political and religious officials—donned in the garments of mourning—to beseech intercession from the prophet Isaiah, while he himself donned the garments of mourning and headed for the house of the Lord. His response was not passive!

Isaiah received the delegation, which relayed to the prophet King Hezekiah's lament and request:

> Thus says Hezekiah, 'This day is a day of distress, of rebuke, and of disgrace; children have come to the point of birth, and there is no strength to bring them forth. It may be that the LORD your God will hear the words of the Rabshakeh, whom his master the king of Assyria has sent to mock the living God, and will rebuke the words that the LORD your God has heard; therefore lift up your prayer for the remnant that is left' (37:3–4).

It is obvious from these words that Hezekiah was under profound conviction of sin. He was ashamed, readily admitting his failure: that despite all Jerusalem's labour her strength is exhausted—she cannot deliver. Will mother and child (Jerusalem and her citizens) perish together? Hezekiah has been gripped by the awareness that by chasing Judean independence without regard for God's will or honour, he has led Judah to ruin. As doom hovers over the city, as Jerusalem awaits her fate, and as God is mocked, a humbled Hezekiah beseeches Isaiah to intercede before the Lord for the remnant that is left.

From Isaiah, Hezekiah will receive no rebuke and no derision. There is no, 'I told you so!' There is no, 'Why didn't you just listen to me?' It has been 34 years since Isaiah prophesied that the waters of the Euphrates (the mighty and many armed forces of Assyria) would flood into Judah and engulf Immanuel's land right up to its neck.[1] Yet Isaiah finds no satisfaction in the fact that his prophecy—for which he had doubtless been subject to 34 years of derision—has finally come to pass. True prophets might be saddened and frustrated by *rejection*, but they are not negatively transformed by it—unlike false prophets, who are inherently self-interested.

---

1 Isaiah 8:5–8.

It was on account of *rejection* that the Islamic prophet Muhammad was transformed from a peaceful preacher and advocate of religious reform and monotheism (inspired by the Judeo-Christian faith) into a vengeful, self-promoting jihadist. Initially the Arabs rejected Muhammad as prophet because his monotheism threatened to cripple Mecca's economy, revolving as it did around the hospitality and merchandising industries that were totally dependent on the traditional annual pilgrimage to the Ka'bah, the rectangular black tent where Arabia's idols were housed. Meanwhile, the peninsula's Jews and Christians rejected Muhammad as a prophet on the grounds that he simply was not credible. Eventually the Arabs would submit, but only after Muhammad Islamised Arabian religion—for example, attributing the Ka'bah to Abraham—and gave the Arabs an ultimatum: convert or die. After massacring many Jews and Christians, Muhammad decided that it made better economic sense to permit them to live as dhimmis (subjugated peoples/second-class citizens) in order that they might be taxed, and their civilisational and agricultural expertise exploited for the benefit of the Muslims. The Sharia laws prescribing death for apostasy and blasphemy are essentially laws prohibiting, punishing and eliminating rejection of Islam.

From the long-rejected prophet Isaiah and his gracious, long-suffering, waiting Lord, Hezekiah receives only welcoming words of comfort. Firstly, God says: 'Do not be afraid because of the words that you have heard, with which the young men of the king of Assyria have reviled me' (37:6). This is beautiful. Leading with the exhortation, 'Do not be afraid', God proceeds to displace Hezekiah's misplaced fear and replace it with his own divine perspective. God refers to the Rabshakeh and his delegation as 'young men', literally servants, lackeys, tools, errand boys. Hezekiah might be intimidated by this over-confident polyglot, this decorated delegation, this 'great army', but God is not.

'Fear not', God says, as he does repeatedly throughout Scripture, for as Oswalt notes,

> the magnitude of the human threat is really not the issue. Whether it be the neighbouring countries or the emperor of the world, God is greater, and that being so, we do not need to live in fear. So although Hezekiah was concerned as to whether

God would 'hear' the blasphemy, God was concerned that Hezekiah had heard it and become frightened.[1]

'Behold,' continues the Lord, 'I will put a spirit in him, so that he shall hear a rumor and return to his own land, and I will make him fall by the sword in his own land' (37:7).

God can say, 'I will … I will …' precisely because he is sovereign. God is in control and he will simply predispose Sennacherib to return home where he will fall by the sword in his own land. That which is presently inevitable—the Assyrian conquest of Jerusalem—will simply not come to pass.

Upon hearing that Sennacherib had left Lachish and was fighting at nearby Libnah, the Rabshakeh departed Jerusalem without the unconditional surrender he had sought or the uprising he had hoped to incite. (37:8)

Then Sennacherib heard a rumour that another Egyptian detachment was on its way (37:9). Just to make sure Hezekiah did not jump to conclusions and settle into a false sense of security, thinking God was about to deliver him, Sennacherib stoked the fire, sending Hezekiah a threatening letter (37:8–13).

Like the Rabshakeh's speeches, Sennacherib's letter is worthy of close examination on account of its similarities with modern propaganda aimed at destabilising Christian faith.

Sennacherib threatens Hezekiah

With the Rabshakeh having failed in his attempt to breach the bond between the masses and their king, Sennacherib now attempts to breach the bond between Hezekiah—whom he now addresses with respect as 'Hezekiah king of Judah'—and his God. Just as the Rabshakeh had sought to tempt the masses into conspiring against their king, Sennacharib seeks to tempt Hezekiah into conspiring against Yahweh after the manner of Ahaz some 34 years earlier.[2] To this end, Sennacherib rants about the useless gods of the vanquished nations. 'All the lands, all the nations, have been destroyed,' he boasts. 'And all their gods were powerless before me.' Like the Rabshakeh,

---

1 Oswalt, p. 647.
2 Isaiah 8:12 (see Chapter 3).

King Sennacherib simply does not understand that Yahweh is not like other gods.

In an attempt to strike a fatal blow against Hezekiah's morale and appeal to Hezekiah's self-interest, Sennacherib asks: 'Where are all the kings?' No doubt Hezekiah knew all the kings named in the letter—'the king of Hamath, the king of Arpad, the king of the city of Sepharvaim, the king of Hena, or the king of Ivvah' (37:13). No doubt he had heard of their fate at the hands of the Assyrians—tortured, disembowelled, flayed alive, decapitated, impaled. Sennacherib is stoking Hezekiah's memory, raising the heat, fanning his survival instinct while asking: 'Is that really what you want?'

But with his mind now liberated from the limiting confines of self-sufficiency and practical atheism, King Hezekiah is able to draw on and apply his faith-energising memories. Yahweh, he recalls, is most definitely not like other gods, the 'no-gods' as he calls them. Hezekiah knows he has brought disgrace to God's name. Now all that matters to Hezekiah is that God's glory and honour be restored.

Hezekiah's prayer

King Hezekiah takes Sennacherib's letter into the Temple and spreads it out before the Lord. He is not informing God of the situation. He knows that God already knows. Rather Hezekiah, who is now walking, thinking and fearing differently, is finally handing the matter over to God (37:14).

'Everything is political here,' notes Jacques Ellul,

the siege, the famine, the war, the carving up of the vanquished, the balance of power between Egypt and Assyria. Everything is political, but the genius and truth of Hezekiah is to have seen behind the political problem the real question: 'Who is the Lord?' To be sure, the question seems to us to be very banal. Every Christian will say easily and smoothly and almost out of habit: 'The Lord Jesus Christ.' But what is needed to make this correct answer a true one is the political dimension. To say that God is the Lord when Sennacherib is about to enslave you and put out your eyes is to say something of real significance.[1]

---

1 Ellul, *The Politics of God*, pp. 169–70.

As Ellul notes, King Hezekiah's withdrawal into the house of the Lord and his crying to him was a political act whereby the truth that God is the Lord is reaffirmed. 'If we are not mistaken,' writes Ellul, 'this is the most difficult course.'[1] It is difficult because it appears passive when reason would dictate that action is most necessary. 'In a war or revolution,' notes Ellul, 'it is much more difficult to pray than to fire guns.'[2]

While prayer might appear passive, it is not. Hezekiah chose to act with radical faith. His prayer, which is the climax of Isaiah chapters 1 through 39, marks a pivotal moment in the history of God's people.

> And Hezekiah prayed to the LORD: 'O LORD of hosts, God of Israel, enthroned above the cherubim, you are the God, you alone, of all the kingdoms of the earth; you have made heaven and earth. Incline your ear, O LORD, and hear; open your eyes, O LORD, and see; and hear all the words of Sennacherib, which he has sent to mock the living God. Truly, O LORD, the kings of Assyria have laid waste all the nations and their lands, and have cast their gods into the fire. For they were no gods, but the work of men's hands, wood and stone. Therefore they were destroyed. So now, O LORD our God, save us from his hand, that all the kingdoms of the earth may know that you alone are the LORD' (37:15–20).

Before the Babylonian envoys Hezekiah was tall, self-sufficient and proud. Now he is prostrate before the Lord. Yet the great Hezekiah has not been reduced—rather, he has been awakened. Shaken and awakened from his fantasy by a terrible existential threat, this godly king offers up a prayer that is essentially a confession of faith wherein God alone is worshipped as King and Creator of all heaven and earth. Yahweh is invoked as Sovereign and appealed to in abject humility. There is no boasting here—no 'please Lord, consider how good and deserving I am,' as in Hezekiah's earlier prayer, when he was seeking deliverance from his terminal illness (38:3)—for Hezekiah knows that he is unworthy and wholly dependent upon grace.

Hezekiah acknowledges in prayer that while the nations have fallen under the kings of Assyria, it is only because their gods were not gods at all. Rather, they were 'no-gods', non-living, the works of human

---

1 Ibid., p. 170.
2 Ibid., p. 171.

hands, without power to save. Yahweh, however, *is* different. He lives, he loves, he is sovereign, he saves, and, what is more, he is 'our God'. And so Hezekiah, knowing his God has power to save, humbly requests deliverance from the hand of Sennacherib, only not for Jerusalem's sake—for he is fully aware of her unworthiness—but 'that all the kingdoms of the earth may know that you alone are the LORD' (37:20).

With Hezekiah now waiting on the Lord, the Lord's wait is over. He who has been waiting to be gracious, now rises to show compassion.[1]

The battle turns.

> Then Isaiah the son of Amoz sent to Hezekiah, saying, 'Thus says the LORD, the God of Israel: Because you have prayed to me concerning Sennacherib king of Assyria, this is the word that the LORD has spoken concerning him ...' (37:21).

And just as Hezekiah's prayer was all about the glory of God, so too, was the Lord's response all about the glory of God. King Sennacherib of Assyria is rebuked for his blasphemous self-exaltation that has culminated in unrestrained cruelty and destruction (37:22–29).

Sennacherib thinks he is supreme—but God has news for him! Sennacherib is not the one in control here—it is the Lord! He sees all, hears all, knows all and will act justly.

> Because you have raged against me
>   and your complacency [sha'anan] has come to my ears,
> I will put my hook in your nose
>   and my bit in your mouth,
> and I will turn you back on the way by which you came
>   (37:29).

Sha'anan, translated in the ESV as 'complacency' is also translated as 'tumult' (KJV), 'arrogance' (NLT, NASB, ASV, RSV) and insolence (NIV). It comes from the root *shä·an'* which means to be at ease, at peace, at rest. Sennacherib's *sha'anan*, which was so offensive to God, was his ability to arrogantly do whatever evil his heart desired—razing, looting, killing, enslaving, perpetrating gross cruelty—without a single pang of conscience. He could only do this because he saw himself as supreme, a law unto himself, answerable to no one. As Ellul notes:

---

1 Isaiah 30:18 (see Chapter 10).

Sennacherib is not condemned because he has massacred thousands of people; he has massacred thousands of people because he has been a law to himself, regarding himself as independent of God and accountable to nobody. This is why God calls him to account.[1]

God will show Sennacherib who is the Lord. Sennacherib reasons: 'I will soon lay siege to Jerusalem—a siege I will maintain until the city falls into my hands.' But God determines: 'No, you will not. You will not enter or even threaten this city, for I am going to send you home before you can even shoot an arrow at it' (see 37:29, 33–35).

God then promises the remnant in Jerusalem a sign, so that subsequently, when all this is over, the remnant might know that it was the Lord who delivered them. While the Assyrian invasion disrupted the harvest and prevented sowing, the people would not go hungry for there would be enough food for the next year from what would grow up by itself. Then in the third year there would be plenty, for sowing and harvesting would proceed in peace. Sennacherib would not return.

Peace is a gift from the Lord that should not be taken for granted. Peace results from God's restraining of wickedness. Every day we have peace, every year we can sow and reap, advance and prosper, we should thank the Lord for his great blessing.

And so it came to pass:

> And the angel of the Lord went out and struck down
> a hundred and eighty-five thousand in the camp of the
> Assyrians. And when people arose early in the morning,
> behold, these were all dead bodies. Then Sennacherib king of
> Assyria departed and returned home and lived at Nineveh.
> And as he was worshiping in the house of Nisroch his god,
> Adrammelech and Sharezer, his sons, struck him down with
> the sword. And after they escaped into the land of Ararat,
> Esarhaddon his son reigned in his place (37:36–38).

How ironic that Sennacherib was assassinated 'in the house of Nisroch his god'. Having blasphemed Yahweh as just another useless god amongst the useless gods of the nations, Sennacherib was struck down as he knelt in the presence of his useless, lifeless god, Nisroch,

---

1 Ellul, *The Politics of God*, p. 176.

who was powerless to save his servant.[1]

Naturalists try to explain away the deliverance of Jerusalem by claiming natural causes—such as soldiers spontaneously dying on mass due to a plague of rats or an outbreak of plague. Those who do not recognise Yahweh do not recognise his miracles.[2] But a miracle it was. There truly was nothing standing between Sennacherib and his conquest of Jerusalem—nothing, that is, but the Lord. And between the Lord and Jerusalem there knelt a humbled king whose faith deflected the wrath of God. Where Hezekiah's 'mere words' of diplomacy and political activism had failed as a strategy for war, his 'mere words' of prayer had succeeded.

'Divine guidance and protection were sought, and God granted them,' writes Herbert Lockyer.

> God's honor had been insulted. He who dwells between the Cherubim had been defied, and Hezekiah pleads with God to vindicate Himself. What an answer to prayer the king received! God sent an angel to deal with the arrogant Assyrians and by the morning light, 185,000 of their corpses lay scattered over the field.
> It is ever fearful for the enemies of the saints of God to force them to the throne of grace. Hezekiah, it must be noted, pleads the sovereignty of God. 'Thou art God alone.' 'If God be for us, who can be against us?' One solitary saint retires to pray—one solitary angel, by order of the Lord, destroys a vast host. The efficacy of prayer is seen in that Hezekiah through his dependence upon God had more power than the armies of Judah and the hosts of Sennacherib.[3]

'Thus,' affirms Motyer,

> the way of believing prayer is the truly practical way of dealing with the harsh realities of this world. What neither armaments

---

1 Sennacherib was assassinated in his temple by his sons in 681 BC. While he led many military campaigns subsequent to 701 BC, he never returned to Judah.
2 The Pharisees were not even moved when Jesus raised Lazarus from the dead, right before their eyes (John 11:38–53).
3 Herbert Lockyer, *All the Prayers of the Bible*, Zondervan Publishing House, Grand Rapid MI, 1959, p. 80.

(36:9) nor diplomacy (30:1–2) nor money (2 Kings 18:13–14) could achieve, prayer has done.[1]

Christians have a freedom the world can only dream of. Because our God is the living, loving, sovereign, saving and eternally faithful God, the Christian is never condemned to fate. Jerusalem was doomed before Hezekiah prayed. But Hezekiah's prayer changed everything. Hezekiah's prayer marks the moment the crown of the Lord of Hosts was put on and the battle was turned back at the gate (28:6).

'The Bible teaches us,' writes Jacques Ellul,

> in effect that God intervenes in the course of events. But, as we have frequently noted, he seldom does so in an explosive, strange, and incomprehensible way. To be sure, one might say that we have here the basis of the theopolitics of Isaiah. God genuinely inserts himself into the course of politics. He acts at his own level, and for Isaiah, miracle is the instrument of this insertion. In each miracle God penetrates into the city. He takes it in hand. He makes himself its Lord. In each miracle he contests the authority of the political power, the political autonomy that man always claims, the independent right of man to make history. In each miracle he gives concrete shape to an epoch of divine sovereignty. He forces man to confront him. God has always the full and perfect freedom to act in this surprising and disruptive fashion, to be the supernatural which shatters the course of the natural.[2]

As Sovereign, our God is absolutely free to break or interrupt the process of 'historical fatality'.[3]

My appeal to afflicted, persecuted and threatened Christians is this: remember the Lord; stay faithful to your king. He is faithful and true.

---

1 Motyer, p. 282.

2 Ellul, *The Politics of God*, pp. 184–5.

3 Ibid., p. 186. As Ellul notes, the ultimate historical fatality—that this whole world should be condemned to death—was broken when Jesus Christ, Immanuel, went faithfully to the cross and offered up his blood so that all those believe in him might not perish but have everlasting life. The crucifixion did not look much like a miracle at the time either. But it was, and three days later the prophesied sign—the resurrection—told all who would believe in him, that God had indeed secured their salvation. (See: Jesus tells his disciples (Matthew 16:21; 17:23); sign of Jonah (Matthew 12:39–40; 16:4); sign of the temple (John 2:19).)

He can be trusted. Put on the crown of the Lord of Hosts and wait for him. For God is totally free—not constrained by social, economic, military or political contingencies. Because God is free, we are free: free from fate, not condemned to repeat history, but free to make history.

—⟨∿⟩—

Jesus Christ, our faithful king

The Davidic covenant, you may remember, has both conditional and unconditional elements. God's (the suzerain's) promise of blessing was conditional upon the king's (the vassal's) faithfulness.

King Ahaz's faithlessness brought disaster to Judah and the nations, particularly Syria and Ephraim (7–8). Subsequently, King Hezekiah's faithfulness brought divine deliverance to the remnant in Jerusalem.

Included in the Davidic covenant was God's unconditional promise that he would raise up David's offspring and establish his kingdom forever.[1]

After Ahaz violated the covenant, opening the floodgates to catastrophe, God promised a son, Immanuel[2] (lit. 'God with us'), who Hezekiah prefigures.

Hezekiah, son of Ahaz, a king of David's line, stood as an intermediary between God and his people. Hezekiah's people were delivered because they were faithful to their king, and he was faithful to the Lord, and the Lord was faithful to his covenant.

Jesus Christ—Immanuel, born of David's line—is our faithful covenant king. He fulfilled the covenant on our behalf and then, as our Great High Priest, interposed his own precious blood between the wrath of God and the elect. We who are faithful to Christ are eternally secure on account of him—our faithful Davidic king—because he has been faithful to the Father who will always be faithful to his covenant.

As Isaiah scholar Avraham Gileadi notes, the story of Ahaz and

---

1 2 Samuel 7:12–16.
2 Isaiah 7:14.

Hezekiah 'presents a message that transcends history'[1] and is 'typological'.[2]

When the Lord's people make improper covenantal choices, they bring ruin to the church and the nations. When the Lord's people make correct covenantal choices, they find that God is faithful to all his promises.

> Ah, the thunder of many peoples;
>> they thunder like the thundering of the sea!
> Ah, the roar of nations;
>> they roar like the roaring of mighty waters!
> The nations roar like the roaring of many waters,
>> but he will rebuke them, and they will flee far away,
> chased like chaff on the mountains before the wind
>> and whirling dust before the storm.
> At evening time, behold, terror!
>> Before morning, they are no more!
> This is the portion of those who loot us,
>> and the lot of those who plunder us (17:12–14).

1 Gileadi, p. 64.
2 Ibid., p. 65.

Questions for Discussion and Reflection

1. In what ways does Hezekiah's prayer (37:16–20) and God's
   response (37:21, 33–38) fulfil the promises of :

   (a)   30:15

   (b)   30:18–19

   (c)   28:5–6

2. Hezekiah did what we so often do: he 'remembered' the Lord only
   after everything else—great cities (Babylon), economic power
   (Tyre), collective security (the western alliance) and military
   might (Egypt)—had failed.

   How much suffering and devastation do you think we bring upon
   ourselves, the Church and the world, because we resist the way of
   faith and are slow to look to the Lord?

   With repentance, recall an example of when you looked to the Lord
   as a last resort and now wished you'd looked to him in faith a lot
   sooner.

3. Considering that Isaiah is more than mere history, and is
   prophetic and typological with a message that is therefore eternal
   and universal, what does the story of Jerusalem's deliverance teach
   for us, today, as we face escalating insecurity and threat?

Prayer

That the battle might be turned back.

O Lord my God,
You are *Baal Perazim*: the Lord of bursting through, Lord of the
    breakthrough! (2 Samuel 5:20)
You are *Yahweh Sabaoth*: the Lord of hosts, Commander of heaven's
    armies!
You are the one who can change everything.

Forgive your Church, O Lord, for the wasted years:
    years spent vainly seeking security in humanity, in cities and in
    humanistic projects;
    in economic power, in collective security and in military might.
We acknowledge with shame and sadness and deep repentance,
    that while we have resisted the way of humble faith—
    preferring instead the way of arrogant works—
    our enemies have advanced bringing much suffering upon the
    Church and the world.
O Lord, please help us make things right;
    may the battle yet be turned back at the gate.

Lord, I pray for my besieged and threatened Christian brothers and
    sisters—
    believers who are wounded, oppressed and heavily burdened,
    facing violent persecution, faith-shattering trauma and immoral
    injustice, simply on account of your name. (John 15:21)
May the Spirit of God sustain and fan into flame the faith that
    flickers in their hearts
    and protect them from the devil's 'flaming darts' (Ephesians 6:16)
    of doubt and despair.
May they look to you without delay,
    and cry out to you without hesitation.
For you, O Lord, will hear their cry
    and answer as soon as you hear it.
Intervene in their reality, O Lord.
Interpose yourself in their calamity.
For nations and neighbours and despots might rage,
    but you—the almighty and glorious Lord of hosts—can change
    everything!

That the battle might be turned back;
    that the Church might be delivered;
    'that all the kingdoms of the earth may know that you alone are
    the Lord'; (Hezekiah's prayer, Isaiah 37:20)
    and 'that the earth might be filled with the knowledge and
    glory of the Lord as the waters cover the sea'; (Isaiah 11:9b and
    Habakkuk 2:14)
I will exalt and glorify the Lord of hosts,
    my God in whom I trust.

Amen.

CHAPTER 12

Choose this day ...
A timeless and universal message

Isaiah 34–35

As spectators in the divine courtroom, we shuddered as God entered into judgement against Jerusalem's corrupt, abusive, faithless, self-serving rulers; and her vain, haughty, idolatrous, self-obsessed citizens (3:13–15). We trembled as the charges reverberated through the chamber. We paled when Yahweh, in wrath and indignation, roared his verdict.

'Guilty!'

They were guilty, so prescribed penalties would *therefore* apply: invasion, occupation, exile and death (3:16–4:1).[1]

How relieved we were that it was 8th-century-BC Judah in the dock and not *us*. How relieved we were that the sins listed in the indictment were hers; that the verdict being issued was against her; and the sentence pronounced would apply to her.

Relieved indeed! For we know full well that our nations and cities are equally worthy of condemnation. Having largely rejected and forgotten the Lord, our nations and cities exhibit the same pride and arrogant self-sufficiency. Our rulers are just as corrupt and just as pragmatic when it comes to injustice. Our societies are just as idolatrous, just as worldly, just as self-obsessed and just as humanistic, exhibiting the same ideological and practical atheism.

---

1 See Chapter 1.

Relieved indeed! And so, we reason smugly as we thumb over Isaiah's pages, while we are prepared to learn the lessons of history, we need not be too concerned for ourselves, for it is not as if the indictment (sin), verdict (guilty) and sentence (death) apply directly to us.

We, however, cannot remain complacent spectators for long, for something very disturbing takes place in chapter 34. Here, at the pinnacle of the oracle series, the death sentence described and handed down against Judah in Isaiah 1–5 is delivered against 'the nations' and 'all their host' (that is, 'their total population'[1]). The nations are the objects of God's wrath. The nations along with all their peoples have been 'devoted to destruction' and 'given over to slaughter' (34:1–3).

The typology of Isaiah

Through the use of shared motifs, Isaiah links chapter 34 directly back to chapters 1–5, thereby equating the nations—represented by Edom—with the Lord's rebellious people.[2]

Harman writes concerning 'Edom' as typifying opponents of God:

> Here Edom is singled out as an illustration of nations in revolt against God. The Edomites were the descendents of Esau [the son of Isaac, and brother of Jacob], and there is a progressive hostility to them marked out in the Old Testament until Malachi, the last of the canonical prophets, speaks of them as 'a people always under the wrath of the Lord' (Malachi 1:4).[3]

Likewise Oswalt:

> Throughout the OT, from Genesis (25:23) to Malachi (1:2–3), Edom is treated as the antithesis to Israel. More so even than the Amalekites, Edom is noted for attempting to block what God was doing for the world in his self-revelation to Israel (Numbers 20:14–21). Thus Edom was typical of those nations which insisted upon their own ways in opposition to those of God.[4]

Motyer also quotes Amos1:11, and Psalms 60:8 and 83:1–8, among others, to demonstrate the identification of Edom as a perpetual

---

1 Motyer, p. 270.
2 Gileadi, p. 55.
3 Harman, p. 226.
4 Oswalt, p. 610.

enemy of God (Motyer, pp. 268–9).

In chapters 1–5 and chapter 34, the destiny of the faithless is destruction. There will be slaughter by the sword (3:25; cf.1:20 and 34:5, 6); unburied corpses (5:25; 34:3); and destruction by fire as in Sodom and Gomorrah (1:7, 9; 34:9–10). Houses will fall desolate (5:9; 34:13) and the land unfruitful (5:2, 4; 34:10b). Travel will cease (3:26; 34:10b) and cities and strongholds will be overgrown with thorns and briers (5:6; 34:13).[1]

If Israel is a type for the nations of the world, then the prophecy of Isaiah concerns not only Judah in the 8th century BC, but all the nations and peoples of the world universally. Thus we cannot remain as spectators, and we cannot read Isaiah simply as history, for while Isaiah is history, Isaiah also transcends history, for Isaiah is prophetic and typological with universal application.

And so Isaiah launches chapter 34 with a blast of evangelistic urgency, calling upon the nations and peoples of the world to draw near and pay attention.

> Draw near, O nations, to hear,
>   and give attention, O peoples!
> Let the earth hear, and all that fills it;
>   the world, and all that comes from it.
> For the LORD is enraged against all the nations,
>   and furious against all their host;
>   he has devoted them to destruction, has given them over for
>   slaughter (34:1–2).

Isaiah does not want the nations and peoples of the earth to be ignorant of their predicament. For the charges have been laid, the verdict has been declared, and the sentence has been delivered: the nations and the peoples of the earth are 'guilty' and sentenced to death, devoted to destruction, given over for slaughter. 'For the wages of sin is death ...' (Romans 6:23a).

Oswalt comments:

> The powerful poem in 34:1–17 depicts the effects of God's wrath upon the nations. In vv. 1–4 the universal nature of the judgement is pictured. Not even the heavens will escape. Then vv. 5–8 particularise the statement by applying it to Edom ...

---

1 See Gileadi, p. 54.

The language here is of sacrifice, reminding the reader that unless someone provides a sacrifice for our sins, we must ourselves become that sacrifice … Verses 9–17 continue the address to Edom as the typical nation, depicting the land as utterly desolate, inhabited by nothing but desert wildlife. This is the end of all humanity grasping for abundance: death and desolation. The rebellion of a whole world against God is not a matter for a tap on the wrist, nor are its natural effects negligible.[1]

Terrifying? Oh yes!

But remember God's promise to Judah? In the midst of woe there will be justice and comfort.

> Woe to them!
>   For they have brought evil on themselves.
> Tell the righteous that it shall be well with them,
>   for they shall eat the fruit of their deeds.
> Woe to the wicked! It shall be ill with him,
>   for what his hands have dealt out shall be done to him
>   (3:9c–11).

We can be comforted by this because, while Judah is a type of the nations of the world, Judah's righteous remnant—those who persevere in covenantal faithfulness, walking in the light of the Lord, trusting him regardless of their circumstances—are a type of the true church that exists in the midst of the nations. For again, through the use of shared motifs, Isaiah links chapter 35, which describes the destiny of the righteous from amongst the nations, directly back to chapter 4:2–6, which describes the destiny of Judah's righteous remnant, thereby equating the Lord's elect with Judah's remnant, again confirming Israel as a type.

In 4:2–6 and in chapter 35, the faithful righteous inherit healing (4:4; 35:5–6) and a land bursting with new life, blooms and shoots (4:2; 35:1–2); sustained by abundant waters, rivers and rain (4:6; 35:6–7). There they may travel freely, with ease and security (2:2–3; 4:5–6; 35:8–10). And as the song of the wicked is silenced, the ransomed of the Lord arise with singing and proceed with everlasting joy; their

---

1 Oswalt, pp. 607–8.

sorrow and sighing gone forever (4:2–6; 35:10).[1]

'Chapters 34–35,' writes Oswalt,

> present a striking contrast between a productive land turned
> into a desert (ch. 34) and a desert turning into a garden (ch.
> 35). As such they bring to a close the collection of teachings
> concerning the nations and God's sovereignty over them (chs.
> 13–35). When all is said and done, the prophet says, the issues
> are clear and rather simple.
> Arrogant, self-important humanity cannot stand before God.
> In our attempts to be independent of him and to build the
> kingdom of Man on earth, we have sinned, and the word is the
> same for all: 'The soul that sins shall die' (Ezekiel 18:4, 20). In a
> real sense, to sin is to forfeit one's life into the hands of God as
> a sacrifice (34:6, 7).
> On the other hand, those who reject the blandishments of
> this earth with its temptations to make their own way, those
> who choose to wait for God, to put themselves in his hands,
> though that be in a desert, will discover a highway which leads
> to a glory not their own. Rather it is something which is freely
> shared by the One to whom the glory belongs. To align oneself
> with the nations of the earth is to choose a desert; to trust
> in God is to choose a garden … In a way similar to chapters
> 24–27, they drive home the wisdom of trusting God and the
> folly of trusting the nations. In this they form the climax to the
> entire segment.[2]

Commenting on Isaiah 34 and 35, Ortlund writes:

> In these two chapters Isaiah leads us by the hand all the way
> out to the brink of future history where time merges into
> eternity. He shows us the seamless connection between what
> we embrace now and what we will have then. He lifts his eyes
> from his own times in the eighth century BC to see how things
> will finally end up 'forever and ever' (34:10).[3]

The eternal and universal principle is this: to trust in the world is to
choose frustration, defeat, futility, judgement and catastrophe: that is,

---

1 See Gileadi, p. 55. See also Isaiah 30:19–26 (healing, new life, waters, travel
  in security) and chapters 24–27.
2 Oswalt, pp. 606–7.
3 Ortlund, p. 196.

the desert. While to trust in God is to choose rest, sanctuary (*miqdas*) and glory: that is, the garden.

So choose you this day …

———✺———

Fortify yourselves and one another

As storm clouds gathered over Judah, God promised the righteous that all would be well with them (3:10). However, he did not promise that they would be delivered *from* the tribulation, *from* the mighty flood of judgement that God would bring against the nation (8:5–8). Rather, after prophesying the defeat of the enemy nations (8:9–10), Isaiah shared with the righteous, God's paradigm for threatened believers: a paradigm for a counter-cultural life of radical faith that would enable the righteous to not only endure, but shine *through* tribulation and affliction (8:11–14).

Likewise, God has promised his faithful church sanctuary (*miqdas*) and eternal glory. However, he has not promised to deliver us from all tribulation, from the judgements that God brings against the nations. Rather, the true church, like the remnant in Judah, shall be saved; only not from tribulation, but through it.

As such, the true church, like the remnant of Judah, will require strategy (including a paradigm for how to walk) and fortitude if she is to endure. And so Isaiah urges the faithful of Judah (himself included)—and by extension the true church universally—to fortify themselves and each other—encouraging one another in the realm of actions (*hands*), stability (*knees*) and conviction (*hearts*)[1]—that they might be prepared for tribulations: readied, fortified; able to stand firm in faith.

> Strengthen the weak hands,
>   and make firm the feeble knees.
> Say to those who have an anxious heart,
>   'Be strong; fear not!
> Behold, your God
>   will come with vengeance,

---

1 Motyer, p. 274.

with the recompense of God.
He will come and save you' (35:3–4).

Mercifully, Isaiah frames his exhortation with promise, so that those who need a 'stiffening of their resolve'[1] may be encouraged by the assurances laid down in the preceding verses (35:1–2) and urged forward, motivated to persevere (35:3–4), by the promises set before them in the subsequent verses (35:5–6b).

Promise

The wilderness and the dry land shall be glad;
    the desert shall rejoice and blossom like the crocus;
it shall blossom abundantly
    and rejoice with joy and singing.
The glory of Lebanon shall be given to it,
    the majesty of Carmel and Sharon.
They shall see the glory of the LORD,
    the majesty of our God (35:1–2).

So Persevere (an exhortation to fortification)

Strengthen the weak hands,
    and make firm the feeble knees.
Say to those who have an anxious heart,
    'Be strong; fear not!
Behold, your God
    will come with vengeance,
with the recompense of God.
    He will come and save you' (35:3–4).

To Attain The Promise

Then the eyes of the blind shall be opened,
    and the ears of the deaf unstopped;
then shall the lame man leap like a deer,
    and the tongue of the mute sing for joy (35:5–6b).

And yes, Jesus Christ is a partial fulfilment of 35:5–6b, for the ministry of Jesus Christ foreshadows the day when the curse will no longer apply and healing will be complete. As we have already noted, more often than not the interpretation of prophecy starts at our fingertips and stretches to the horizon, having immediate, future and eschatological

---

1 Ibid., p. 273.

application. So while chapter 35 is doubtless referring to the return from exile, and to the incarnation of Jesus Christ, and to that future day when affliction, tribulation and death will be banished forever, it also has application for the 21st-century church.

Our need of endurance

Having chosen to trust in God, the church's most immediate need—if we are to advance in the hope of what is promised and not shrink back in the face of tribulation and persecution—is our need of endurance. As the writer of the epistle to the Hebrews notes:

> For you have need of endurance, so that when you have done the will of God you may receive what is promised. For,
> 'Yet a little while,
>   and the coming one will come and will not delay;
> but my righteous one shall live by faith,
>   and if he shrinks back,
> my soul has no pleasure in him' (Hebrews 10:36–38).

So what practical steps can we take and what strategies can we employ to meet this need for endurance? How might we strengthen hands that are weak (Hebrew: *rapheh*, i.e. drooping or slack) and make firm, knees that are feeble (Hebrew: *kashal*, i.e. stumbling, tottering, giving way)?

To this end, the Epistle to the Hebrews makes a wonderful New Testament companion to Isaiah 35:1–6. For not only does the writer of the epistle echo Isaiah's exhortation—'lift your drooping hands and strengthen your weak knees' (Hebrews 12:12)—but he fleshes out the call with some very practical strategies.

Following the pattern of the prophet, the writer of Hebrews frames his exhortation in promise.

Promise

Our salvation is secure and assured—it shall be—on account of who Jesus is and what he has done (Hebrews 1:1–10:18).

So Persevere (an exhortation to fortification)

Therefore we can draw near to God, set our sights on the goal, fortify ourselves and one another—'lift your drooping hands and strengthen your weak knees,'—and persevere: 'run with

endurance the race that is set before us …'
(Hebrews 10:19–12:17).

To Attain The Promise

Then, though God shake the heavens and earth to bring down
all that is false, limited and mortal, we need not be afraid. For
we have come to a kingdom that cannot be shaken: Mount
Zion, the City of God,[1] the heavenly Jerusalem filled with
angels, all the saints and Jesus our Saviour
(Hebrews 12:18–28).

After establishing that though our salvation is secure we still have
need of endurance (Hebrews 10:36–38), the writer of Hebrews
takes us by the hand and introduces us to a vast company of men
and women of radical faith. These are ones who have gone before us
and endured tribulation so that they might rise again to a better life
(11:35b). He is feeding our faith-energising memory so that we who
are presently on trial in this world might draw strength, confidence
and courage, as well as motivation and inspiration, from this great
multitude of witnesses who surround us like a cloud. 'You have need
of endurance,' he says, 'so remember! Remember Abel. Remember
Abraham and Sarah. Remember Moses. Remember the Exodus out
of slavery, the parting of the Red Sea and the day the walls of Jericho
fell. Remember Rahab. Remember Samuel and David. Remember
the martyrs. Remember their faith. Remember their endurance.
Remember, remember, remember.' And in the strength of that faith-
energising memory, press on!

> Therefore, since we are surrounded by so great a cloud of
> witnesses, let us also lay aside every weight, and sin which
> clings so closely, and let us run with endurance the race that is
> set before us … (Hebrews 12:1).

Far too many Christians today have absolutely no idea that they are
surrounded by so great a cloud of witnesses because they are totally
ignorant of, and disconnected from the history and present reality of
the church. While this lack of faith-energising memory is a serious
problem, the remedy is simple: attention to history and heritage, and
engagement in global Christian mission and ministry, in particular

---

1 cf. Isaiah 26.

the ministry of intercessory prayer for the repressed and persecuted church struggling at the front line of the spiritual battle.

Not optional

The absolute necessity of engagement with the persecuted church

Without a doubt, sometimes hands are weak (drooping, lifeless) and knees are feeble (tottering, unstable) on account of laziness or inattention: these Christians are simply unfit. However, it is often the case that hands are weak (drooping, lifeless) and knees are feeble (tottering, unstable) because the believer is simply dispirited and exhausted, worn out from endless struggle and on the verge of collapse.

No one should be surprised to learn that persecuted believers often feel distressed and defeated, as if all is hopeless and they might as well just drop their hands and give up. No one should be surprised to learn that persecuted believers frequently buckle at the knees, burdened as they are by grief and stress. It is no small thing to cling to Christ when the cost is high: crippling poverty, violence, enslavement, homelessness, imprisonment, torture, exile, death—especially if that price is also being paid by your loved ones; by your children.

We must never trivialise or romanticise the spiritual struggle that assails persecuted believers. They will find themselves asking: 'Why is God not coming to save me?'[1] They will find themselves thinking: 'God doesn't seem to see me, nor does he seem to care about me.'[2] And humanly speaking, there is not much else to say when your pastor has just been bludgeoned to death by sectarian zealots; or your children have just been burned alive by Islamic militants; or your wife has just been kidnapped and raped by Muslim fundamentalists with the tacit approval of the state; or your husband who is in prison on account of his faith has just been brutalised sexually for the umpteenth time; or your elderly parents have just died of starvation and disease in the jungle after being expelled from their village because your faith was

---

1 Psalm 10:1: 'Why, O LORD, do you stand far away? Why do you hide yourself in times of trouble?'

2 Isaiah 40:27: 'Why do you say, O Jacob, and speak, O Israel, "My way is hidden from the Lord and my righft is disregarded by God"?'

deemed to have upset the ancestral spirits.[1]

Our 'adversary the devil prowls around like a roaring lion, seeking someone to devour' (1 Peter 5:8b). And just as exhausted, wounded gazelles make easy prey for a hungry lion, so too can exhausted, wounded believers make easy prey for the enemy.

So it is not without reason that the scriptures exhort us: 'Bear one another's burdens, and so fulfil the law of Christ' (Galatians 6:2), and of course the 'law of Christ' is love:

> But when the Pharisees heard that he [Jesus] had silenced the Sadducees, they gathered together. And one of them, a lawyer, asked him a question to test him. 'Teacher, which is the great commandment in the Law?' And he said to him, 'You shall love the Lord your God with all your heart and with all your soul and with all your mind. This is the great and first commandment. And a second is like it: You shall love your neighbor as yourself. On these two commandments depend all the Law and the Prophets.' (Matthew 22:34–40)

If we are to be obedient to Christ, and to the law of love, then we simply must get alongside the persecuted church. We can do this by going (as missionaries or visitors); by giving (i.e. by financially supporting Christian aid and advocacy groups); and through intercessory prayer, which is both partnership in the gospel[2] and advocacy to the highest authority.

Intercessory prayer is a very simple yet practical way in which we can bear one another's burdens. Yet many Christians resist, believing they could not possibly bear more burdens. Pastors can be especially resistant, concerned that serious attention to and engagement with the persecuted church might negatively impact the mood of the service, unduly upset the congregation, challenge a triumphalist theology, or even threaten the finances.

But surely this too is a matter for faith. If God calls us to bear one another's burdens, then we simply must do it as a matter of obedience, in trust. Of course we must exercise wisdom, discernment and sensitivity, but for this and for everything else, we are to seek and

---

1 These are not fictional persecutions. They relate to cases I wrote on in the early months of 2011, from India, Nigeria, Egypt, Afghanistan and Laos.
2 Romans 15:30 (NIV): 'join me in my struggle by praying to God for me'.

271

trust the Lord. It really is that simple. We have no grounds for anxiety, for when God calls us to give generously, go fearlessly, pray without ceasing, and bear one another's burdens, we can rest assured that he is not calling us to meaningless self-destruction. Our God can be trusted!

Furthermore, it has been my personal experience, that when we, in obedience and love, take on the burdens of the persecuted church, they do not compound our own burdens. Rather, they displace them. And while it sickens me to be pleading for prayer for the persecuted by appealing to self-interest, my personal testimony is this: to bear the burdens of the persecuted is a great privilege that is not only inspiring and empowering, but profoundly liberating.

Let us not be ashamed of chains

Sadly, many free and prosperous churches are actually ashamed of the persecuted church. No stranger to this phenomenon, the Apostle Paul wrote from prison to urge his young protégé Timothy not to be ashamed of the gospel or of chains—not his own chains, should he find himself in them, nor the chains of others who are being persecuted on account of the gospel (2 Timothy 1:8). Paul was not ashamed of his chains (2 Timothy 1:12). But in what must be one of the most painful verses in all of Paul's epistles, we read: 'You are aware that all who are in Asia turned away from me …' (2 Timothy 1:15).

From a worldly perspective, it is quite understandable that the Christians of Asia[1] would turn away from Paul, even if he was their spiritual father. Paul was hardly an icon of worldly success. Furthermore, he was a convicted criminal; any contact with or support for him would doubtless impart guilt by association, leading to an increase in government surveillance and repression, if not outright violent persecution.

So all the believers of Asia turned away from Paul in his hour of need— all, that is, except Onesiphorus, the only one who was not ashamed of Paul's chains.

> May the Lord grant mercy to the household of Onesiphorus,
> for he often refreshed me and was not ashamed of my chains,
> but when he arrived in Rome he searched for me earnestly and

---

1 'Asia' in Paul's time was much of the western portion of modern-day Turkey.

272

found me—may the Lord grant him to find mercy from the Lord on that Day! (2 Timothy 1:16–18).

Likewise, the Christians of Philippi, in Europe, were not ashamed of chains—not their own and not Paul's. Writing from prison to thank the Philippian Christians for the gift they had sent, Paul explained that it was only right and natural that he should feel deep affection for them, for they were partakers with him in both gospel ministry and persecution.

> *It is right for me to feel this way about you all, because I hold you in my heart, for you are all partakers with me of grace, both in my imprisonment and in the defense and confirmation of the gospel.'*
> Philippians 1:37

When a free and prosperous church, Christian organisation or individual believer turns away from the persecuted church—whether it is because they are ashamed of chains and embarrassed by suffering, or because they simply do not care, or because they have become politically compromised—they are actually dismembering themselves from the Body of Christ. And a dismembered member is not only unhelpful, it is also unviable and so cannot make a claim to health and wholeness, no matter how big and how full its auditorium; no matter how grand and lofty its offices; no matter how advanced its technology; no matter how rapturous its singing; no matter how powerful its alliances; and no matter how fat its coffers.

Separated from the Body, removed from the great cloud of witnesses, the dismembered member will struggle to endure. We need to be connected to the Head and we need to be connected to each other.

Looking to Jesus

Ultimately, however, we are called to run the race set before us (Hebrews 12:1),

> looking to Jesus, the founder and perfecter of our faith, who for the joy that was set before him endured the cross, despising the shame, and is seated at the right hand of the throne of God. Consider him who endured from sinners such hostility against himself, so that you may not grow weary or faint-hearted (Hebrews 12:2–3).

273

When we have need of endurance, we must look to Jesus.

Jesus is our *means*, because not only is he the founder but the perfecter of our faith. He is a faith-perfecting God! He not only begins the work, but he brings it to completion (cf. Philippians 1:6). He is our steadfast anchor within the veil.[1]

Jesus is our *goal*, because one day it shall be just as Isaiah prophesied: 'your Teacher will not hide himself anymore, but your eyes shall see your Teacher' (30:20b). 'They shall see the glory of the LORD, the majesty of our God … Then the eyes of the blind shall be opened …' (35:2c, 5a). Yes, one day we will be with him, face to face.

Jesus is our *role model*, because he himself set his eyes heavenward and for joy that was set before him endured immense persecution, even unto death. So when we have need of endurance, we should look to him—consider him[2]—and follow him in his example.

> *He is no fool who gives what he cannot keep to gain that which he cannot lose*—Jim Elliot, missionary and martyr

And so the writer exhorts us to fortification and urges us forward, to run the race set before us with eyes fixed on Jesus. Meanwhile, he warns us not to be like Esau, the father of the Edomites, who in haste traded his inheritance for some immediate temporal relief (Hebrews 12:16b–17).

Be strong, fear not

Finally, Isaiah exhorts us to encourage those of anxious heart with these words: 'Be strong; fear not! Behold, your God will come with vengeance, with the recompense of God. He will come and save you' (35:4).

'He comes', writes Oswalt,

> is a powerful statement throughout scripture … To the heart which cries, 'He is too far away, I cannot reach him', the answer is, 'You do not have to reach him; he comes to you.' So God has been coming to us across the millennia: through the process of revelation, in the acts of his providence, in the first coming of

---

1 Hebrews 6:19–20.
2 E. Kendal, 'Easter Reflection: Consider Him', RLPB 104, 20 April 2011.

Christ. And he will continue to come until that last day when we will be united with him forever.[1]

Motyer observes that by exhorting believers to be strong and fear not, Isaiah has employed 'Joshua's verbs'—be strong and courageous (Joshua 1:6, 9, 18)—as if he was wanting to encourage his hearers and readers to remember Joshua and even adopt him as a role model—Joshua, who stepped forward in faith to lay hold of the Promised Land despite the obstacles.[2] 'It is a call to fortitude of faith,' notes Motyer, 'not grim determination but believing determination.'[3]

What is more, Motyer adds, this God is your God, 'the God who is still prepared to be "yours", notwithstanding all your weaknesses'.[4] And this God, your God, has vowed to come with vengeance (i.e. lawfulness and justice[5]), and with recompense (i.e. compensation).

So choose you this day ...

Summary, conclusion and call to faith

While King Ahaz typifies abject faithlessness, King Hezekiah typifies the godly, immensely successful leader, or the pastor or believer who falls prey to pride which then expresses itself in arrogant self-sufficiency. God—the one from whose hand all blessings flow—is forgotten while humanity's wisdom and might are exalted. Today, multitudes of peoples, including multitudes of Christians, are suffering the horrendous consequence of decisions made in faithlessness and arrogant self-sufficiency.

Meanwhile, God waits to be gracious. He waits for us to wait for him, having promised to respond to the sound of our cry (30:15–19).

While this word relates specifically to the grand geopolitical drama Judah found herself embroiled in during the latter part of the 8th century BC, it is far more than mere history: it is prophecy and as such it transcends history; it is typological and as such it is eternally and universally applicable.

---

1 Oswalt, p. 623.
2 Numbers 13–14; Joshua 1.
3 Motyer, p. 274.
4 Ibid.
5 Harman, p. 227.

Judah's fifty years of peace and prosperity through the first half of the 8th century BC produced not humble gratitude and worship, but pride and arrogant self-sufficiency wherein God was forgotten. Eventually, the consequences of folly and sin mounted and Judah found herself facing a major geopolitical crisis and existential threat.

Nevertheless, in grace and mercy, as foreign invasion, occupation, siege and exile loomed large, God spoke directly into the Judean crisis, calling his people to return and trust him. All of a sudden, through the words of the prophet and the witness of the remnant, God was back on the radar, back in the news and back in the chatter as the call rang out: 'Choose you this day whom you will trust.'

The Judeans, thinking themselves sufficient for the task, decided to handle matters all by themselves, without God, thank you very much. They put their trust in limited defences: weapons, walls and water; military might, political diplomacy and alliances with power. Practical atheism was the order of the day.

So God waited to be gracious. He waited as the law of cause and effect progressed and the consequences of faithless folly were realised. He waited as the mighty Assyrian army advanced into the Levant. He waited as Judah's fortified cities were razed and her towns and people decimated. He waited as her allies were annihilated. He would wait until the people—as represented by their king, Hezekiah—were prepared to wait for him. And so he waited and waited until King Hezekiah, in an act of radical faith, bowed humbly before his true Sovereign, and in repentance and faith sought grace and the glory of the Lord.

Until the moment that prayer passed Hezekiah's lips, nothing stood between the indomitable army of King Sennacherib of superpower Assyria and the remnant forces of King Hezekiah of provincial Judah holed up in Jerusalem. But Hezekiah's prayer marked the moment the crown of the Lord of Hosts was put on (28:5). For as soon as Hezekiah's cry touched the ear of God, he answered, just as he promised he would (30:19), and the battle was turned back at the gate (28:6). For God, who is absolutely free, interrupted historic fatality so that that which was inevitable—the Assyrian conquest of Jerusalem—did not come to pass.

Similarly, during the second half of the 20th century, the world in general, the Judeo-Christian West in particular, and even the church, enjoyed relative peace and unprecedented growth and prosperity. But generally speaking, this has not resulted in gratitude and worship. Rather, we have forgotten God and grown proud and arrogantly self-sufficient. We think that we do not need God's wisdom, yet corruption, injustice, violence, conflict, hardship and persecution are skyrocketing. Meanwhile, God, in grace and mercy, is calling the nations and peoples of the 21st century to return and trust him. All of a sudden, through the words of the prophet and the witness of the true church, God is back on the radar, back in the news and back in the chatter as the call rings out: 'Choose you this day whom you will trust.'

The nations and even the church (largely), thinking themselves sufficient for the task, are inclined to handle matters all by themselves, without God. As persecution escalates, people put their trust in their defences, military might, political diplomacy, in humankind, in alliances with power—and in the City of Man along with all its vain projects. Alas, practical atheism is still the order of the day.

Like the remnant of Judah in the 8th century BC, the church must return to the Lord and stop regarding and exalting humanity. We must seek God's perspective and inquire of him, so that instead of 'kicking against the goads' we might conform to and advance his will. We must adopt God's counter-cultural paradigm: walking, thinking and fearing differently to the world. We must put on the crown of Christ if we are to 'turn the battle back at the gate'. For Christian security is not found in humankind. Nor is it found in the City of Man or any of its vain and spiritually rebellious projects wherein social transformation is sought without spiritual transformation (contrary to Isaiah 2:1–4). And Christian security is not found in alliances with power, for these invariably turn out to be covenants with death. Most of all, Christian security can never be found in practical atheism, for what God seeks is faith.

Meanwhile, our faithful Lord is waiting to be gracious to us, waiting for us to wait in faith for him. He will wait as our limited defences crumble. He will wait as our diplomacy and politics prove futile. He will wait as our allies betray and fail us. He will wait until we caste off our idols as useless. He will wait until we are prepared to look to him, trust him, wait for him and give him all the glory.

He is *Baal Perazim* (the Lord of bursting forth).
He is *Yahweh Sabaoth* (the Lord of Hosts and the Commander

277

of Heaven's forces).

He will surely be gracious to us at the sound of our cry.

Remember, believers are never condemned to fate, because God is absolutely free to interrupt historic fatality through the insertion of miracles. Even today, that which seems inevitable need not be. This is why we pray!

The church is not to be pacifistic when it comes to aid, advocacy and raising awareness. Help must be extended, advocates must speak out with a prophetic voice, while ignorance is a bulwark to be blown apart. But means matter, and God will never bless covenantal betrayal and conspiracies hatched in faithlessness against him. The issue is trust: in whom or in what will we trust when our lives and liberties are on the line? What God seeks from us is faith.

For the purpose of fortification, let us find time in our private and corporate worship for this proclamation of faith:

> Our God can be trusted.
> He can be trusted indeed.
> For this we know: God is for us.
> In God we trust![1]

—⁓⁓—

I would like to close with a personal appeal to all Christians— whether you are facing tribulation now or not (for one day you will be)—and to all Christian leaders whose decisions impact many; and to all Christian peace-makers and religious liberty advocates who are devoting their lives and energies to serving the Lord's suffering, persecuted, threatened, besieged church. And just as Isaiah employed Joshua's verbs, I would like issue this call to faith by employing Joshua's challenge: 'choose you this day ...':

> Now therefore fear the Lord, and serve him in sincerity and in truth: and put away the gods which your fathers served on the other side of the flood, and in Egypt; and serve ye the Lord. And if it seem evil unto you to serve the Lord, *choose you this day whom ye will serve*; whether the gods which your fathers served that were on the other side of the flood, or the gods of

---

1 See Psalm 56.

the Amorites, in whose land ye dwell: but as for me and my house, we will serve the Lord. (Joshua 24:14–15, KJV).

Trust the Lord! Seek him, inquire of him and serve him. Resist the temptation to walk, think and fear in the way of the world. Be different! And if it seems ridiculous to you that we should trust the Lord, then you choose, right now, for yourself, whom you will trust; whether it be humans with their cities, military might, political influence, advanced technology, wealth and celebrity or any one of the various spiritually rebellious vain projects in which humanity invests its hopes.

Yes, you choose for yourself in whom or in what you will trust But as for me and my house, we will trust the Lord.

Questions for Discussion and Reflection

1. God is in the process of bringing down all the false idols that humanity exalts and trusts in so that God alone will be exalted (2:6–4:1 and chapter 34). Like the righteous of Judah, the righteous of our day will be delivered (2:2–4; 3:10; 4:2–6 and chapter 35)—not from suffering, but through it.

   What must we do to fortify ourselves so that we might be strong and firm in our faith through persecution and seriously testing times?

2. How does engagement with the suffering persecuted church work to strengthen:

   (a) those who are facing persecution?

   (b) those who are doing the interceding and extending the hand of fellowship and assistance?

3. Promises like those in Isaiah (2:2–4; 4:2–6; 11:6–9; 19:16–25; 30:19–26 and chapter 35)—along with so many others passages that point to global revival—seem out of reach, even unimaginable, especially when the enemy is at the gate. But he who promised is faithful (Hebrews 10:23)! He is *Baal Perazim* (the Lord of the breakthrough), he is *Yahweh Sabaoth* (the commander of heaven's hosts). And because *he* is free to intervene, defeat is never 'inevitable'.

   What must we choose to do if we are to see the battle turned back at the gate in our own day?

Prayer
That we might endure.

Dear Father,
In the beginning you poured out your creative spirit in generous abundance,
and in the end you will judge all creation in righteousness and justice.
In these last days—
as you shake this world to bring down all that is false and as defeated principalities and powers fight to resist their inevitable end—
oppression and persecution are escalating against your Church.
Awaken our faith O Lord, and convict our hearts concerning what we must do to fortify ourselves
that we might endure and turn back the battle
that is raging at our gate.

Lord, I commit this day to feeding on your word,
drinking of your Spirit,
walking in your light and giving thanks in all circumstances
so as to plant myself firmly in the rich, deep, faith-energising and sustaining knowledge and memory of God.
May the Holy Spirit work powerfully in my heart
to alert me and convict me of seditious, creeping sins,
such as dangerous pride, laziness, self obsession and worldliness.
Lord, I commit myself to the whole body of Christ, acknowledging that as one body, all members need each other.
I acknowledge that the body of Christ is suffering this very day, as multitudes of believers face crippling discrimination, violent persecution, oppression and terrorism,
simply on account of the name of Jesus.
Lord, I commit to doing for them as I would have others do for me.
(Matthew 7:12)

Rejecting laziness and self-interest, I will extend my hand to those whose hands are drooping.
Through aid and encouragement I will help them press on.

Rejecting the luxury of blissful ignorance, I will seek out and take

upon myself the burdens of whose knees are weak.
Through relief and solidarity, I will help them stand firm.

Rejecting the silence of selfish disinterest, I will speak words of hope
    to those whose hearts are anxious.
Through caring and compassion, I will help them find peace.

For our strength is greatest when we are strong together—
    one body whose hope, strength and crowning glory is the Lord
    of hosts.

That we might endure;
    that the battle might be turned back;
    that the Lord might be exalted and glorified;
    and that the nations would come, (Isaiah 2:2–4; Psalm 22:27)
    may the Church choose to trust in the Lord.

Amen.

BIBLIOGRAPHY

Journals and Institutes

Defense & Foreign Affairs Strategic Policy. The International Strategic Studies Association. www.strategicstudies.org.

Foreign Policy Research Institute. www.fpri.org

Blogs

Kendal, Elizabeth. Religious Liberty Monitoring blog http://elizabethkendal.blogspot.com

Kendal, Elizabeth. Religious Liberty Prayer Bulletin blog http://rlprayerbulletin.blogspot.com

Religious Liberty Prayer is a ministry conceived in 1997 by Australian Ron Clough, a member of the World Evangelical Alliance Religious Liberty Commission. It was established to facilitate informed, strategic intercessory prayer for the persecuted church and for religious freedom in the world. It is not inconsequential that one of its side effects is that those who pray benefit just as much as those who are being prayed for. Elizabeth Kendal began writing these prayer bulletins for the Religious Liberty Commission in July 1998. When she resigned from the World Evangelical Alliance in April 2009— some 500 prayer bulletins later—Ron Clough and she established the Religious Liberty Prayer Bulletin in order to continue the ministry in an independent capacity.

Books

Bright, John, *A History of Israel,* 4th edn, Westminster John Knox Press, Louisville KY, 2000.

Brueggemann, Walter, *Deep Memory, Exuberant Hope: Contested Truth in a Post-Christian World,* Fortress Press, Minneapolis MN, 2000.

Brueggemann, Walter, *The Prophetic Imagination*, 2nd edn, Augsburg Fortress, Minneapolis MN, 2001.

Caldwell, Christopher, *Reflections on the Revolution in Europe*, Doubleday, New York, 2009.

Dearman, J. Andrew, *The Book of Hosea*, in The New International Commentary on the Old Testament, Eerdmans, Grand Rapids MI & Cambridge UK, 2010

Edwards, Jonathan. *The Works of Jonathan Edwards*, (2 volumes), Hendrickson Publishers, Peabody MA, 2004.

Ellul, Jacques, *The Meaning of the City*, Eerdmans, Grand Rapids MI, 1993.

Ellul, Jacques, *The Politics of God and the Politics of Man*, Eerdmans Publishing Company, Grand Rapids MI, 1977 (1972).

Foxe's Book of Martyrs, prepared by W. Grinton Berry, Baker Book House, Grand Rapids MI, 1978.

Gileadi, Avraham, *The Literary Message of Isaiah*, Hebraeus Press, New York, 1994.

Harman, Allan, *Isaiah*, Christian Focus Publications, Fear, Ross-shire, 2005.

Hillers, Delbert R. *Covenant: The History of a Biblical Idea*, The John Hopkins Press, Baltimore & London 1969.

Horton, Michael, *Introducing Covenant Theology*, Baker Books, Grand Rapids MI, 2006.

Johnstone, Patrick, *Operation World 21st Century Edition*, WEC International, Paternoster Lifestyle, Carlisle, 2001

Kidner, Derek, *The Message of Hosea*, The Bible Speaks Today series, InterVarsity Press, Nottingham, 1976.

King, Phillip J. *Amos, Hosea, Micah: an Archaeological Commentary*, Westminster Press, Philadelphia PA, 1988.

Lewis, C.S. *The Screwtape Letters*, Barbour and Company Inc. Uhrichsville OH.

Lockyer, Herbert, *All the Prayers of the Bible*, Zondervan Publishing House, Grand Rapids MI, 1959.

Mangalwadi, Vishal, *The Book That Made Your World: How the Bible Created the Soul of Western Civilisation*, Thomas Nelson, Nashville

TN, 2011.

Morton, Sue (ed.), *Angels in the Rafters. Reflections from the* MCS *community following the attack on Monday 5 August 2002,* Murree Christian School, Chiang Mai, 2002.

Motyer, J. Alec *The Message of Amos,* The Bible Speaks Today series, InterVarsity Press, Nottingham, 1974

Motyer, J. Alec, *The Prophecy of Isaiah: An Introduction and Commentary,* InterVarsity Press, Downers Grove IL, 1993.

Ortlund, Raymond C. Jr. *Isaiah: God Saves Sinners,* Preaching the Word series, Crossway Books, Wheaton IL, 2005.

Oswalt, John N. *The Book of Isaiah (2 Volumes),* The New International Commentary on the Old Testament, Eerdmans, Grand Rapids MI, 1998.

Pink, Arthur W. *An Exposition of Hebrews,* Baker Book House, Grand Rapids MI, 2006.

Sanders, J. Oswalt, *World Prayer,* OMF International, Littleton CO, 1999.

Schaeffer, Francis A. *Death in the City,* Crossway Books, Wheaton IL, 2002.

Schaeffer, Francis A. *True Spirituality,* Tyndale House Publishers, 1971, 2001.

Spurgeon, C.H. *Treasury of David,* (3 volumes), MacDonald Publishing Company, McLean VA, n.d.

Thomas, I.D.E. (ed.) *Golden Treasury of Puritan Quotations,* Moody Press, 1975.

Tozer, A.W. *This World: Playground or battleground? A Call to the Real World of the Spiritual,* Harry Verpleogh (ed.), Christian Publications Inc., Camp Hill PA, 1988.

Trofimov, Yaroslav, *The Siege of Mecca: The 1979 Uprising at Islam's Holiest Shrine,* Anchor Books, New York, 2007.

ABBREVIATIONS

ASV American Standard Version of the Holy Bible

EU European Union

KJV King James Version of the Holy Bible

MILF Moro Islamic Liberation Front

NASB New American Standard Bible

NATO North Atlantic Treaty Organization

NIV New International Version of the Holy Bible

NKJV New King James Version of the Holy Bible

NLT New Living Translation of the Holy Bible

OIC Organisation of Islamic Cooperation (formerly known as the Organisation of the Islamic Conference)

RLM Religious Liberty Monitoring
– elizabethkendal.blogspot.com

RSV Revised Standard Version of the Holy Bible

RLPB Religious Liberty Prayer Bulletin
– rlprayerbulletin.blogspot.com

UDHR Universal Declaration of Human Rights

UK United Kingdom

UN United Nations

US United States of America

UNHRC United Nations Human Rights Council